]

Tune

Joseph M Lalsala

Also by Joseph M Labaki

Inconscient Et Sexualite

A
Riffian's
Tune

An autobiographical novel

JOSEPH M LABAKI

CLUNETT PRESS

Published by Clunett Press, UK, 2013

First published in Great Britain in 2013

ISBN: 978-0-9926484-0-4

All names of the individuals in this book are fictitious
but the story is based on reality

ACKNOWLEDGEMENTS

I am indebted to many friends whose encouragement and support have helped me through this journey. Particular thanks to Selma Johnson and Jean Cavanagh for being the caring critics that every writer needs. Thank you.

I wish also to thank Philippa Donovan at Smart Quill for her guidance, Belinda Cunnison for her persistence and artist Stuart Polson, for capturing my imagination and making it real. To everyone at Palimpsest Book Production Ltd, you gave 'A Riffian's Tune' its wings. Thank you.

Many thanks to my daughters, Maryam and Ruth, for their creative input, their never-ending enthusiasm and their love. I am blessed.

Special thanks to my wife, Sherry, my editor, typist and above all, my love, for her endless patience and support throughout the years it took to write this book, for those late nights and for bringing form to the deepest memories of my past – without her this book would never be. From the bottom of my heart, thank you.

For My Mother

GLOSSARY

Bab Ftouh:	Huge city gate to Fez, built in eleventh century by Prince Al Foutouh
Bab Guissa:	City gate to Fez; built in twelfth century
babouche shoes:	traditional Moroccan leather slippers with very pointed toes
Darija:	oral dialect spoken in Morocco; mixture of French, Spanish and Berber languages
funduq:	built in a square around a courtyard, it shelters pack animals and horses and hosts merchants and travellers
hafiz:	one who knows the Koran by rote
harira:	thick Moroccan soup made of chickpeas, onion and barley
jellabah:	a long, loose garment with a hood and long sleeves
Kariat:	village
kashaba:	a Moroccan robe with no hood and short sleeves
kattala:	a 'killer' snake; very poisonous
Lalla:	Madame
mahboul:	mad; mentally disturbed

Melilla:	a Spanish exclave on the northern coast of Morocco
Saharaui:	a native of the Sahara
salham:	cloak
samsar:	broker
Si:	a title given to one who knows the Koran by rote
Sidi:	a title meaning 'My lord'
surah:	a section of the Koran
tagine:	Moroccan stew
Tarifit:	unwritten language of the Rif region of Morocco
ʒid:	keep going or don't stop

I

I was born around 1950 in the Rif Mountains, northern Morocco, into the Kebdana tribe. For this reason, I have always been called 'Kebdani' and never my proper name, 'Jusef'. I grew up in a huge Berber family in this rugged and rural setting. Together with my parents and eleven sisters, we all shared a room in my grandfather Hashi's overcrowded house. The house was within a spotting distance of Europe, yet with all the flavour and constraints of Africa.

It was majestically situated on a thoroughfare on a high hill like a camel's back and was surrounded by fig, olive, apricot and peach trees, as well as pomegranate and prickly pear trees. Built from brown and grey stone, the house was rectangularly shaped with a courtyard full of huge boulders on which the wives and their children perched to gossip and plot in the afternoons when the sun started its descent. At the front of the house was a large pond, which in winter brimmed like a glinting mirror with an orchestra of frogs, but in summer was reclaimed by the deep cracks of the hot, dry earth. A few hundred metres away, a hundred hives for cultivating bees provided a steady background hum to the days' activities.

Looking north, the sky and the Mediterranean Sea magically

met. Looking south, the hill was dwarfed by two looming mountains: Makran and Tassamat. Makran overlooked the hill, but Tassamat towered above them both. In the spring, the mountains wore a patchwork of greens and were blanketed with the rich aromas of wildflowers, but like everything else in the region, were brown and dry throughout the summer. From Tassamat, I could almost watch what was happening across the sea in Malaga with its many cars and shoppers.

The two mountains were split by a huge, fertile valley, famous for its wild animals: rabbits, porcupines, foxes, hyenas, snakes, wild cats and dogs. Farmers had been known to fight and occasionally kill each other over tiny pieces of this land.

Life in Hashi's house was hell. Cruel and hated by his wives, he had three of different ages and from different tribes and regions. The animosity among them, their children and grandchildren was rife.

His three wives, seventeen sons and nine daughters, their wives and husbands, along with a passel of grandchildren all lived in a single dwelling, both love and terror filling each room. As all the grandchildren looked alike in size and colour, miscalling us was a common mistake. Within the house, with loyalty to our grandmothers or mothers, we formed three competing and warring tribes.

My sisters, my parents and I all lived in one single room divided in two: a sleeping area and a utility space. The wall was dotted with wooden hooks on which hung rawhide sacks made from animal hide, either goat or sheep. A tall jug of water was permanently behind the door, and beside it a smaller jug that everyone shared. After use, everyone had to remember to replace the lid, made of prickly pear, as if it were left off many cats would swarm to dunk their heads into the jug.

Water was an ever-present problem. It was always a struggle to keep thirst's dry fingers at bay, especially among these desiccated lands it claimed as its own. To fetch just one or two jugs of water, my sisters Salwa or Sanaa, or both, had to travel at least four kilometres to the well. The carriers were women or donkeys, never men. A donkey could carry two clay jugs; a woman, one jug on her back. Often a woman, bowed with the weight, would carry a jug on her back and a child on one arm, with a few more children following. Donkeys and women were the engines of this community life. Women gave birth and fed children; donkeys carried water, ground the grain and ploughed the land.

At dark, with practically no exception, all the foxes on the mountain and owls in the area started their nightly chorus, edging ever closer to the house. Their unpleasant shrieks were very distressing and deeply disturbed all my sisters. The thick, impenetrable darkness and the cries of all the animals brought fear and anxiety to our hearts. Sunset had only one meaning: it was time to return home. With the feral moans heavy in the air, no one was brave enough to stay out later. I was fascinated by the owls' eyes and hoots, but frightened to step out into the darkness and investigate.

My mother warned, 'You will be picked up by the *Iwaj Ben Inak* (the Mutated Twisted Giant), one hundred metres tall, with long arms, skinny fingers, and always starving. He stalks at night and gobbles every human he can catch, be it child or adult. Because of his height, he cannot get into houses, so stay inside! The *Iwaj Ben Inak* can carry dozens of men on his back while chewing others!' Though petrified, I wished I could see him through the window.

There was rarely anything to eat before bed; if there was anything, it was cooked barley, but never enough to fill so many hungry tummies. The nightly ritual began like a religious ceremony: like a school of sardines stuffed into a tiny tin, we would lie down, and my mother would throw a heavy hand-made rug on us. We neither wore pyjamas nor cleaned our teeth, but slept just as we were. As the family grew, the rug got shorter and shorter, and no one liked to be at the end of the line, as it could be cold, especially in the winter. There was always a tug of war. As the night dug in, however, silence took over, just what my weary mother needed.

I spent a lot of time tagging along behind one or another of my sisters, sometimes wanted, often not. Unwanted whenever my sisters were invited to a social event or wedding, I was forced to detach myself and create my own little world. I populated it with miniature people carved from pieces of wood and dressed with tiny scraps of cloth. As if in a play, I used different voices to have conversations and moved them through events from my dreams.

Small and thin with no brothers, I was ambushed on a daily basis by my older cousins, Mohamed and his brother Ahmed, who lived across the courtyard and waited for me to go out to play. The fighting was sometimes spontaneous, but frequently engineered by other cousins, mainly Abdullah, who was older than all of us. Whenever I faced one of them, the other attacked me from behind and tried to strangle me.

Crying, I asked my mother for help. She told me that I would have a brother to help, but this promise was never realised. She promised an angel would help me, and I watched for an angel to drop from the sky, but that didn't happen either. Only once was I saved – by a swarm of locusts that came in a thick cloud, covered the sky, stormed us and broke up the fight I was losing. My face constantly carried scratches. As children the only way we knew was fighting, not surprising as we had so often heard my mother and the other women describing the fights between Hashi and Marosh, a barbarous neighbouring tribal head. Praise was measured only in terms of vengeance, bloodshed and cruelty. Like other boys, I aspired to be a cruel hero.

A few miles away from my grandfather's house lived Mrs Robbi. She was short, broad, buxom and had a large mouth with a booming voice to match, always looking to make a joke of someone. She particularly hated girls. She worked as a midwife and had been trained by the local butcher. She prided herself on never losing a mother and never hesitated to use her scissors to sacrifice a baby for the mother. I disliked her because she always teased me.

'Your ears are growing like a donkey's,' she would say with a laugh, implying I was getting more and more stupid.

She was respected for what she could do and feared for what her tongue might ignite. She could split couples and even families, bickered incessantly with my sisters, and was a source of pain for my mother. When not barking at my sisters, she was guffawing loudly, ensuring she could be heard for miles around.

Mrs Malani, a gifted herbalist, lived a few miles south and

was a complete contrast to Mrs Robbi. She was a strikingly beautiful young woman: tall, with deep blue eyes, thick mahogany hair and an unfailingly cheerful disposition. I always felt safe whenever she was around. While my mother was very fond of Mrs Malani, my father preferred Mrs Robbi.

*　　*　　*

MY SISTERS DIDN'T MAKE LIFE easy for me, my mother or, in fact, anyone else. Mrs Robbi never missed an occasion to say how unworthy of husbands they were. To make this worse, two of my elder sisters, Salwa and Sanaa, were determined, against my mother's warning, to tattoo their faces.

Endless bickering and quarrelling ensued. My mother was consistent and persistent in her attempts to dissuade them. Puzzled, tired, and disappointed she wearily delineated Salwa's physical beauty, 'You are tall and slender with olive skin, honey-coloured hair and long legs. What more to wish?'

Although happy to hear their mother's compliments, nothing could change their resolute determination to be tattooed. My mother's words washed over them without effect. 'While it might look fine when you are young, as you get older, it will look horrible,' she implored. 'Look at me!'

Bad-tempered, the two sisters threw everything they could grab, slashed the door, kicked the wall and spat on my mother. Frightened, watching and expecting them to hit her, I cried in the hope of stopping the tantrum. When Sanaa became aggressive, shouting and getting closer to my mother's face, I pelted an onion at her. Angry, she cut the onion in two and rubbed each half on my eyes.

'You can cry louder now!' she thundered in my ears.

My eyes stung like fire, and I couldn't open them. When I finally did, I found myself alone. I looked for my mother, and she wasn't in the room. As I went out, I found her sitting in the shade in the courtyard, braiding Sanaa's hair, talking and laughing. I took my hurt away to play outside the compound.

Defying my mother's advice, my sisters went to Mrs Himo, a tattoo artist living on a distant hill. She spent the whole day poking their faces with dull needles. When they came home in the evening, no one could recognise them. Each one came back with five tattoos: one on the forehead, one on each cheek, one on the chin and one on the tip of the nose. Mrs Himo's disfigurement of their faces worked against their burning desire to win a husband. Shortly after this mutilation of their faces, Mrs Robbi started to refer to them as 'the twin piglets' (there was only one year of age difference between them and the tattoos on their noses were strikingly prominent).

As the gibes of Mrs Robbi started to bite, and the decoration did not turn out as expected – the lines were not as straight as they were supposed to have been – my sisters began to wonder if there were a way out.

Despite their hatred of Mrs Robbi, they went to see her to ask if she could erase the tattoos. She answered jokingly, 'We can burn them off!' knowing the cure would be more defacing than the disfigurement.

*   *   *

MY LIFE OUTSIDE, AWAY FROM Hashi's house, was sometimes fun. My cousins and I spent hours and hours trapping birds.

Uncle Masso sold me two bird traps in exchange for four eggs that I had stolen. I set my traps under a fig tree or on the top of a hill; traps had to be hidden under the soil, but allow for the movement of the tiny worm trapped in the middle and wriggling to free itself, ironically, movement that would attract the birds. What euphoria whenever a bird was caught! The hunting was never just for fun; it was for food, but trapping birds was a competitive sport where skill and luck were combined. I always felt proud to come home with a bunch of birds hanging around my neck. Small though they were, their contribution in feeding my needy family was great.

'You are a born hunter, my son! You catch far more birds than your cousins!' exclaimed my mother.

One summer's day, I was outside playing by myself, as usual, when two strong men grabbed me and carried me inside the house. One of them put my legs, as tightly as he could, between his own and presented me, like a sheep about to be shorn, to an old man. All I could see were a pair of scissors in his hand, a knife beside him on his right and an egg yolk on his left. He grabbed my penis, and in a second I was cut and bleeding all over my legs and toes – circumcised. Then everything was a blank. Unconsciousness brought sweet relief.

Pieces of dried, dead skin fell off, but the joy of scratching prolonged the healing. I waddled like a duck for weeks.

I asked my mother if I would need a second circumcision. It was a relief to hear, 'No, no.' But I didn't believe her. Fear of being grabbed by a man kept me on the lookout whenever I was outside. Though the physical experience was once in a lifetime, it was never so in my dreams. The nightmare haunted me for many years to come. Wary and untrusting, I became suspicious of every man.

The only scar that haunted me more than circumcision was hunger.

2

Drought struck. The beautiful valley, hills and mountains became desert. Even the sea shrank. The foxes' howls died, but the owls' hooting filled the sky, as they predicted the house would be abandoned and become dilapidated, ruined and haunted by vultures. Dead fish washed up on the shore, and those who were lucky enough to be near the sea lived on their dead and diseased remains.

I asked for bread but there wasn't any. I searched the house; I couldn't find any. Day and night passed without food. I thought bread and dreamed bread, and I wasn't the only one. Coming into the house at midday, I found my mother, sickle in hand, digging at the wall, chopping and eating the soft stone, cracking it with her teeth. I saw her struggle to swallow it. I did the same until she stopped me.

As if struck by a spell, Hashi's dwelling became a haunted house. Overnight, seventeen sons and nine daughters, with all their children, disappeared. My father's fate was the worst. With my mother, he decided to take us to Algeria, the French colony, in the hope of teaching the Koran, but my father had no practical skills to draw upon or youth to plough with. He was a simple *hafiẓ* but in a land of abject illiteracy, he was a consultant.

At sunrise we started the journey. Two of my sisters were tricked into staying behind and abandoned to their fate. I was about five years old and barefoot, as I had been since I was born. I was given useless Spanish shoes with tyre soles, twice the size of my feet. I threw them over my shoulder, but thirty minutes into the journey tossed them as a bother.

After two days plodding along, we spent the night in a cave on the bank of the river Moulouya, 'The Twisted', a river notorious for unpredicted flooding, sweeping trees and claiming human lives. The cave was inhabited by a mentally disturbed hermit, who was tall and too thin, with very long, matted black hair cascading down his back. His wrinkled, leathered face was hardly visible under his beard and moustache. He had not one single tooth and looked demented, deranged, dirty and dangerous. The cave was narrow and exceedingly deep, with a cold blackness that hung in the air. A man called Bourass was already inside with his wife, elderly mother and son. I refused to go in.

'Get in!' shouted my father. Then from inside, he called, 'Come in!'

I ignored him. Hearing my father shouting, the hermit came up behind me. Terrified of him, I rushed into the cave and cried, 'Let's go back! Let's go back!' My pleading fell on deaf ears.

It happened that Mr Bourass was also a *hafiz*, so a quick pact was struck between him and my father . They conversed in the complete darkness of the cave. His wife and my mother didn't exchange a word. The same night while everyone was sleeping, Mrs Bourass crawled to our rawhide bag and devoured a good portion of our barley loaf. The cold, miserable morning started with a dispute. My father and Mr Bourass, like hedgehogs, listened passively.

'You ate my bread!' my mother accused Mrs Bourass.

'A lie in your face!' Mrs Bourass retorted. Confronted, challenged, humiliated and interrogated like a criminal, she broke down and ran to throw herself into the river. I watched her with horror. No one called her to come back or followed her. When she reached the river, she meditated over the cold, running water and changed her mind. She slunk back and squatted on the ground alone.

It was early on that cold morning that we came face to face with the river. It marked the division between our Spanish-occupied north and the French colony, the south of Morocco. French customs and police patrolled the border and were mortally feared. Ruthlessly, they stripped illegal immigrants of everything – even a loaf of bread – and turned them back to die.

The river looked alluringly quiet and was half a kilometre wide, but only experts knew how and where to cross. They would never go straight across, but would zigzag to avoid whirlpools, of which the river was full. Hidden undertows were everywhere. My father had no knowledge of either the depth or the undertow. Mr Bourass, far younger than my father, took his clothes off and rolled them around his neck. Watching him, I saw heavy bones with no flesh.

He shouted, 'Cross in pairs! Hold hands! If one sinks, the other should pull!' We trusted his advice and his technique sounded safe.

I was tied to my mother's flimsy belt to keep me from going under. The water reached my chin and got into my mouth. I choked and coughed, but still managed to stay afloat and guide my mother across.

We all crossed except Mr Bourass' mother. She was left until last. Mr Bourass escorted her, held her hand; she rolled her clothes up, half-naked, and they crossed side by side. Mr Bourass' mother was old, short, frail and heavy-boned, but with no flesh, like her son. He decided in the middle of crossing to take a short cut, as she was tired and struggling. She suddenly slipped into a sinkhole and started to sink in the mud. Her son, trying to pull her out, yelled at her.

I watched in horror, biting my lip. Naïvely, lured by the shallow depth of the water, I ran into the river. My mother yelled, 'Stop!' She grabbed me by the hair before I got in too deep.

'I am coming!' shouted my father as he waded into the water only to get stuck in the mire. There were a few people on the other shore, including the hermit who was running in circles like a whirling dervish and flapping his arms like an owl. Mrs Bourass sank quickly. The only sign of her was a bubble on the surface of the water. Mr Bourass stood in the middle of the river and refused to come out, but he was also afraid to dive under the water. A scarf emerged toward the shore. It was obvious that Mrs Bourass would never surface again.

I thought my father, mother and sisters would moan and cry, but no one did. Stripped of our inner dignity, all that was left was a façade of humanity.

Soon, it got colder. I was soaking wet, and my teeth chattered so hard that I couldn't speak or feel my tongue. The Bourass family was left behind, and mine moved on.

Still full of fear and horror, we took an offshoot path, less known and much less safe, but surprisingly, full of moving migrants of all ages – old and young, men, women and children, making up mass columns that stretched into the distance. This slow and steady exodus included some families just like ours, and occasionally, some individuals who appeared to be struggling on their own. Everybody was carrying a rawhide bag.

Migrants were scattered everywhere like tired and hungry sheep. We followed a few columns, and the road was prickled with small sharp grey stones. Moving on, we heard an amorphous cry. I listened and asked my mother, 'What is it? Listen!'

It sounded like a distressed child's voice, but too raw to be human. It stopped and started, a constant sound of distress. I spied a young girl alone, abandoned, small and very thin, about three or four years old. At first she looked like a wild cat. Her whole face was covered with long, dark, dirty hair. We stopped to see if her parents were about, but there was nobody around except a dark, dying dog. Not far away on a gentle hill, there were some wild pigs. When we stopped, she staggered, crying constantly, toward us.

'Why is she here?' I asked my mother. She gave me no answer. I stood, transfixed, glassy-eyed, staring at the girl. While we stopped, other migrants were passing by, their faces as well as their hearts dried and dead. No one stopped, looked or asked questions about this abandoned girl.

'Does anyone want this girl?' I asked my mother.

'No, no . . .' she answered.

'Not even her parents?' I asked. Then I thought of my two sisters left behind and concluded that my parents didn't want them. I feared they might leave me as well if I couldn't keep up with them.

We moved on, and her cry became louder. She tried to follow us, but being weak and hungry, she couldn't. Bit by bit, the distance between us and the girl became bigger and bigger until she disappeared. She was left to die or live with only the company of a starving dog.

Trudging on, my toes were sore and calloused, I felt my knees might buckle, and I asked my father to carry me.

'If you can't walk, stay here,' he responded.

I stopped and squatted on the ground, but they continued moving without looking back. As they got farther and farther away, I realised I was being left, pushed myself up and ran to catch up with them.

Three days later, my sister Miloda started to feel ill, unable to move or stand up. She soon developed diarrhoea and could not stop vomiting. Passing an empty, derelict shack, we huddled inside and found a hidden place to make a fire so we wouldn't alert French customs or the police. Together we foraged for tinder and wood scattered in the path and managed to find enough for a small fire. My father lit it and my mother put Miloda on her lap, both facing the fire. My father drew a talisman and my mother hung it around Miloda's neck.

I asked my mother, 'Why didn't my father draw a talisman for the girl we passed?'

She ignored my question, as she often did.

For a while, Miloda looked as if she were sleeping, but later, she started to gurgle. 'She's dying,' my father whispered in a panicked voice.

'Don't say that!' hissed my mother.

As time went on, Miloda's body grew colder and colder, her breathing shallow and laboured. Then my mother succumbed to the horrible reality that Miloda was dead. The climate of despair and horror grabbed me, and I thought I would be next. My mother was crying, holding and cradling Miloda, her tears running freely like a river. My father sat hopelessly upon a large stone.

'Why don't we cross the valley and find someone?' I whispered into his ear, watching him grieving and lost.

My father and I went across the valley looking for help. As we ventured deeper, we happened on a few sheep. 'There must be someone near,' I said. I looked around, but saw nothing, no sign of life. As we went farther, a small house appeared like a matchbox in the distance. There were a few trees here and there, and we were relieved to see a house or something that looked like one. Without hesitation, we headed straight to it. I wondered how we would find our way back.

We got closer to the house, but before we reached the door a big, fierce black dog emerged, growling and baring its teeth. It was impossible to get past. My father shouted, 'Mohammed! Mohammed! Mohammed! Is anyone living here?'

The front door opened hesitantly and an old woman appeared. Badly myopic, she craned her neck right and left, and called in a brittle voice, 'Is it you? Is it you, Ahmed?'

A few seconds later, an old man with a white beard came out. He tried to talk, but his voice was gentle and weak. The frenzied dog made it impossible to hear or understand the man, who advanced toward us as he waved the dog off.

'Do you need some bread?' he asked. 'Some water?'

'No, thank you,' answered my father.

'I do!' I whispered.

'What is troubling your heart?' asked the old man.

'I am from the north of Morocco, taking my family to Tassan, and one of my daughters has passed away. Could you help me to bury her? Could you show me where the nearest Muslim cemetery is?' asked my father in a rasping voice.

'Unfortunately, there is no Muslim cemetery nearby. There is no land left for a cemetery. The French own the land and the sky,' said the old man. 'As you can see,' he continued, 'I am an old man. I cannot walk fast, and I cannot carry any weight. My shoulders are stiff and constantly in pain, but I will call my nephew.'

He called on his nephew, living in the house with him, to fetch a man called Mr Kadour. 'Mr Kadour,' said the old man, 'is young, strong and very helpful. He doesn't live very far away from here.' Turning to his nephew, he said, 'Go to Mr Kadour and tell him we need a pickaxe and shovel.'

'Where is your family?' the old man asked.

'Over there . . .' my father motioned and described the place.

'Go back and wait for Mr Kadour to arrive,' the old man told us.

A while later, the old man arrived on his own, limping and

tired but talkative and eager to help. As he moved around the cramped hut, he murmured, 'God, You are the Almighty. God, You are the Almighty . . .'

Mr Kadour arrived, pickaxe and shovel on his shoulder. The old man's nephew joined him shortly after. Mr Kadour asked the old man if he knew us. 'No,' said the old man, 'They are migrants – victims of poverty and oppression. We have seen a lot of them this month. God bless us all. Once the girl is taken care of, buried, they will move on . . . that's all.'

Mr Kadour explained how far and difficult it was to get to the cemetery, but that said, in the last few years two or three people had been buried on the top of a high hill nearby. I watched Mr Kadour dig the grave. In the middle of the large opening, he dug a smaller slot-like hole. My father carried Miloda to the gravesite where they laid her deep into the hole as if she were a gift to the earth, and covered her with large stones like a roof. Mr Kadour shovelled the fresh earth on top of the stones.

I had watched Miloda stop breathing. I had touched her cheek and found her cold and stiff. I had seen my mother weeping and had watched Mr Kadour sweating and digging and, all alone, I had felt pain and sorrow, but I didn't understand death. I didn't know if it were the end of pain or just the beginning of it.

3

After eight days of crawling along with the sky as our only shelter, sleeping rough and hungry, we reached Tassan, a small village with two short and modest streets facing each other. A cemented space dotted with a few trees split the streets.

It was midday. I looked right and left, saw no one, and then heard a church bell, but it stopped as suddenly as it had started. I spied two women crossing the street; both were wearing black, their heads covered with veils, entering a big building.

'Can we join those ladies?' I asked my mother, while hoping for shelter and a place to rest.

'That is not for us,' my mother answered.

I wished one of the women, who looked strong and energetic, were my mother and could save me from my miserable and tramp-like life. I wished one of them would kidnap me.

Fifteen miles from Tassan, we joined a ghetto filled with destitute people just like ourselves. We stepped into a shack, one single room built with wicker and mud, crumbling, infested and leaking. The local community was composed of labourers and peasants – people impoverished in their homeland. Their houses, which were no more than huts, lay scattered on the sides of two rolling hills with a gentle creek snaking between them. The hillsides were barren except for a few trees battered by the wind at the very top, but the banks of the creek were dotted with fig trees.

Starving, walking barefoot with my toes bleeding and my heels turning into hooves, I hated the shack, the ghetto and the locals. I wondered why my father had brought us here and why he had left my two sisters behind. Running away from death hadn't improved our lives or ended our pain.

Within a few weeks of our settling, the ghetto and the rural community were struck by a mysterious plague. Our neighbour, young, strong and newly married, died within eight days. A week later, his mother passed away, and then his father the week after that. A collective cry filled the air. Age made no difference.

Because he was a *hafiz*, my father was hired to give the dead their ritual washing. As no one else wanted the job, he enlisted me to help him. Lifting the dead from their bedding proved to be hard on me. I had neither the physical strength to do the job nor the inclination to touch the cadavers. Once they were put on wooden slats, I held the jug and poured the water on my father's hands while he gently washed the naked bodies; his hands swabbed them while I watched. My father showed no feeling.

One morning, I was deeply disturbed by the body of one brawny man in his late twenties, looking strong and solid as if he would awaken, lying naked to be washed. I could never shake off this image from my mind. As the body was too heavy for my father to move, I pulled it by the arm to move it onto the slatted platform to be washed. My father washed his entire body except his genitals.

'Father, you missed his penis,' I reminded him.

He said, 'We skip that.' Then, I understood there were some parts of human beings so private, no one should touch them, dead or alive.

'Who killed him, Father?' I asked.

'God,' he answered.

'Does God kill?' I asked.

'Yes,' he responded.

Sad, I went back to the shack and wondered on what basis God had made his decision.

My father was hired as a Koran instructor for children. On the side, he drew talismans for the sick, the dying, the troubled and those possessed by demons. He drew a talisman for a woman whose son was dying. While waiting for her to pick up her talisman, I opened it and looked at it. I saw nothing but scribbles on the piece of paper. I ran to my mother and said, 'I can do the same. If anyone wants a talisman, tell them I can draw one!'

My father's remuneration was in kind: a few kilos of flour, a meagre amount of oil and some sugar.Everything was voluntary on the part of the community; every family was supposed to make its contribution, but hardly any of them could. To be paid in kind, to collect two or three kilos of flour and a small amount of oil proved to be a difficult and humiliating task. Like a beggar, going from shack to shack to collect some flour, my father started to cry when everyone apologised for not having any. People did not own any land, and there was no industry or tourism; all they could do was work as cheap labour for the French farmers who owned the land, exploited the locals and despised their culture.

To visit an old family friend who lived far away, my father borrowed our neighbour's donkey. He rode the donkey and I was seated behind him. We started on a sunny day, the road was long and dusty and the journey was boring. Before we reached the house, two Frenchmen in a white car caught up with us. Neither my father nor I heard the car. It crept up behind us, and bit by bit, it got closer and closer and tagged the donkey. I jumped off, and my father was left on the donkey alone. I grabbed the reins and tried to pull the donkey out of the way, but it was slow and stubborn. Wherever I dodged, the car followed us. It was half an hour of horror, expecting my father to be crushed. The French driver didn't want to kill us, but was having good fun. They terrified me, traumatised the donkey, revved their engine, finally passed and sped away. One of them opened the window and shouted at me, 'Ah, ha, haaaaaa, *attention!*' as he passed, his face twisted with the remains of his mocking laugh. I wished I had a gun to chase them as he had chased us, but they were in a car and I was dragging a borrowed donkey.

Puzzled, I later asked my father and mother, 'Why do French people have cars, tractors, houses and food to eat, but we don't?' I wanted a serious answer or explanation, but I didn't get one.

'They have this world, and we will have the next, the eternal one,' my mother answered with conviction.

I disliked this answer. 'I want a car!' I said, 'or a bicycle.'

'In heaven, you'll get a horse!' my mother replied.

'I'd prefer a car,' I retorted. 'The car does as I wish, and the horse does as he wants.' I rained questions upon my parents. 'Why do French people have all they want to eat, and we don't? They eat meat, and we don't? They eat fish, and we don't? They laugh, and we don't? They play, and we don't?'

'In heaven, we will have honey and dates,' answered my father.

'Can I swap?' I asked.

'If you swap, you will go to hell!' threatened my father, eyes flashing.

Still unconvinced, I persisted, 'Why are they able to build cars and tractors, and we can't?'

'They learned, and we didn't,' answered my father, with an air of acceptance that I didn't understand.

'What has stopped us learning?' I asked.

My father refused the challenge, got angry, exploded in a temper and shoved me. 'A devil in your head!' my father reprimanded, looking ready to smack me.

Watching the middle finger of his hand approach my mouth, I darted out of the shack. If my parents had been French, I could have joined those happy, well-dressed and fed French boys and girls. Children coming out of school with jotters and pencils was, for me, the most enviable position in which to be, and made me burn with frustrated jealousy. I had no choice but to live in my own world – a world where books didn't pay their way. To occupy myself, I went to a spot where there was wet clay in the earth, and made cars, tractors and lorries and left them to dry in the sun.

As neither our housing nor our material possessions improved, my father was persuaded to join a gang of professional thieves. He hesitated at first. 'I am an old man . . . and a *hafiz*,' he said.

'Join us. You are just as hungry as we are. You won't need to do anything hard.' The reward was too tempting for my father to resist.

The gang was efficient, well-organised and dangerous. They swooped down on a different farm every night. Rich French farmers were their targets. The operative gang 'collected' the goods overnight, by moonlight. They had no rifles, but had elaborately crafted fakes made of bamboo covered with dark cloth – a useful trick to deter anyone trying to stop or follow them.

The stolen goods were crops: grapes, potatoes and wheat. While men ravaged and brought crops home during the night, women hand-threshed the wheat with pummels. Sadly, my mother was among them. Storage was in remote, hidden, cavernous pits, far from the prying eyes of the local police. Emboldened by their success the gang graduated to stealing animals, mainly cattle. Under the light of the full moon, they poached a massive brown bull. Not able to hide it and seized with panic, they spent the entire night butchering, packaging and dividing it democratically. Watching them destroying the bull, I wished the police would catch them. They bribed me to be a lookout and stay awake the whole night in the darkness, one kilometre from the house. I went to the junction, sat down in the darkness and the next thing I knew, it was morning.

The gang's camouflage was sophisticated, but not perfect.

The excess of digested grapes created a hygiene problem. As there were no sanitary facilities, personal waste floated everywhere. Half-digested grapes among the human waste formed sickening piles. The police could have easily discovered what was going on.

The land of opportunity turned out to be a pit of misery. My mother was constantly ill, lying on the floor. My sisters caught malaria; I sat on them to stop the shivering, but the convulsions rocked me. They lost their hair, and I, left alone, wandered just outside our ghetto and suffered racist abuse from Algerian boys.

After two years, thanks to my mother, we decided to return home to the Rif mountains. One beautiful sunny morning, when not a single cloud interrupted the vast expanse of perfect blue, we started the long journey home, just as poor as we had arrived. Mr Morui, a family friend and Riffian native, took us to Maghnia. He had a wagon with two dark horses and worked as a transporter of goods: potatoes, tomatoes, fruits, vegetables and sometimes people. It was a long flatbed wagon, and other people were cramped in the back.

The journey started slowly and happily, the trotting of the horses creating a mellifluous drumbeat that was uplifting to hear, but as we neared Maghnia we came to a very steep descent into a valley, at the foot of which was a railway. Mr Morui, sitting at the top, driving and talking, had completely forgotten to ratchet up the brake, so the wagon lurched forward, pushing the two horses and knocking them onto the tracks. Like emptying a sack of potatoes, we were jettisoned from the wagon in every direction. Landing on my left side onto cement a few metres away from the wagon, I was horrified to see my father struggling to stand up and my mother on her back like a tortoise, flailing her arms and legs in the air. The whistle of the train pierced the valley, and a few seconds later, a freight train whizzed past. The two horses were killed instantly. Men, women and children screamed and cried.

'It could have been worse,' said an old woman, consoling Mr Morui.

'I wish it were,' he replied.

'Do you want us all to die?' I asked, shocked by the event and perplexed by Mr Morui's wish.

'You don't understand my living pain,' he replied, crying.

'Jusef, Jusef, your hand, your hand!' shouted a frail, old woman stuck on the ground beside me. I stretched both hands to pull her, but her weight and my strength failed us both.

'She must have broken something!' shouted my mother.

Shaken, leaving Mr Morui behind, we resumed the journey on foot to the train station. The old woman, limping and crying, leaned on my right shoulder; my left was badly bruised.

At the station, a colourful water-seller, weaving through the crowd like a king, accosted us and barked, 'Water!' He was dressed in a long red robe with a large golden belt around his middle. A rawhide bag full of water was strapped across his shoulder, and from this and other straps that crisscrossed his body, a myriad of little golden bowls were strung. A large sombrero fringed with red and yellow tassels shaded his entire face, but it was still possible to see his big, bushy moustache and matching eyebrows that hid his eager seller's eyes. He energetically shook a rattle to draw attention to himself, but he needn't have bothered. I stared at him.

In the midday sun at the hot, dry station, people were thirsty and followed him like a pied piper wherever he went. I had never before seen such exquisite-looking clothes. Laden with all his golden goblets on display and in his beautiful costume, *the water-seller*, I thought, *must be extremely wealthy. Why doesn't my father sell water like he does? Should I think of becoming a water-seller when I grow up?*

The train arrived, a juggernaut looking like a giant, steel snake with huge clouds of smoke billowing from it as if it belonged in the depths of hell. I felt both terrified and excited. I had never dreamed such a thing existed. There was no queue and there was no order. Travellers swarmed and blocked every entry door with no respect for women, consideration for age or care for the frail or disabled.

'Push! Push!' shouted everyone surging forward en masse like a wave.

Pushing and shoving, we climbed into the train, but not everyone made it before the doors were slammed shut. All seats were occupied by French soldiers, armed with rifles laid across their laps, looking tense and sweaty. The aisle was overcrowded with men, women and children all sitting on top of each other. To escape the ticket controller, an old man stepped on me as I sat cross-legged in the aisle. One middle-aged man was dangling from the ceiling like a monkey and trying to pass from one compartment to another. A morose French soldier was irritated; he pummelled the man with his machete and burst his bowel. The man fell on me like a bird shot from the sky. Nobody mourned him or wiped up his blood. He was shoved to the door and left in the corner to bleed to death. I was surprised and shocked to see that my father was not bothered by the dying man.

A passenger asked my father to write a complaint. 'To whom are you going to complain?' my father asked.

'I don't know,' answered the man.

'Well, you don't complain about the governor to the governor. This is the way it is, my brother,' said my father, resigned. At the next stop, the mortally wounded man was shoved off the train.

The train journey ended in chaos, as before reaching Oujda, a border town, the train's whistle went off and the train slowed. Hundreds of people took a risk, jumped off the train and ran into the desert. I watched as one man, limping and carrying a heavy bag on his shoulder, struggled to keep up. Falling down, he picked himself up and fell down again. Yet, he carried on.

As the deafening noise of the whistle continued and people kept jumping off, I asked my father, 'What's happening? Why are we not jumping?'

'They are contraband smugglers,' he answered.

The whistle crescendoed until a train engineer arrived and tightened a tiny screw on a box on the wall just above me.

4

At Oujda, my father didn't want to pay for a seat for me on the coach. 'He's too young! And too small!' he argued.

'He's over thirteen kilos,' the coach driver insisted.

To end the argument, they decided to weigh me on a baggage scale. I was thirteen kilos. Provided I sat on my mother's lap, my father didn't need to pay. My mother and I were squashed into each other most of the way from Oujda to Zaio. When her knees got tired, I sat on the floor at her feet, but with her restless feet, she kept kicking me, sometimes hard.

We spent the night in Zaio with my uncle Hamidi, my mother's brother. He asked my parents if they would let me stay with him to be his shepherd. It was an evening I will never forget. They talked and bargained over me; they were deciding for me, and I wished they would stop. I didn't want to be a shepherd; my memory went back to the French boys coming out of school, and I wished I were one of them. While my uncle and mother bargained, my father was absent. I wished he had said no.

We left in the early morning, and I was carrying a bag twice my weight on my back. My toes were bleeding and my back was aching. After a tiring journey, we arrived at Hashi's house. There was no door to knock upon, no dog to bark nor donkey to hee-haw. The house had aged, and us with it. My two sisters appeared. They didn't know who we were, nor we who they were. They looked scruffy, dirty, thin and disengaged. They had survived on *aiarni*, a white bulbous root that grows under the soil, has to be dug up, chopped, dried and then baked. It is extremely bitter and horrid to eat as it sticks in the middle of the throat and cannot be swallowed in one single swallow.

The first visitor I saw was Mrs Malani, who dashed to hug me. Warm hugs had been very rare in my life. She stroked my head and checked my scalp for lice; she found many, and she cried, but I didn't know why. Mrs Robbi came days later, and I wondered what had happened to her. I remembered her as big and fat, but no longer. The change was stark. She looked older, less agile and less happy, but maybe more wise. She had lost her sharp tongue and her front teeth, and she seemed to listen more. She was aware of the gap in her mouth and often closed it before finishing her sentence or put two fingers in front of it. She tried to hide her crumbling body and missing teeth, but no disguise could mend what time had eroded. I looked at her, and she looked at me as if she were saying something to herself.

After I'd spent months of complete boredom, my sister Sanaa dragged me to the mosque. We fought, and she won. On a high hill facing the sea, the mosque was a very small stone building, L-shaped with two tiny rooms, but with no fence, no trees, no water or sanitary facilities in or around the building. I was shoved through the door into a small room. A middle-aged, skin-headed man with a long beard, thick moustache and a sapling branch in his hand ordered me to sit cross-legged on the bare floor at the very back of the room. I disliked him immediately; just the look of him was terrifying. The other boys in the room all looked ragged and bored; some were older, and others were younger. They didn't know who I was or where I had come from, but perked up at having a new arrival join them.

The moment I sat down, my freedom was stolen. I wasn't allowed to move, stand up or leave the room. Each time I tried, the *hafiz* shook the sapling branch over my head as a threat. Like a mouse, I remained terrified. I was handed a big piece of polished wood on which he wrote a bit of the Holy Koran. My task was to memorise it, but he realised I didn't know the Arabic alphabet. He wrote the alphabet on the piece of wood and asked another boy to teach me how to pronounce the letters. My only real learning ended with the alphabet. All that came after that was memorising. Because the text of the Holy Koran was in Arabic, we memorised it in Arabic, even though I didn't speak or understand it.

We were beaten morning and afternoon on a daily basis for trivial reasons, like passing wind, whispering, or not reciting in a good strong voice. To save time and energy, the *hafiz* would corner three boys and whip them all at once with the supple green branch of a sapling. Whoever tried to escape would get the worst. He often called me up and pulled my ears. Anyone passing must have heard crying and begging for mercy, but no one ever bothered to stop.

One local *hafiẓ* was particularly violent and bad-tempered. I broke his cane, but he brought a new one the next day. I broke that one too.

'Who broke the cane?' he asked the boys.

'Jusef,' they said.

He sent me to a tree nearby and asked me to bring a long, supple stick. Enthusiastically, I climbed the tree and cut a stick as long as I could, two metres long and an inch in diameter. He sat me in a corner so that I couldn't move and whipped me with it. The pain went all over my body so I didn't know which part he was hitting. I went home with a swollen neck and welts all over my body, but I didn't tell my mother or father. I knew they would do nothing about it. I watched my mother assess my wounds, but she only turned her head as if she hadn't noticed. It was as I expected.

I hated the *hafiẓ* and if I could have poisoned him, I would have done. Failing that, I ran away to escape a beating the following morning. Sanaa spied me taking the path away from the mosque and called Salwa. They ran behind me, grabbed me and struggled to stuff me, like an oversized ferret, into a big potato sack. I was no match for their strength and could hardly breathe. Sanaa threw the bag over her back.

As punishment, they took me to Seva, a deaf mute who lived alone in an isolated hut perched on a hill, far from anyone. She was demonised, believed to be a nasty witch, and children of my age and even older were terrified of her due to the piercing, high-pitched shrieks she made while flailing her arms around as if conducting an invisible orchestra.

As I had feared, she moaned and screamed with wild eyes,

her long, straggly hair flying as she energetically swayed with extravagant motions of her arms. The look of her disturbed me. I stood petrified; a warm trickle down my legs was the only movement I could make. When she saw I was afraid, she inched forward, stretched her arm toward me, stroked my head gently and smiled. She dissolved my fear and disappointed my sisters.

To escape the beating, the torture and the humiliation, I realised I had to be a *hafiẓ* myself. Though endowed with a good memory, I woke myself up at four o'clock every morning while everyone else was sleeping and memorised the required text by candlelight. I got angry with myself if I didn't get up promptly and asked my parents to buy me an alarm clock. They always promised, but never did. I nagged them to wake me up; again they promised, but they didn't do that either. I tried to guess the time by measuring the shadows the moonlight created on the wall.

In the absence of the moonlight at the end of every lunar month, I relied on the roosters, especially the brown one. It was big, constantly chased the hens, was very sensitive to the dawning light, and when it started to crow, it didn't stop. It was getting old, and my mother was afraid that its meat would become too tough if it were left to live longer, so she decided to slay it for dinner. I was deprived of a good timekeeper.

At dawn, without any breakfast or anything to eat, I picked up my slate and went to the mosque. My mother gave me one or two spoons of sugar and said, 'That will help you to remember.' It might have done, but it also entirely rotted my teeth, and I was toothless at an early age.

Upon arrival, I sat down on the bare floor and started the memorising process with the other boys, all sitting cross-legged and terrified, in a semicircle around the *hafiz*. At seven o'clock, the *hafiz* tested us to see who could recall the *surah*. Called by name, each boy went individually, squatted on the floor and faced him. If the *surah* were recited with smoothness and confidence, the *hafiz* would give his order to wipe the text off the slate for the next *surah*.

Those with good memories would wipe their slates with water, paint them with chalk and expose them to the sun to dry. They always took a while to dry, especially during the winter. Those whose memories failed were abusively beaten, and I was in this position more than once. The *hafiz*, Hajout, an elderly man, acting like a Spanish bull charging a toreador, whipped me with a cane, and a searing pain spread all over my body.

'If beating me would help, I would have done it myself!' I shouted, as if I were facing a reasonable and intelligent man. But Hajout knew no logic.

Mr Brosso, a violent, middle-aged *hafiz*, picked on boys and beat them at random. He turned the local mosque into a torture chamber, and alleviated his depression by brutalising us. My classmate Zine had a good short-term memory, but poor retention. He memorised quickly, but was unable to recall text three or four hours later, so when called by Brosso, he failed to remember. Held by two big boys, he was beaten by Brosso with several sapling branches at once. Traumatised and bleeding, Zine screamed, lost water and consciousness. Watching him, I cried, felt his pain and deplored his humiliation.

After a particularly brutal afternoon when Zine and I were tortured, I convinced Zine that we should run away from home and the mosque to escape Brosso's grasp. We left, but not knowing where to go, we crossed the valley, headed east, toward the mountain and walked until it started to get dark. Zine began to cry from hunger and twisted his ankle on a tree root, as we were both barefoot. I helped him walk to a shrine nearby.

We spent the night there in pitch darkness, hungry and terrified. We stayed through the following day but then, thrown out by the caretaker, had to return home.

When I finally dragged myself home, my mother looked surprised at my weary state and said, 'Jusef, you look horrible! Didn't you sleep well at your sister's?'

Avoiding her gaze, I answered, 'I wasn't at my sister's. Zine and I ran away from the *hafiz*. He beat us. I would have run away for good if Zine hadn't twisted his ankle.'

Under her deep conviction the *hafiz* held the gate to heaven, she told me, 'Beatings are of no benefit to the *hafiz*, but they are to you!' With that, she shook her fist in the air and turned away from me.

It was the first time I truly felt like defying my mother, but knew that I wouldn't. Instead, I pondered her reasoning and vowed never to be like her. *If she were not illiterate herself, if someone had taught her . . . if she hadn't fallen under such a spell of conviction, she would know the* hafiz *is ignorant and illiterate and would go with me, stick in hand, to take revenge.*

A few months later as I sat on the floor with a few other

boys, slates on our laps, Brosso pointed to my group and said, 'You! Go outside and wipe your slates!'

We scrambled to get outside, gathered around a very small jug and jostled with each other to put our hands into it, each extracting a fistful of water to wash his slate. Everyone pushed and grabbed until the jug broke and shattered on the ground. We all scattered. Crouching on the ground around the corner of the mosque, I cleaned my slate with my dampened hand, then wiped it on my *jellabah*. With a piece of chalk in my hand, I covered the slate with a white glaze, then, bored with the process, doodled some Arabic numerals on my slate with my finger.

Hafiz Brosso came out the door, sauntered to a bush to relieve himself, then spied me engrossed in my slate. He walked over to see what I was writing. Finding numbers, he flew into a rage and yanked the slate out of my hands. He hurled it into the brush and boxed my ears savagely. Whip always at the ready, it found its way to the side of my head, above my right ear. Blood gushed from my head and I screamed.

Brosso, raging and spluttering, shouted, 'Never! Never write numbers! Not mixed with the holy *surah*! Get out of my sight before I kill you!'

I got up, stumbling from dizziness, and ran, holding my head, blood dripping, dripping down my arm.

At home that night, my father and mother whispered in the corner. I heard my mother say, '*Hafiz* Brosso is too harsh. Jusef has a gash above his ear; he could have been deafened. I hope he can hear.'

My father answered, 'He has to learn to do as he's told.'

The next morning, half of my face was swollen. My mother put powdered sugar on the open wound.

'I won't go back to the mosque, Mother. *Hafiz* Brosso will kill me. I won't be a good *hafiz* if I'm deaf or dead!' I told her.

'Yes, *Hafiz* Brosso will be gone soon. You can do your work here at home until he's gone, but then you must return,' she responded.

Sitting under a pomegranate tree by the house, I repeated, hundreds and hundreds of times, the same *surahs* of the Koran until they became a part of me. When everyone celebrated the departure of *Hafiz* Brosso, and the new *hafiz* was hired, I returned to find he had come from exactly the same mould.

I took a small flute that I had made from a reed and played it before the *hafiz* arrived. Hearing the flute from his home, he rushed to the mosque. He pushed me to the ground, trampled over me and my flute, stamped and kicked me, and asked a boy to hold me. The boy, bigger and stronger than I was, grabbed me by the waist and whisked me off the ground. I wrapped my arms around his torso to stop myself from falling. The *hafiz* stretched my legs onto a boulder in front of me and whipped them with a stick.

'Music is evil! I'll beat the devil out of you!' he sputtered, going red in the face.

He stopped me from playing music just as his predecessor had stopped my learning about numbers. I laughed to myself and thought, *I will never succumb! Music and numbers aren't evil. I'm paying this price because ignorance is in charge. It's the real evil!*

Fortunately, I became a *hafiz* in an exceptionally short time compared to many people. I was given the title *Si* – a title given only to those who know the entirety of the Holy Koran by heart. In theory, I was as qualified as any of the *hafizs* but, like them, I was still unable to read or write. The language I spoke was Tarifit, an unwritten language of the Rif region. Of the Arabic language, all I knew was its alphabet after three long years in Koranic school.

5

A few weeks before starting my shepherding, I checked out the local bingo club. Old and young men congregated under a tree or squatted against a wall to shelter themselves from the summer sun or the cold winter wind and played bingo the whole day long. Baghdad, the most trustworthy, was the official caller. He thrust his hand into the small hand-stitched bag on his lap, picked out the numbers and called them in a gravelly voice, 'B1 . . . N4 . . . O2 . . .' He played the game himself and filled in his own bingo cards. I was thrilled to join the club and leave the mosque behind; I felt a change of status. I played regularly and sometimes won, but mostly lost. Each time an aeroplane flew overhead, Baghdad stopped the call, jumped up, put his left hand to his brow to shade his eyes from the sun and peered nervously at the passing plane. When it had passed and the noise had died down, he sat down and told us that the aeroplane was from 'Japan! Japan!' Interrupting the game for aeroplanes annoyed me and provoked anger among the players.

I soon discovered that bingo was a dull, numbing game, and shepherding was the only occupation facing me. My older sister Rabbia had been waiting impatiently for me to take the reins. She handed me her slingshot and staff and suddenly, I found myself running barefoot behind sheep and cows, across hills, mountains and valleys seven days a week, rain or shine.

To be a good shepherd took skills I didn't have. Sheep, cattle and goats were like oil and water. They didn't mix, had souls of their own and I just didn't understand them. My first weeks were tiring and frustrating. Sheep needed freedom to graze freely; I kept them close to each other, and so prevented them from searching for food. Instead of being at the front, I stood behind them, which kept them running from me without stopping. Instead of letting them relax, I made them anxious. We were in a battle of wills. They wanted to run free to look for grass, and I wanted to keep them safe, for I knew that foxes were everywhere and could strike at any time.

Coming out of the house one drizzly morning Rabbia shouted, 'Wrong! Wrong!' and called me for my first lesson in shepherding. 'Never stand at the back,' she said. 'Be at the back only when you want to take them into their pen.'

'But they run in different directions!' I complained loudly.

'Try to whistle and throw stones so the sheep will know you are present. Never be in the middle, for they will run in all directions. Once you arrive at your destination, stand at the front so they never pass you. Know that animals have a simple soul! They appreciate being fed, taken to the mountains, knowing you are between them and the foxes, but they fear being caught and slain.'

The lesson was hard to put into practice, but with experience I developed a rapport with my animals, and started to be able to predict their movements. Days were long and very lonely but I no longer needed to wake before dawn, which was an improvement. There was no chance of coming home at midday, and the days were very hot, so I took the sheep under a tree to sleep and waited for the sun to cool. At sunset, but sometimes later during the summer, I took them to their pen. Once at home, there was nothing for me to do but sleep or recite the Holy Koran for fear of forgetting it. My mother would come, sit on a sheepskin, listen carefully and rock back and forth. Her presence embarrassed me.

I learned the skill of how to live in peace with my animals. To protect them from going too far or getting lost, I sat between them and the high hills. Like a demented person, I started to talk to my sheep. Whenever I spoke, they stopped eating, raised their heads to listen and seemed to understand me. If I held something in my hand and called them, they all ran to me. Some of them were so confident that they rubbed against me. I became a part of the animal world and nature. The tree seemed to call me, and the call was so powerful that I was compelled to sit under it and listen to the music of the leaves swishing in the wind. The high mountain, Tassamat, looked like a staircase to heaven. I loved to reach the top and look at the trees, valleys, and the distant sea. I wondered what was behind it all. But despite the peace of nature and the company of my sheep and cows, I felt abandoned and lonely. I thought I had a second soul that was empty and needy, and I didn't know how to fill it.

Fooling around, I found a reed and made a flute out of it. I laboured intently, cutting and burning the holes just so, and lovingly looked upon my finished flute. Chaotic at first, my fingers started to dance to find a tune, and the flute sang, to the enjoyment of myself and my animals. Being in the high mountains surrounded by valleys, the music and the echo of the flute permeated the surrounding area. People from far away could have listened to my music.

One Friday afternoon my uncle, Mimoun, climbed the mountain and beckoned me. *Why is he here?* I wondered. Happily, I ran to meet him with my flute in my hand.

'Show me your flute,' Uncle Mimoun demanded. Proudly, I did. Uncle Mimoun raised it high over his head and smashed it against a green stone. Admonishing me, he added, 'Playing the flute is neither part of your father's tradition nor your grandfather's culture!' Shocked and surprised, my jaw dropped. *Uncle Mimoun acts just like a* hafiz, *except he doesn't trample or step on me. They all look different, but at heart, they drink from the same fountain. He has destroyed my flute, my friend and companion.*

I thought I could do without my flute, but soon discovered it had kept me sane and my sheep and cattle happy. Because of my flute, the valley had been more than just a hollow space. As I played, it had echoed my soul and mirrored my need.

It took me a long time to find another perfect reed. Before I started to make a new flute, I went to Uncle Mimoun's wife, Mimount, and complained. 'Uncle Mimoun tricked me and smashed my flute,' I told her.

She stood calm and poised. At first, she didn't understand what all the fuss was about. She knew that I played the flute. She had heard it. She showed real compassion and promised that she would talk to Uncle Mimoun. Like my mother, she had many daughters. To alleviate my anger, she teasingly promised me one of her daughters to marry when I was ready. I felt belittled. I had come to complain, and Mimount was trying to distract me. This was about my flute, not marriage.

A few months later, my father embarked on a new shepherding transaction. Two neighbouring families passed their goats to me to shepherd. Out of the blue, the number of animals in my care more than doubled, even though goats and sheep didn't mix well. My life became hell. Early each morning I had to take my animals and go to collect Mr Himo's and Mr Shabony's goats. Collecting them was not a big problem, but keeping sheep and goats both safe and within view became soul-sucking. Those goats were devil incarnate. They didn't stay with the sheep, they didn't stay together, they climbed anything, cliffs, low trees, onto roofs, they ate everything and they ran fast and far. I needed help. I explained the problem to Rabbia, but she had never had to look after goats, so I was left wondering what to do. The goats kept my mind away from my flute for a while.

I thought our dog Dargan, being big and colourful, might be a help. I bribed him with some food, and he followed the sheep, just like one of them. It took me about twenty minutes to shepherd them from my house to Mr Himo's and Mr Shabony's houses to collect their goats, and then half an hour from their homes to the mountains. During this trip, the dog was an angel. Once we reached the mountains, the sheep, goats and cows all started to graze.

Just as the animals settled, the dog began barking. *He is either hungry or thirsty*, I thought, but had nothing to give him.

He was an untrained dog. Nothing could shut him up or make him do what I wanted him to do – go after the goats and bring them back when they went too far. His own bark and its echo in the valley excited him. He barked constantly and chased the sheep for fun, making them scatter in every direction. I took him along for a few days, and then decided I was much better off without him. Nothing else that I tried worked with the goats. They never got tired and nothing, not even a high cliff, could contain them.

One early morning it was cold, misty and damp. The whole landscape was covered with thick fog, and the wind played with it. All the sheep and cows were hunched down, and the goats were hungry. The cold weather and dampness didn't affect the running mood of the goats. It was only in the late afternoon when I was gathering the sheep and goats to go home that I realised Mr Himo's big black buck was missing. The buck didn't actually belong to him – he had borrowed it to mate with his does. I looked around for a long time, and it was getting dark. As I came close to a thicket, I saw several happy foxes playing, jumping around and climbing on each other. To my horror, I found the buck lying dead with his throat ripped out. For a moment, stunned, I was not able to move. I didn't know what to do, and worse, I didn't know what I would say to Mr Himo.

I gathered my thoughts and checked if there were any more animals killed, but luckily there were not. It was my habit to take Mr Himo's and Mr Shabony's goats home before my sheep. This time, I decided to take all the animals to my own pen first.

Alarmed at the terror on my face, my eyes red and puffy, Rabbia asked, 'What's the matter?'

'The black buck is dead,' I answered.

'No!' she said, her hand flying to her mouth.

I took Mr Himo's animals home with the bad news. He was outside his house. The absence of the black buck was the first thing he noticed.

'Go and bring the black buck!' he shouted.

'The black buck is dead,' I said.

He exploded in a tantrum, and his wife was worse. 'Donkey!' she shouted at me.

'The ass is you!' I replied under my breath.

Mr Himo took his two sons with him and went to Tassamat to check for himself. They found the blood and what was left of the buck in a bush, and brought the remains home for his wife to cook.

Two days later coming home from the mountain at twilight, I was ambushed by his two sons, one my age (about ten) and one older. The younger one punched me in the face. I punched back, and my fist landed on his throat. Instantly, he couldn't talk and abandoned the fight. I fought with his brother for half an hour. He bit my shoulder; I grabbed a stone and hammered his head to free my arm. It was not a glorious fight for anyone, but Mr Himo wanted revenge.

Coming down from Tassamat late one afternoon, I was accosted by Mr Himo at the foot of the mountain. As he often wandered the valley, I thought nothing of his presence. He beckoned me with a calm voice. I hurried to meet him, but when I faced him, his face swelled and his eyes bugged out.

With a long stick in his hand, he brought it down over my head. I grabbed his stick and discovered just how fragile he was, and how strong I was. 'Shame on you, Mr Himo,' I said.

He yanked the stick out of my hand and tried again to hit me. I grabbed his stick before it met its mark. *The days of being beaten are over*, I told myself. I hurled the stick into the brush and left him behind. *He is neither strong nor wise.*

I didn't report the incident to my parents. I knew it would escalate into a fight and increase the already burgeoning animosity.

Mr Himo no longer wanted me to shepherd for him. He refused to pay my father for the shepherding already done, and I was glad to be rid of him and his animals.

As well as keeping my animals safe from foxes, I had to keep them from grazing on other farmers' land. Mr Ismach was different from Mr Himo. He had no animals of his own and allowed me to shepherd on his land. I was there one day in the middle of August when he arrived at midday with his assistant, Omri, to start crushing a massive mountain of wheat, bigger than a house. The sun was vertical; it created silent music that filled the air and deafened my ears. I listened to it, but I couldn't write it down or capture it. The heat pressed between the two hills created a colour unknown to me. If I had been an artist, I would have been tempted to try to paint it.

On the hillside, I heard Mr Ismach and Omri shouting. Forgetting my animals, I joined them.

I noticed something strange and unusual — it looked — like an earthquake. The entire pile of wheat was shaking. We quaked with fright and backed off.

Gaining confidence and curiosity, we inched closer to the pile; Mr Ismach with a pitchfork, Omri with a hoe and me with an axe. All of a sudden, a snake with a girth as wide as a barrel, fangs lashing and eyes burning, lurched out of the pile toward Omri. He shrieked, yelled and ran down the valley alongside the dried creek bed, but the monstrous snake chased him. Mr Ismach and I followed behind.

'Zigzag! Zigzag to confuse the snake!' I shouted.

Deafened with horror, Omri kept sprinting straight. Ismach, old and overweight, couldn't keep up. With the axe still in my hand, I chased the snake. Headed to his house, Omri came to a steep ascent, which he scaled. The snake followed uphill, which afforded me an opportunity to throw my axe at it. Hit, bleeding and confused, the snake circled. I then pelted stones at it. With Omri still running off, it took Ismach and me the rest of the afternoon to finish it off. Hearing the news, farmers turned up to see for themselves what their valley contained. The monstrous dead snake remained in the dry riverbed for a month and created an enormous stench, which attracted rats, vultures and all sorts of scavengers. The story was told far and wide.

Baghdad told the bingo club that I had killed the snake, an African rock python, and this was the first time I had ever heard anything good said about me.

I defied Uncle Mimoun's wish and managed to find an ideal reed to make a new flute. I laboriously polished it. Playing the flute allowed me to reconnect my feelings to nature. I looked after all my animals well, and counted them at the start and at the end of each day. Farmers heard the flute either in the valley or on the high mountain. I played it all day long, and the music lulled me to dream of a beautiful imaginary girl-friend, Nora, to alleviate my loneliness. I imagined her dancing to my music, but all too soon, the reality of baaing sheep jolted me.

Mrs Malani heard me playing my flute and told my mother that these were her favourite times to go to the valley and the mountain to search for and harvest medicinal herbs for her clients. I could see her and would meet her in the valley or on the peak of the mountain two or three times a week. I felt it comforting that she was nearby. I sometimes felt compelled to neglect my animals and go and speak to her.

She was always smart. Even while searching for herbs, she was dressed beautifully. The wind played freely with her long, dark, curly hair. I saw her crush the leaves between her fingers to test the aroma before pulling a herb or picking a leaf. Shape, size, colour and smell were indicative for her. Whenever I saw her in the valley or on the peak of the mountain, I felt the land had a mother's soul.

At home, whatever energy was left after shepherding I spent with Rabbia, experimenting in sorcery. My father had a mountain of notes: very old, crumbling, hand-written texts with illustrations and a few words I could decipher which could only be handled with utmost care, and printed books teaching supernatural science. Making a young groom impotent, restoring the virginity of a widow, and finding hidden treasure and lost parents or children were the most common subjects. I believed I could succeed in sorcery and charge a high price, freeing myself from shepherding so that I could go to school.

I tried to perform a spell to summon demons. Upon their arrival, I believed I must not look at them or talk directly to them, for if I did, I would be struck mad, deaf, blind or dead by their lightning power. I imagined they were stick-thin, wore black clothes, and I believed they were sexually immoral, unrestrained, lacked leadership, jumped around and leap-frogged over each other. I'd heard they hated to be summoned or given orders, as they were constantly busy. They hated the sorcerer as they didn't like to obey, but the spell forced them to do so. They were, by definition, saboteurs. To distract me, they might pretend to fight among themselves and throw plumes of fire upon each other. I hid behind my father's trunk and watched and watched, but saw nothing and concluded they were present, but invisible.

Rabbia's ambition was to charm, to look the most beautiful, sweet and attractive of all the girls. When I returned from shepherding, tired and hungry, she jumped on me. 'Are you ready?' To please her, and also to get her off my back, I scribbled the Beauty spell on a large dried leaf with the lizard's blood she had provided. Rabbia crumbled it and dropped small pinches wherever there was a gathering of young women. We believed the spell would make every other girl look like a toad, and Rabbia stunningly beautiful, sweet and the centre of attention.

Tired and exhausted one day, I found Rabbia ecstatically happy, for she had been at a wedding and had felt confident, beautiful and pursued. A woman had asked her if she would like to marry her son. This was the first offer Rabbia had ever received. She had a crush on a young man who didn't like her.

She pestered me to write a spell. After hours of digging in my father's trunk, I found one that would work. Being a miser, Rabbia didn't want to pay. She only agreed when I reminded her that the fee was part and parcel of the spell.

I wrote the spell with a quill and the blood of a hen on a piece of dried cat skin that Rabbia had handed to me. Rabbia hung the talisman on a branch of a tall tree facing the main door of the man's house for seven days to rattle in the wind. We anticipated that a special group of demons and spirits would inject love into his heart and steer his eye and emotion toward Rabbia.

After seven days of the talisman's flapping in the wind, Rabbia brought it down, carried it carefully and buried it in a path where the man would walk over it. If he did, his eyes would be blind to any other girl. Rabbia kept spying on the path to see if he would walk over it.

As she achieved no result, she got at me. 'You are no sorcerer! All your time in the mosque was a waste! I want my money back!' And she was right.

*　　*　　*

MY SHEPHERDING CAME ABRUPTLY to a halt one pleasant spring night. I fell ill. I had no idea where I was, how much I had slept or if I needed water or food. My mother tried to wake me up in the morning and couldn't; I was unresponsive. Shouting loudly at me made no difference. Angry, she tried to sit me up and couldn't – I doubled over. My eyes were red, my ears were swollen, and so was my neck. Touching my fiery forehead, my mother gasped, 'Fire!' As I was useless, she let me sleep.

I developed diarrhoea and vomiting. I tried to stand up and couldn't, so my younger sister, Amina, helped me go outside to relieve myself. Severe headaches, delirium and constant pain followed.

An elaborately carved talisman encircling my head and Mrs Malani's concoctions were my only hope. She dripped elixirs gently onto my unresponsive lips. Anxious waiting followed before the heartbreaking revelation that the mixture hadn't worked; it was clear I was on the brink of death, holding onto life by shallow, rattling gasps.

I heard Mrs Malani say, 'Where there is breath, there is hope.'

Fever, nightmares and thirst continued for weeks. Neighbours with whom I had never spoken poured in. One day I opened my eyes and found my brother-in-law Mustafa, Sanaa's husband, beside me. He lived far, far away, and I couldn't understand the reason for his visit. As my illness had made me weaker and weaker, everybody thought it was just a matter of days before I would die. To my surprise and horror, I awakened to find Mr Tabari, my second cousin who lived across the riverbed, taking measurements for my coffin.

'He's small and thin. The grave will be child-size,' I heard Mr Tabari mutter.

'How many metres of cloth will we need to wrap him?' asked my father.

'Four should be enough,' answered Mr Tabari.

I overheard them talking about my burial. I struggled to open my eyes and saw both my mother and Mrs Malani crying. I did not panic – I was too ill to care, and could not imagine myself under the ground; I did not think of hell or heaven even after the grave was dug, the cloth bought, and all that was keeping everyone whispering was that I was still breathing. I kept them waiting.

Even with no medical help, no doctor nor medicine, my body began to recover. Out of bed, colours looked strange and mixed. My memory troubled me for a time, and some words I had known were forgotten. Just as I felt disconnected from my goats, cattle and sheep, I lost faith in the family values and culture.

6

It was a rainy winter with no dry days. I longed for August, but it was far away. Creeks were flooded, but all water was lost to the sea. Soon, the spring came with great fanfare. Makran, Tassamat and the hills were cloaked with grass, yellow, red and purple flowers. Then, like a glorious cavalier, summer arrived in a hurry. To herald its coming, to allow for expenses and quieten my sisters – to buy clothes and allow them to go to weddings – my father decided to sell the black bull that I had worked very hard to fatten. As he was too frail, he asked two of his sons-in-law to take it to the biggest livestock market at Nador to sell. They happily agreed and requested I go with them to take care of the bull.

We started the journey at midnight, under the moonlight. During the trip, my two brothers-in-law rode together on a mule, followed by the bull, and me on foot, a stick in my hand, behind the bull. As if it knew its tragic destiny, the bull resisted from the start. My task was to keep it walking straight and fast to keep up with the mule.

All the way, my brothers-in-law spoke about nothing but prostitutes. They talked about the best sexual positions,each one boasted about the number of women he had slept with, and each claimed to have seduced and slept with more than the other. My presence didn't deter them.

On the outskirts of Nador, we came to a shallow creek, and the bull refused to cross. At first, I thought I could force him to cross, but the more I whipped him, the more nervous and stubborn he became. Changing tactic, I crossed first and tried to pull him by the cord around his horns. As I pulled, the bull suddenly snorted, jerked his head and yanked me into the middle of the muddy creek. The water was not deep, but it was black, thick and dirty. My clothes got wet and completely covered with mud. I kept yelling for help, but my brothers-in-law were busy discussing where to find whores.

A man on horseback passed by, heading towards Nador, and shouted, 'Struggling, boy?'

'Yes!' I replied, unashamedly. Like a cowboy, the man on horseback drove the bull across the creek while I pulled on the cord.

'Are you all alone here?' he asked.

'No, I am not.'

When I caught up with my brothers-in-law, they realised I had been left behind. 'What an ugly sight!' exclaimed Salwa's husband.

'You should have waited for me! Can't I ride, and one of you walk behind the bull?' I asked.

'Look at your clothes! You'll dirty the saddle,' replied Salwa's husband.

'The mud will dry,' I replied.

'Let it dry first,' he answered.

Before my clothes could dry and the mud fall off, we were

in the town. We reached the market just before it closed at four-thirty. The bull was tired and looked dull, but was quickly sold to a Spanish dealer. 'Couldn't we have asked for a little more?' I asked.

Salwa's husband shrugged, 'Don't be greedy.'

The moment the bull's rope was handed over, we scurried to a hotel. My brothers-in-law washed their faces and combed their hair before rushing to a local restaurant. I stayed the entire night alone in the room; they later boasted they had spent the whole night going from one hotel to another, from one street to another hiring prostitutes and whistling at every woman they passed. It had been a big night for them, thanks to the sale of the bull, but I felt a real sense of betrayal. But then, I didn't know how the night had been for my sisters.

That summer, I met a man in the village who told me about a school in Fez called Kairaouine Educational Complex, established in the year 859, which was a primary and secondary school as well as a university. The more I learned about this school, the more desperately I wanted to go. I became excited, anxious, nervous and impatient, but had no idea how to get there. From sheep to school, there was no bridge. I talked about it and became a laughing stock.

I heard the school was huge, dark and cold in the winter, and the town was big, like piled chicken coops, with a river running through it. I also heard there was an entrance examination.

In a hurry, with a few coins in my pocket, I rushed to Zaio to find a bookshop, but there wasn't one. Moving up and down in the street, peering through a glass window, I saw an old man with a beard twice the size of his head, squinting and trying painfully to read a book. Inside his shop, I expected to see books lining the walls. What I found was a basket of bananas, potatoes and eggs.

'Do you know where I could buy one or two books for beginners?' I asked the old man.

He looked puzzled and lost in thought. 'Ah! Ah! I know what you want. I have two at home, but they are very, very old. I will sell them to you if you wish,' he replied. He closed his shop, went home and brought the books.

I bought both. One explained Arabic grammar and the other dealt with religious matters and the liturgy. They were yellowish in colour, over-sized, and had explanatory notes in the margins. They were too big and awkward to hold while reading, let alone understand, so the most comfortable way to thumb through them was to lie on my stomach, a position in which I could not stay very long. Candlelight rarely illuminated the entire page.

Neither book was of any real use to me. Trying to understand a grammar book of a language – Arabic – which I did not speak, did not know, had only heard, was like playing blind bingo.

I thought my father could help me. 'What does that mean?' I asked. Sadly, I realised that his pretence – 'I am learned' – was an empty façade and self-deluding.

'I'm going to school!' I told my mother early one morning.

'Mad!' she said. 'Enough is enough.' She huffed out of the room.

My mother loved her sheep, her goats, and the hill on which

we lived. Her only desire was to keep her family around her and the hill actively alive with goats, sheep, and cows moving back and forth.

I had no relatives in Fez for help. I didn't speak the language, Darija, that was spoken there. I spoke Tarifit. To survive in Fez, I needed a place to stay. To find accommodation, I needed someone to share the expense. The more I thought about it, the more frightened and nervous I became. Even if I managed to get there, I didn't know if I would be accepted. Fortunately, the bull had been sold, and I knew my father still had some money left, but not very much.

When I repeated my wish to be educated and requested some money, my father exploded with a roar, went berserk, stood up and shouted in my face, 'Will you be educated if I give you one thousand francs?'

'Father, education is time-consuming,' I told him.

He kicked me, and I stormed out of the room.

Late August was unusually misty, foggy and enjoyably refreshing. Still wondering what to do, I tried to get some money from my five brothers-in-law. My wish to go to school was mocked and described as folly. It was particularly hurtful and humiliating when their comments reached me through my sisters. I had no choice but to go back to my father and mother to plead again. I was determined not to spend any more time lost in the valley tending sheep and goats, and I was also determined not to become a member of the mind-numbing bingo club. I used every argument I could think of. I had done my shepherding and looked twice my age – wrinkled and dried by the wind and sun. I had already lived rough and tough; I didn't sleep on a bed or mattress covered with cotton sheets, but directly on the floor, wherever I could find space. Cockroaches, scorpions, and spiders didn't frighten me; I had observed them moving, mating and fighting with each other.

As a despised shepherd, I had learned how to live alone, my flute mirroring my soul. I had learned not to expect gifts or look for miracles and had accepted that my views of the world were simply those of a shepherd. The echo of the valley and the endless sky said something about God, but I could never quite say what, and I thought it was much better that way.

I not only needed my parents' help, I needed a companion. I tried to sell the idea of school at Fez to my half-cousin Abdossamad who was twice my age, twice my size, whom I had helped during my Koranic days. Like a singer who could only sing with a group, he could only remember when reciting with me. Amazed and puzzled, my cousin's mouth opened and his lips trembled. 'I am engaged,' he said.

'I didn't know that,' I said. 'To whom?'

'My cousin, Boshra.'

Boshra was a little girl, not yet ten years old. Confused by my suggestion about school, he suddenly started to describe how beautiful she was.

'Wouldn't it be better for you to wait until she is grown up to see what she will be like?' I asked. 'Her beauty might change,' I added, thinking of my sisters.

'No,' he said. 'My mother advised me to grab the opportunity. The engagement itself was expensive: a big crowd was invited and many chickens and eggs were needed to feed them all.'

That week, I went to the village, Arkmane, and shopped in *Sidi* Moha's. The shop was built in a Spanish style with double doors, and very large. *Sidi* Moha was an old man: tall, pale, bald and always smiling. The shop was basic. He sold sugar, olive oil, salt and matches. I bought sugar and olive oil as my mother had instructed me.

'What else have you to do in the village today?' *Sidi* Moha asked me. 'Why are you looking so anxious?' he added.

'I am hoping to find company to go to Fez,' I told him.

To my surprise and delight, he mentioned *Sidi* Hadj Bahbout. Bahbout was a known figure in the village, rich and a person of influence. He had a big shop, twice the size of *Sidi* Moha's. He had many children, both boys and girls, and wanted to give some education to his favourite son, Maroine, who was good-looking, articulate, and the most intelligent.

Wasting no time, I stepped into *Sidi* Hadj Bahbout's shop and came upon two men who looked alike, big and well-fed. The only difference between them was one looked younger than the other.

'May I speak to *Sidi* Hadj Bahbout?' I asked.

'He is not here!' shouted the tall one.

In fact, *Sidi* Hadj Bahbout was sitting far back in the shop, drinking tea with some men. 'If *Sidi* Hadj Bahbout is here, I would like to speak with him,' I shouted loudly.

Hearing me, he stepped forward. His long black-and-white beard impressed me. He was wearing white clothes and a brown turban. As I inched closer to him and shook his hand, everybody stopped talking to watch, as though I were about to commit a murder. I knew I had to be quick and precise and said, '*Sidi* Hadj, my name is Jusef. *Sidi* Moha told me that your son, Maroine, wants to go to Fez. I am going if he wants to go with me.'

He shook my hand again, firmly this time, and all the other men clambered to follow suit. He asked me to take a seat in an old chair that could have fallen apart at any time and ordered three pots of tea from the coffee shop next door. *It is a good start*, I thought to myself, but I was afraid that he might ask some details, such as how I was going to finance the trip and the schooling, but he didn't. He asked me to come back next week, and his son, Maroine, would be with him.

It was getting late in the afternoon, the sun was setting and the temperature was falling. It had been an extremely hot day and it was past time to go home. It had taken five hours of walking to get to Arkmane from home, crossing several valleys and mountains, and it would take more than five hours to reach home, as I was tired and hungry.

Along the way, I passed two important shrines where men and women went to spend days and nights seeking help. *Sidi* Yahia was a shrine for those who had sight trouble. People sat inside the shrine, close to the grave of *Sidi* Yahia, and shouted for help. They dug the soil from the tomb and sprinkled it around their necks and chests.

The *Sidi* Mimoun shrine was famous as it was believed to be the more potent. People, rich and poor, came from all regions, towns and villages to be exorcised of their demons. The shrine was situated in a beautiful place on a river in a valley full of trees. One could almost be deafened by the carols of different birds.

Possessed men and women were taken there, chained to the trees and left to shout and cry for days. On the way home, I did not want to go past the *Sidi* Mimoun shrine, but it was late and there was no alternative. As I came near, I heard a lot of confused yelling, making my heart sink and palpitate, but I still had to pass the shrine. For a moment, there was complete silence. I thought what I had heard was just normal visitors, but as I approached the shrine, which was on my left, and looked into a wide, open courtyard, I saw two men and one woman chained to the trees. They were far apart, but facing each other. As I slowed and watched, they realised that I was passing. They all jumped and shouted, but were chained by both legs.

'Son of bitch! Son of bitch! Come and make love!' the woman shouted at me. 'You will like it! Try it!'

The two men screamed at her, 'Shut up, you slut! Shut up!'

As I hurried away, they turned to insult each other . . . and the shrine itself.

Late, I arrived home tired, but with high hopes. Falling asleep almost immediately, I felt the night was very short. Rabbia awakened me in the morning to do the shepherding as Amina was pretending to be ill. 'Yes,' I said, but then went back to sleep.

As there was no sign of my moving, Rabbia came and shook me again. 'Get up! It's getting hot, and soon no one will be able to move.'

Disoriented, I got up and threw a few handfuls of water on my face. This helped a bit. Only half awake, I picked up a small stick and whistled to let the cows, sheep and goats know that we were moving. Whistling and whirling the stick in the air was enough to get the attention of all the animals except the donkey. For all the other animals, the stick worked like a magic wand, but the donkey had to feel it. It was turning into an unhappy day. I usually didn't take the donkey with me to the mountains, but that day it was not needed for any work at the house, so I took it to graze with the rest of the animals.

The morning was sunny and warm. High on the mountain, I felt the fresh breeze permeate every cell of my body as though I had been born at that precise moment. Every animal was happy and busy grazing on whatever it could find. The goats were jumping and running everywhere, but the donkey was always standing still. It was midday, the sun was just above my head, and I felt I could reach it if I stretched out my hand. It was time for the animals to quench their thirst. I whistled and signalled the move toward the trough.

The goats and sheep understood the whistle, the time and their need. They raced to the trough, and the goats were ahead. The cows and donkey plodded behind. While the bull was drinking, the donkey arrived and crowded beside it. To my horror, the bull whipped his head to one side and gored the donkey with all its strength, piercing its neck and shoulder with its long, strong, sharp horn. In the blink of an eye, blood spurted from the wound. I ran to see what had happened, and found the shoulder of the donkey split in two. While the donkey was bleeding to death, the bull went back to drinking dirty water full of dead flies and mosquitoes as if nothing had happened. I had no choice but to drive the animals home. The donkey was practically unable to move. I found it crying, tears trickling down its face.

When I arrived home, everybody was shocked; they blamed and criticised me for the bull's aggression. The house was full of opinions and theories. I checked constantly on the donkey, and the deep wound was oozing steadily. It shivered each time I touched its shoulder. Desperate, I went to see Mrs Malani and explained what had happened. Swiftly, she reassured me the donkey would be all right, grabbed a bottle of water and came with me.

The donkey was under the tree, and I took her directly to it. I hoped she would give a prognosis, be it good or bad, but she said nothing. She examined the wound, pressed her finger against the shoulder to see how painful it was, and cleaned it. She gave a good shake to her bottle and sprinkled the liquid all over the wound, then gave me the bottle, and instructed me to sprinkle the liquid over the wound every three hours.

I followed her instruction religiously, hoping and strongly believing the wound would heal and the donkey would recover. Several days passed and there was no change. Then its neck started to swell, followed by the shoulder. Tiny, white worms swarmed all over the wound, and the donkey was not able to stand.

I walked to the village of Zaio where there was a veterinary nurse with very basic skills. I explained the situation to the nurse, and he seemed to understand me.

'I need to see the donkey,' he said.

'The donkey is lying down and can't move,' I responded.

'If you hire a taxi for me, I will go with you,' the nurse said.

'Hiring a taxi is beyond my reach,' I answered.

He shrugged, turned around and walked away. Deeply disappointed, I ran back home to think what else I could do. Before reaching home, very close to the valley where I had killed the snake, I heard commotion and shouting. As I hurried to see, I found farmers and shepherds (very young girls and boys, no older than ten) stoning the donkey to death. By the time I got close to the donkey, it was dead.

I looked at it and chased the shepherds away. Numb, I walked home and thought, *people of all ages, all kinds, boys and girls, can be just as cruel as death itself.*

*   *   *

MY MIND STILL SIMMERING, pondering the fate of our donkey, I went to see *Sidi* Hadj Bahbout and his son, Maroine. Though I left before light, I was not the first to arrive in the village; the butchers were first. A cacophony of bargaining activity was going on among them, but quickly the noise died down and the butchers bought all the animals they needed, healthy or ill. The animals were slaughtered, butchered and sold on the spot – the blood, hot and alive, was left to dry. The animals' heads were piled on top of each other, and shoppers bargained on heads, bowels, brains, hooves and skins. On my way to *Sidi* Hadj Bahbout's shop, I found a small boy about five years old, crying, tied to a hook and left alone in the middle of the road to fry under the sun. The boy was crippled – probably suffering from polio. The belief was that someone with miraculous healing power might spot the boy, have mercy on him and heal him. 'First, crippled by nature, second, tortured by his parents – poor boy,' I murmured to myself.

With mixed hope and fear, I stepped into *Sidi* Hadj Bahbout's shop and asked his elder son, 'Are *Sidi* Hadj Bahbout and Maroine here?'

I knew little about Maroine other than he was about twenty years old and married. 'Come to the back of the shop and wait for them,' Maroine's brother said. This was unexpected hospitality.

Time passed and there was no sign of them. I could not sit still and wait, so I left the shop and went to the café at the end of the street. *Sidi* Hadj Bahbout was there, surrounded by a group of men, talking, laughing, drinking tea and smoking all sorts of tobacco. He called me to join the crowd. 'This is Maroine, my son,' he said. Maroine did not move. He sat indifferently on his chair next to his father. The crowd left, and just the three of us remained. We changed tables and *Sidi* Hadj ordered fresh tea. Moving tables gave me a chance to observe Maroine.

He was tall, very thin, his eyes covered by a fringe of hair and he wore jeans (known as 'American trousers'). His father was wearing the same clothes as last time, a brown and pink turban, white *jellabah* and *salham* (cloak) and, contrastingly, smart brown loafers. While talking, his hands were waving constantly in every direction, and he was continually struggling to roll up his sleeves. Listening and watching him, I was busy trying to find out what kind of boy Maroine was. Could we share a room? Suddenly, Maroine thrust his hand into his pocket and brought out a pack of cigarettes. I couldn't read, and Maroine told me they were called Camels. 'They are much better than Bastos,' he said. He generously offered me a cigarette with his left hand and in his right hand, he held a lighter.

'No, thank you. I don't eat cigarettes,' I said.

Maroine insisted. His father smiled, looked at me first, then at Maroine. 'Maroine,' he said, 'Jusef has never smoked. If he had, he would say, "I don't smoke", not, "I don't eat".' They both chuckled; I turned red and started to sweat. Kindly, *Sidi* Hadj Bahbout began talking about Fez and the trip.

Sidi Hadj knew nothing about the journey as he had never ventured south. Nevertheless, he warned, 'Once you're in Fez, be constantly on your guard. Everybody cons everybody.'

The meeting was brief, but the essential achieved. Maroine was going. 'We'll meet at the start of September and set off the following week,' Maroine and I echoed to each other and shook hands.

On the fifth of September, I went to see *Sidi* Hadj Bahbout and his son, Maroine, to confirm the departure. I met them in their shop and was anxious about what we might face – accommodation, registration, the journey, and possibly a test. Since I had no idea what the test might contain, my ambition went beyond my ability, and I didn't speak Arabic, French or Spanish. Neither *Sidi* Hadj nor his son Maroine wanted to discuss anything concrete, but they confirmed the departure for the tenth of September.

Ecstatic, I went home. The moment I set foot in the house, I was assigned a task: water, water, water. 'Couldn't my brother-in-law get water?' I asked in a whining voice, as he, my sister and their family had been living with us for over a month.

My mother ran toward me and shouted, 'Don't disgrace me!'

I had no choice but to ride our young, new, untrained donkey five kilometres, adding to the day's already long journey. As I went to the spring, I felt the days were still expanding and the nights contracting. On my way, I marvelled at the night sky. Millions of stars were crystal clear, and sometimes I saw a shooting star. I wondered what all that was about. However, it didn't take long for me to come back to where I was: not in the sky, but on earth, not on the bright moon, but in the dark valley on my way to the spring just one week left before I was due to leave home. Nearing the house I heard the family feasting, voices like waves filling the air.

In the courtyard of the house, I joined the family sitting on homemade rugs, admiring the moon and the stars, with two lights lit nearby. My mother was busy going in and out, cooking and keeping her cauldron alive, as the fire kept dying and her eyes watered with gentle smoke. 'Jusef!' she called me in. 'Because you insist on going to Fez, we will give you some money,' she said, hoping my madness would fade.

'Where did the money come from?' I asked.

'Don't ask,' she replied, paused, and looked down thoughtfully. But then she added, 'The bull.' Thrilled, I divided the money into piles and hid each part in different quarters of my clothing, and the largest part went into a tiny pocket in my trousers below my abdomen; I stitched it in.

'Could I have a blanket?' I asked her.

'Yes,' she replied. With the money sewn in my pockets and the blanket, I felt confident about the move from north to south to seek my education.

On the tenth of September, I was about eleven years old when I asked my father to accompany me to Arkmane to meet *Sidi* Hadj Bahbout and his son, Maroine, so he could see for himself that I knew what I was doing and where I was going. It was from there that Maroine and I were supposed to start the journey. I had packed the blanket into a duffel bag and my few items into a small case. The donkey was just strong enough to carry the bag, the case and my father.

Temperamental, the donkey tried to reject the load. He wriggled, his head down. My father was unwell, and I was constantly anxious he might fall, so I walked behind him as we wended our way to Kariat Arkmane.

*   *   *

KARIAT ARKMANE WAS A small village on an inlet of the Mediterranean Sea and had only three small streets forming part of a square. The main building was a police station, and there was neither a school nor a hospital, just a prison. Once a week, like a volcano, the village erupted, then died. One could buy and sell potatoes, tomatoes, barley, grains, bird traps, mousetraps, perfume and women's make-up side by side in the open air. Herbal doctors sold all sorts of weeds and magical elixirs. The few cafés were crowded by men, but never a woman. It was in those cafés that men loved to gossip, share ignorance, talk politics and arrange marriages. Magicians often came to the village and entertained the mixed crowd. Snake charmers came to show their power over their snakes. With their flutes, they demonstrated how a big and dangerous snake could be seduced, tamed and pacified. The village was meaningful to my father and grandfather. It was here, many years ago, that my grandfather had been tortured by Spanish police for leading a guerrilla rebellion, and an order had been issued to arrest my father.

On that hot Wednesday, like all other Wednesdays, the village was entirely besieged by thousands of donkeys – all tied up with no trees to protect them from the almighty heat and the power of the sun. Donkeys brayed everywhere, and as soon as some stopped, others took over. Hungry and thirsty, they lost their bold and blind sexual aggression. They could only express themselves by stomping the soil with their heads wilted. There was no water or food – the whole village was without water. Café owners had to go miles to fetch it and store it in a barrel for months, if not years.

My father and I arrived at Kariat Arkmane in the early morning and, like other shoppers, tied our donkey against a few heavy stones, anchoring it like a ship at sea. There were only two coaches a day from Arkmane to Nador: one in the morning and the other in the late afternoon.

Reaching the building and before entering *Sidi* Hadj Bahbout's shop, I said, 'Father, you can pick up my correspondence from this shop. Kariat Arkmane, Number 17.'

My father lifted his head, looked above the door for the number, and squinted. I realised he needed glasses. 'Good,' he breathed a legato sigh with scepticism playing on his face. I entered the shop with my father behind me. Immediately, I smelled a rat; there was neither welcome nor smile from *Sidi* Hadj Bahbout. Maroine was sitting far back in the shop, smoking a cigarette and playing dominos with his friends. I went straightaway to *Sidi* Hadj Bahbout.

'This is my father,' I said, proudly, but he did not look at me.

He pulled his beard up in the air and grumbled, 'Maroine is not going.'

'Not going?' I bellowed with anger and shock. A sudden vertigo chilled me. *One could count the hairs in his beard, but not his lies*, I thought to myself.

'This is not a man's word!' shouted my father loudly, facing *Sidi* Hadj Bahbout.

Chin up, *Sidi* Hadj Bahbout kept combing his beard with his fingers. Horrified that my father's short temper might erupt into a fight, I grabbed his hand and said, 'Let's have a pot of tea.'

There was a café just next door with tables scattered outside and people shouting to each other, enjoying the tea and the sea breeze. There was just one little table free, with one single chair. My father took the seat, and I went inside to grab another chair for myself. Returning, I found him angry, talking to himself, shaking his head and gesticulating. I wouldn't have gone near him if he were not my father. Furious, he tried to persuade me to return home, but I knew a second chance wouldn't come.

While my father was talking, I listened. 'It's because of anomie like *Sidi* Hadj Bahbout's that we are oppressed,' he said. 'We are taxed shamefully,' he added, 'on our donkeys, pomegranates and prickly pears. In return, they built a prison for us. Look!' he said, indicating the prison, which was only a few hundred metres away. A long, narrow cement building, it looked like a chicken coop and was very low in height, with no visible windows and only a few breathing holes, as though peppered by machine gun fire. Prisoners weren't able to stand up. God only knew who went there and came out straight.

'Other boys are going as well,' I said.

'Where are they?' he asked.

'Nador,' I answered. I could tell by looking at my father's face that he knew I was lying.

Time always passed slowly in the village; it was measured not by hours, minutes and seconds, but by sunrise and sunset. Waiting for the afternoon coach, I felt time frozen, but like a sclerosis, very painful.

7

An old red Spanish coach was stationed in the street, and many people, including children, were moving around it like a shrine. Every minute that passed made me more nervous. My father accompanied me to the coach and boarded it with me to look for a seat. None were free. They were all marked with stones and sticks: 'Reserved'. Every traveller tried to reserve a seat for himself, his friend and a spare. The coach looked like a graveyard. The driver and his assistant, both raging, marched on and threw out every stone and stick.

'Seats free!' they shouted from inside the coach. I went to the very back, the cheaper seats. My father stood behind me until I sat. I kissed my father's hand, not knowing it was an *adieu*. If I had known, I would have kissed it twice.

A few seconds later, a snake charmer boarded and was refused a seat by the other passengers. He carried his snake, rattling and making hissing noises, in a narrow, long white bag. Provoking a ruckus on the coach, he was, at first, quite arrogant. 'Big men!' he shouted, 'Are you afraid of my snake? Ha! Ha!' He soon realised the strength of feeling and objection. He changed his tune, became humble, and pleaded to have a seat in the coach. 'My snake is harmless,' he said.

Immediately, a passenger jumped and shouted, 'Liar! Liar! Not long ago, you were telling the crowd in the village square how poisonous your snake was!'

The driver and his assistant, fists raised, ordered the snake charmer to sit at the very back. The crowd parted, and he sauntered to the back and sat beside me. I didn't feel comfortable. Now and again, the snake became agitated with the excessive heat of the coach, and the man tapped its head. Passengers kept turning their heads to check that the snake charmer and his snake were still at the back. Some of them were so afraid that they didn't put their feet on the floor for fear the snake would escape and crawl up their legs. To alleviate my fear and anxiety, I asked its owner, 'What's the attraction of carrying the snake?'

'The snake is my asset and livelihood,' he said.

'But poisonous,' I said.

After a moment, he smiled. 'I took its fangs out,' he said. 'It can't bite. But you never know,' he added, 'they might grow back again.'

'How did you pull its fangs out?' I asked.

'Simple. I caught the snake from the back by surprise. I moved my hand until it was two centimetres behind its mouth, and held it very tight as though I would choke it. As it was choking, it opened its mouth. Then I pulled its fangs out with pliers.'

'I didn't realise it was that simple,' I said, but, in fact, I was terrified just by listening. I asked if the flute really hypnotised the snake.

'No,' he said. 'It hypnotises people.'

'I have a flute,' I said.

'Do you know how to play it?'

'Yes,' I answered.

'Play something.'

I played a simple tune to words I heard in my head:

No two days in the valley are the same,
No night is ever without dreams.
No journey is ever too long or too short.
Listen to your heart but also to your God.

Everyone in the coach jeered at me. Some thought I was also a snake charmer or an apprentice. At the transfer point, I was glad to get out of this coach for the next one.

On my arrival in Nador, I discovered that I had missed the next coach to Oujda. Looking around, I found suddenly that everything was different. The slow pace of life I was used to had become aggressive – all push and run. *It's just the nature of this town*, I thought. Nador was the commercial centre of the region and a melting pot for all tribes and villages. Listening to the voices and accents of the people, I wondered from which tribes or villages they had come. The town was renowned for its smugglers. Luxury items such as watches, shoes and jewellery could be bought on every corner, in shops and on the streets. Adding to the social complexity, Nador was not far away from Melilla, a Spanish territory in Africa.

Finding a place to stay was both difficult and dangerous. Before looking for a place, I needed to store my bag and suitcase, and this task proved impossible. I asked shopkeepers everywhere if I could leave my bags with them, and they all refused. Carrying my baggage made my movement slow, clumsy and difficult. I knew that my cousin Mimo lived in Nador and worked as a barber. I went to the nearest barber and asked, 'Do you know a young barber called Mimo?'

'He works in the street three blocks down,' the barber responded.

I made a beeline for the salon, and there he was. Mimo had to jostle his memory to recognise me, and it was not his age that had wrinkled his brow, but life in this town. He rarely saw people from Makran and Tassamat and wanted to hear the news and gossip about his stepmother and sister.

'I missed the coach and need a place to stay tonight,' I said.

'I rent a small room. It's no bigger than a grave, but you could stay with me.'

I was saved from being a vagabond that night. Mimo had no clients and since his boss was not there, he offered to cut my unruly hair – a bonus.

It was getting dark, the street was practically deserted and it was time for him to close. I bought a loaf of white bread, some butter, some tea-leaves, solid sugar and mint, and we climbed up to his room in the middle of a shantytown on the top of a hill overlooking the Mediterranean Sea. Small boxes were built on top of each other, like a basket of stones – no road, no lights, no water, no sanitary facilities. I wondered how people knew the way to their houses and how they could figure out which one was theirs.

Mimo and I used two spindly candles to prepare our dinner and boil water for tea. He had no fork, spoon or knife. He didn't stop talking all night about his wicked stepmother.

Dawn ended the night and Mimo accompanied me to the coach station where the air was thick and black – each coach had its own shelter that announced depature time and destination. I bought a ticket and sat at the back. From the coach, I looked out the window at people looking like ants hit by an earthquake with no fixed destination, no order, just people crashing into each other, helpless and mindless. Armed police patrolled the station constantly. The coach moved, and the noises faded with it.

The travellers were of great diversity: Moroccans, Algerians, Spanish and some French. Every group spoke a different language, wore different clothes and smoked different cigarettes or cigars. This diversity was not, for me, a source of peace, but of anxiety and fear. Sitting in my seat, all I could see were the travellers' heads, looking like a line of fat prunes. I felt overwhelmed by such a huge coach, the likes of which I had never seen before.

As the coach was moving faster and faster, farther and farther away from Nador, it was suddenly stopped in open desert by armed police. Some had simple pistols and others had small machine guns. Two of them moved around the coach, and the other two boarded.

They stood in the front and everyone was terrified. They examined faces, showed authority, spread horror, moved around the seats and looked underneath and above them. I kept silent and wondered, *Will it be a massive or selective execution?*

'Your identity card!' shouted one policeman to a woman a few seats in front of me. He then turned to me. 'Identity card, boy!'

I handed him my card, which was an official piece of white paper, typed by a male secretary who had used just two fingers and had left many spaces between words and letters. The paper stated my name, 'Jusef, son of Sarir,' but with no date of birth.

A policeman with a severe face asked, 'The name of your grandfather?'

'Hashi,' I answered.

A second policeman looked at me and asked, 'Do you know the father of your grandfather?'

'Yes. Mohamed.'

'Your wallet.'

'I have no wallet,' I said.

'No wallet?' one of them murmured. 'Show us your money then.'

I showed them what was easily accessible, but not what I had sewn into my trousers.

'Where did you get this money?'

I replied, 'From the sale of our bull.'

While I was being questioned, two more policemen were involved in a row with a woman. She had a bag under her seat. 'You're carrying gold here! Come off the coach!'

Everyone was ordered to vacate the coach. The driver and his assistant were made to bring down all the travellers' luggage. The two policemen picked several cases, asked their owners to open them and they fiddled with the contents like a burglar at midnight. They took away the woman with the case, and no one opened his mouth or moved a finger, as though she had never been with us. Like rabbits ambushed by a fox, everybody jumped back into their seats and we moved on. A complete silence reigned over the coach. The driver detected the atmosphere and put his radio on, but it played melancholy music that didn't suit anyone's mood and failed to revive life inside the coach. Neither talking nor whispering was heard anymore. Shocked by the harshness, I wondered what might become of the woman.

A few hours later, the landscape changed from desert to fertile land. Signs of civilisation and modern life sprouted: electrical pylons and telephone lines. Voices shot through the air, 'Oujda. This is Oujda.' The coach went into a deep tunnel where crowds of luggage porters and children were impatiently waiting. Children were there for easy pockets to pick, but for the luggage porters, it was their livelihood. Bags were thrown to the ground, and the luggage porters grabbed them in mid-air. Snatching from each other was followed by swearing, 'Curse be on your father's house!' or 'Curse on your mother!'

Hearing these words, I realised that I was not only in Morocco, but also a bit of Algeria. Whenever a luggage porter put his hand on a piece of luggage, it became his. He wouldn't ask, 'Where are you going?' but would demand, 'Follow me . . .'

'Where?' shouted a confused, angry passenger. Like a crocodile taking its victim deep into the water, a luggage porter would grab the luggage, take it away, and the owner could only follow. Once the traveller was isolated from the rest, the bargaining would start at the porter's leisure and pleasure.

I was of no interest to the luggage porters. I was a child rather than a rich traveller, and not worth fighting over. While everybody rushed out, chasing luggage porters to find out who had their luggage, I stayed inside. I searched for a coach to Fez, but there was no sign of one. No coaches were coming or going. This was not like the *Parada* (coach station) in Nador – nothing like it – there was no rushing or pushing. Nador was the New York of the North. In Nador, I had heard people and understood them; I understood nothing here.

Soon the coach station became deserted. Only a few boys and porters paced in and out. They all craned their necks to stare at me. I wondered if they often used their necks this way, making them so long, or if it was something to do with me. *Probably they're wondering what a strange creature I am – they think I'm* mahboul *(mentally disturbed)*. I scared them off, and they gave me peace. There were so many boys outside, young and old, big and small, short and tall, and they were all jumping around like monkeys. *What would I do if they were to snatch my case?* The thought made me nervous.

I was standing still, confused, trying to find my way onward. It was one o'clock in the afternoon. The cement in the street was cooked by the sun, and the street was semi-deserted. As I went out, an old man in a chariot pulled by a donkey passed by. The donkey stopped in the middle of the street and stretched its neck down to smell a dropping from another donkey. I yelled at the man for directions to the coach station to Fez. He gave me directions, but they were very difficult to follow – so many lefts and rights – that I failed to remember them all. I followed the directions scrupulously, which took me about three-quarters of an hour. After that, I didn't know where I was or where I was going.

Suddenly a herd of women came out of a house and swept

past me. They were all wearing white clothes, their heads and faces covered, only one eye showing. Some looked fat, others short and pregnant. One hand was holding the headdress, and the other hand supporting the belly. I had never seen anything like it. Neither my mother nor my sisters nor anyone I knew had ever dressed in that strange way and tried to walk. I advanced toward them and they stirred away from me. 'Where is the coach station, please?' I asked them.

They all shouted at me, 'Clear off!'

I wondered if I looked like a thief or a pirate. Certainly they couldn't think I was looking for a woman, could they? They moved like a herd of sheep and seemed to think I was a fox. I stood still and watched as they waddled like penguins past me.

By that time, it was nearly two o'clock. The street became suddenly flooded with pedestrians. People emerged from every hole, every building and every door. *How were all those buildings able to hold that enormous number of people without exploding?* I wondered. They came in a rush, as if escaping from a fire. Two o'clock was a social phenomenon. After a heavy meal and a short, disorientating siesta, the people waddled back to work.

I wished I had not followed the old man's directions. The street became swollen with cars. Mercedes taxis passed by, but their fares were beyond me. Car drivers shook their fists at anyone or anything that stopped or slowed their movement. Maniacal drivers were angry, threw their cigarettes out of the windows, and shouted at the driver of a small chariot pulled by a dark donkey sandwiched between cars. It was fortunate that it was a donkey, as a horse wouldn't have tolerated all the beeping of horns. Neither the driver nor the donkey seemed disturbed by all those agitated drivers, and he turned out to be the same man who had gotten me lost. He was an old-looking man whose face had been disfigured by sun and hard work. The sun had dug into his face and folded his skin, but it hadn't killed his toothless smile. He recognised me and pulled over.

'Quick! Quick! Put your luggage in and jump on!' the old man yelled to me.

Not sure where I was going or where the man was taking me, I felt an immediate relief from carrying the heavy luggage. I didn't speak to the man, didn't trust him completely and was uneasy about his charge. The old man drove his chariot straight to the coach station, and just before coming to the front door of the garage, he lifted his hand and said, 'Here it is! Goodbye!'

I picked up my luggage, jumped out, and said, 'Thank you, sir. How much do I owe you now?'

'Nothing.' he said.

8

With its lack of light, the coach station reminded me of the cave at Moulouya inhabited by the disturbed hermit, and the one between Makran and Tassamat. The floor was cement and darkened with huge stains of dried petrol and oil. Now and again, here and there, dim lights went on and off. Lines of coaches of different colours and sizes were carefully manoeuvring in and out. The pungent stench of gasoline penetrated my nostrils and my eyes watered. Nausea grabbed me and I wondered, *Am I on the right path?* Stifling my doubts, I roamed around like a vagabond making sense of it all, trying to find the coach to Fez. Everybody but me seemed to know where they were going.

People had their heads tilted, looking up. I thought they were praying, but in reality, they were figuring out the signs. By searching and asking the way, I found the pigeon-holed ticket desk for the coach to Fez.

'I'd like to buy a ticket to Fez, please,' I asked, feeling relieved.

'No tickets left,' a man with a low, gruff voice answered.

Shaken, I shuffled backwards. Just behind me, a young ticket-scalper whispered in my ear, 'I have a ticket.'

'How much?' I asked.

'Double price.'

'Too expensive,' I replied.

'No! It's a ticket for the front of the coach!' he exclaimed and went away with a grumpy face.

I raced, caught up with him and bought the ticket. With the ticket in hand, I went back to the ticket desk and asked for the departure time.

'The coach leaves at one o'clock in the morning,' murmured a middle-aged man, his eyes fixed on the floor.

A myriad of voices bombarded my ears. From one corner came what sounded like an echo of a chorus: 'a, a, o, o, i, i, n, n'. At six o'clock, the crowd deserted the station. Looking for a safe corner, I heard again the repetitive 'a, a, o, o, i, i, n, n'. The source of the singsong was three boys. One, older than the other two, was conducting and the others were repeating, like parrots.

Noticing me listening curiously to them from a distance, the oldest boy jumped up and shouted, 'Is my teaching correct?'

I said, 'Yes,' but the truth was that I had no idea what it was all about. I edged closer to their encampment and sat on my duffel bag to listen.

Delighted with himself, the boy returned to his teaching. From time to time, he would become aggressive toward his brother. The irony was that he taught Arabic grammar, but didn't know the language itself. He spoke Tarifit. Whenever he got tired of teaching grammar, he switched to liturgical matters such as hygiene and women's clothes, as they could be sexually provocative.

Just as nervous as I was about the journey, one of the younger boys asked me, 'Where are you going?'

'To Fez,' I said, 'At one o'clock. A long time from now.'

'That's where we're going, to school,' he answered quickly.

'Where is there to wait until one o'clock?' I asked.

'In a café,' one said.

'No, they're closed,' I replied. 'We should rent a room in a hotel,' I suggested.

'Good idea,' responded the oldest boy, whose name was Kamil.

We picked up our luggage, left the station and headed to the *medina*, or old town; a poor, crowded area. Unfortunately, wherever we went, the hotels were full. Also, our looks worked against us. I had unruly hair, wide trousers and a *jellabah*. Kamil limped, had a skinned head and wore a woollen hat that looked as if he had knitted it himself. His brother, Moussa, was thin and short, but with the voice of a middle-aged man. Samir, their cousin, had no hat, was wearing glasses, didn't open his mouth, and looked just like a cat trying to jump on a mouse.

The problem was exacerbated by the Algerian war. Refugees had flooded the town and occupied every room. We scurried up and down the dark streets, looking like demented patients escaped from a mental institution. Desperate, we took a risk and ventured into the darkest slums of the town where we came upon a hotel in a narrow, twisted street.

It was a terraced house with a very tiny low door. To get inside, one had to step deep down. The hall was spacious and had five or six rooms, mostly on the ground floor. All the doors were wide open, some for air, others for the occupants to see who was going in or out. Radio noise was pouring from every room. Music from different channels shook the walls, but no one seemed bothered. Famished and needing to escape our hired hell, we dumped our bags and went out to look for a place where we could have a meal.

Looking for a restaurant, we came to the main street; it had an ornate Catholic cathedral in the middle. Deciding what to eat was not a problem for us. Anything solid would be tasty and appreciated. Aware of our budget, we danced up and down the street looking for a bargain. To attract clients, restaurants had their menus posted outside on mannequins. Menus were written in French; what was written in Arabic and Moroccan dialect didn't make sense to us either. Moussa started moaning; he wanted to get a meal quickly, but he refused to pay the posted price. Embarrassed, his brother told him to shut up, but to no avail.

One waiter met us outside and asked, 'Can I help?'

This was a good sign of Moroccan hospitality, we thought, and rushed inside. The interior was chic, and the aroma of onions cooking whetted our appetites beyond our ability to resist.

The entrance opened into a bar, full of people drinking, sitting on high stools. I wondered, *How can anyone sit on a wobbly high chair, dangle his legs and drink?*

The restaurant was nearly full and most tables were occupied by French clients. In one corner sat a French family with a Franciscan priest. He was drinking wine, smoking a long, thick cigar and looked as though he had a bottle in his mouth with smoke coming out. He was wearing a brown rug-like gown with no underclothes, I thought. Moussa wouldn't stop talking about how strange the man was. I was appalled to learn that the man was a priest. Drinking and smoking was, for me, the last thing a religious leader should do.

We hoped to be treated like everybody in the restaurant, but the waiter seated us in a back corner, isolated from the rest. He brought the menu and slapped it on the table. 'Five minutes to decide!' he said.

'We came in as clients, and end as hostages,' I said. 'What would you suggest?' I asked the waiter five minutes later.

'Soup or salad, *tagine* or fish,' he said, nose in the air.

We all shouted at once, 'Soup and *tagine*, please.'

We knew what to expect – we were Moroccan. Moroccan soup, *harira*, was renowned for its taste and nutritious value. It was thick, made of chickpeas, onion and barley. White flour and sometimes a few pieces of meat – chicken, lamb or beef – were also added. The onion and meat were first boiled, then simmered over a low fire for a long time. This was supposed to allow ingredients to release their flavour and mix with each other. Seasoning was unsophisticated: a little salt, cumin, ginger and often pepper.

Tagine was the tastiest common Moroccan meal. Like *harira*, it varied from region to region and often from family to family. It could be made with either meat or vegetables. The meat had to be thoroughly washed and dried, then mixed with olive oil before being put into the pot. The meat was never thrown into hot olive oil, but fried very gently on its own, with onion, tomato, peppers and garlic added to it. When the meat, the onion and the peppers looked brown, a small amount of water was added, but never boiling or hot water. It had to be room temperature. The amount of water added could either make it or spoil it. The safe measure was one and a half centimetres above the surface of the food. The seasonings were usually cumin, pepper, coriander, almonds, olives or prunes, and salt. Potatoes, chopped in half, were often added to the *tagine* at the same time as the water. The fire was slow, the pot was covered, and when the water boiled down to the surface of the meat, it meant that everything was done. It had to be cooled naturally. Bread was served with both *tagine* and *harira*.

Nothing resembling what we knew was served in this restaurant. The soup was just lukewarm, salty water. I complained; the waiter gave me a mocking look and said, '*C'est du potage*, boy.' (He meant French soup.)

The waiter brought a few pieces of bread, but with no substance, white and misleading to the eye. They looked good, but were in fact full of air. I grabbed a piece, and it disintegrated between my fingers, as it was old. The waiter brought a brown pot, locally designed, and dropped it on the table. 'Here is your *tagine*, boys,' he said.

I picked up the ladle and stirred the *tagine*. All I could find were two bony pieces of meat, more suitable for a dog than for hungry boys. The rest was mushrooms, gravy and salt. Intimidated by the waiter and the owner, we just asked for more bread. The waiter was unhappy and said he would charge extra.

'I've never seen people as hungry as you!' he said.

To crown the meal, the waiter brought a dessert as part of

the fixed menu: four small mandarins, old, shrunken, and two of them were rotten inside.

'Can you change these two oranges for us?' I asked.

'Sorry,' he said. 'Not every number you pick for the lottery wins you the prize.' He made a U-turn and marched away. We divided the two edible mandarins, paid and left. The waiter was happy to see our backs.

Bemused, we headed back to the hotel room; we were anxious about the time and worried we might miss the coach, the only one linking Oujda to Fez. Moussa was a slow walker, and Kamil shouted, 'Don't you know where you are? Move your legs and hurry!'

As we stepped into the hotel, the owner rushed out of her room and shouted, 'Boys! Where were you?'

Music was bellowing from every room, and we were not sure if we had heard what she said. Her voice melted into the music, she charged toward me and peered at each one of us. 'Where were you, boys?' she shouted with a louder voice.

The toughness of her voice and the harshness of her attitude didn't match her elegance and beauty. Unlike many women that I had come across in my rural life, she was sparklingly beautiful. She wore a skirt and low-cut top. She was tall and elegant. Her head was covered with golden hair, and her breasts were planted on a broad chest. To see such a woman was, for me, a gift from heaven, but also a wicked witch from hell. My confused expression inspired her to ask more questions. 'Where were you?' she asked for a third time.

'We were in a restaurant,' I replied.

'Which one?' she asked.

'The one with a posted menu on the corner.'

'Bad choice,' she said. 'Are you related?'

Kamil quickly answered, 'This is my brother, and this is my cousin.'

'No one could guess you are brothers. You have different noses. One juts out and the other is flat,' she chuckled.

'He's my half-brother,' Moussa cut in even before her mouth was shut.

'How many wives does your father have?'

'Four,' Moussa said.

'Do they all live in one house?' she asked.

'Yes,' he replied.

'In one room!' laughed Samir.

'*Lalla* (Madame),' I said, 'we are travelling to Fez and our coach is at one o'clock in the morning.'

Not happy to be interrupted, she sized me up and down and said, 'I think you are running away from home. What have you done?'

I refused to answer her questions, as I didn't want anyone to know that I had been a shepherd. Agitated, I repeated, 'We need to go.'

Outraged, she bellowed, 'I have the power to cancel your coach trip or make it late. I am the chief witch of Oujda and Magnea, in Algeria.'

Moussa, who talked all the time and had no gate between his mind and his mouth, said, 'Witches and witch doctors go to hell.'

She smiled and said, 'Boys, boys, you have a lot to learn. Our task is to help and guide lost souls. Religious people take care only of themselves and we take care of those whose dark nights have no end.' She said to me, 'I know you are anxious. Pick up your luggage and hurry.'

'Thank you,' I said.

She looked at me and said, 'I will ask all our members to burn the demon eyes for you so no demons will haunt you. Our congress will be held shortly in Rabat-Sale.'

'Why Rabat-Sale?' asked Moussa, curiously.

'That is where our wizard prince lives,' she said, her eyes focused on me. 'If you go to Sale, ask for him by name – Sfruy. Tell him *Lalla* Zahra will attend the congress, and she sends warm greetings . . .'

'Why not write to him?' I asked her.

'We never write or phone,' she said. 'We communicate viscerally, telepathically or by word-of-mouth, call it what you will.'

'What if someone lies?' I asked.

'We know what is a lie and what is true. In fact, lies die before they reach us. We are rarely disturbed by lies.'

I grabbed my bag and case and said, 'Goodbye. We must be going.' Everybody followed at lightning speed, leaving Zahra in mid-sentence. I couldn't forget Zahra's image, the way she had dressed, behaved and talked to us.

'Who was that woman?' Kamil asked loudly.

'She's a witch,' I answered.

'No!' said Moussa. 'She's mad!'

'She can't be a witch,' argued Kamil. 'She didn't turn stones into figs or dates. She didn't even know where we were! She is neither mad nor a witch.'

Exploding loudly, Samir accused us of being naïve. 'She's a whore!' he said. 'She showed her best – breasts and legs!'

'No, she isn't,' we all indignantly jumped to her defence.

'Do you really believe anything she said?' asked Samir.

'No,' I answered, trying not to sound naïve. Because of her, we nearly missed our coach.

The coach, engine revving, was already stationed in the street and waiting to pick up late arrivals. Two-thirds of the coach was full and most travellers were foreigners, mainly French and a few Americans, to judge by their clothes: Western and casual. We watched them with some envy and jealousy, but also with some self-pity. The French, in all kinds of cars, dropped their relatives and friends at the station. They looked very well-fed and well-dressed, and we looked skinny and like tramps.

The coach was a massive and imposing Volvo. The driver was a young black man whose voice was thunderous. He could pierce an eardrum with just a few angry words. Passengers called him *Saharaui*, which meant he came from the Sahara. His assistant kept us well at bay and believed we had no tickets.

'Chancers,' he murmured. 'Your tickets!'

Tickets, for us, were our passports, something too precious to lose. With the flick of a finger, each of us handed him a ticket. They had been in our pockets like guns – to be drawn in an emergency. He examined each of them and read its content with utmost care.

'Your luggage,' he shouted abruptly. 'How many kilos does your luggage weigh?'

'This is my luggage,' I said, 'but I don't know about kilos.'

He lifted my case, expecting it to be very heavy, but to his disappointment, it was very light. Nevertheless, he was determined to weigh it. 'Over nine kilos, you must pay,' he said.

The conductor was watching and eavesdropping. He butted in and said, 'It doesn't need to be weighed.'

'I am still going to weigh it,' said his assistant. The relationship between the assistant and the conductor didn't look friendly. The conductor slunk away. The assistant took my case and put it on an earth scale. Fortunately, it weighed less than nine kilos. I noticed French passengers didn't go through the scrutiny we had.

'Could we all sit together?' I asked.

'Your ticket decides,' the assistant said, morosely. With no more questions, we boarded the coach. Kamil, Moussa and Samir took their seats near the back of the coach, but beside each other. My seat was further forward. It was, somehow, a privilege because of the double price I had paid. I found myself surrounded by French-speaking travellers. The few Moroccans in the front mishmashed French and Moroccan dialect.

My seat was by the window, with one empty seat beside me. The moment I sat down, a French woman arrived. She was three times my size. Her round face, short hair and black leather jacket gave little indication of her sex. It was only by gazing at her legs and shoes that I was sure she was female. The heel of her shoe looked as thin as a pencil and as high as a ladder. I wondered how she could walk without tumbling on her face. *Can she run if she needs to?* I wondered.

She sat beside me, flashed me a broad smile and said something, but I didn't understand it. As she settled in, she pulled a bunch of magazines from her bag and plunged her head into the middle of one of them. I wished I could do the same, lose myself in reading. I leaned over from time to time to see what was in her magazine, but all I could understand were the beautifully-coloured photos.

It was the first time I had been close to a European woman and the first time I had seen a woman's legs and knees. I admired her sense of freedom and wished my mother were more like her. Looking at her, I was convinced that God did not love me more than her, or that I was going to heaven and she to hell, as I was already in hell. I doubted the veracity of what my mother had told me in Algeria – 'Hell for them and heaven for us'. Philosophical questions grabbed me, but I lacked words. I had only feelings. Nothing seemed to me to be rational. If it were, my parents would have organised my life and I wouldn't be here. But not everything was absurd; if it were, I wouldn't be wending my way to search for a school, thrusting myself into the unknown. *Neither does it swing from rational to absurd*, I realised. A vague guilt seized me. I shouldn't poke at my faith, for it was all I had.

The road from Oujda to Fez was pretty rough with plenty of bends and holes in the road to make some travellers motion sick, and leaving at one o'clock in the morning was unsettling for most. The coach left the station; only a few dim street lights were visible before plunging into full darkness. The light in the coach was switched off, and I felt as if I were floating through the air. There was loud, collective yawning, sometimes with a leader.

There was nothing to see, nothing to talk about. The coach

seemed to lose all gravity, and the travellers seemed to lose connection with their heads, which were bobbing forward, backward, right and left. Unfortunately, one girl was very sick over a couple. Harsh words were exchanged, but finally all was settled with dignity. The driver was asked to slow down, but no one knew if he did or not.

Everybody snoozed. The French woman fell asleep and blocked the aisle despite her desperate effort to keep herself awake. I saw her struggling with herself and, without thinking, put my right hand on her shoulder and pointed to the window. In a zombie-like state, she thought there was something I wanted her to see. In fact there was nothing but darkness. As she looked puzzled, I stood up and invited her to take my seat in exchange for hers. She gave me a real womanly smile mixed with French charm and gratitude. She mumbled a few words that didn't make any sense to me.

Happy to exchange, she rested comfortably against the window and leaned back in her seat. That didn't resolve the problem of her overflow. She became uncoordinated, spread her legs and pushed me out of my seat. There wasn't enough space to rest her arm, and whatever space there was, she occupied. I felt like a dwarf. To change her position, she laid her head back and, a few seconds later, her mouth opened wide. She started to emit some amazing noises. They reminded me of the braying of the donkey I had left behind. I couldn't resist my curiosity, and my discomfort forced me to turn and look at her. Her chin was moving up and down like a yo-yo. Her mouth looked deep and dark, but it was lit up by a number of gold teeth in the back of her mouth. To have teeth built with gold meant, to me, that she was rich. In Kebdana tradition, gold was the most important component of a dowry, which was exchanged for virginity.

A massive woman sitting diagonally two rows in front of me kept turning around and peering at the French woman. She could have been Jewish or Egyptian; her clothes were neither French nor Moroccan. She was wearing a long skirt and her head was wrapped with a black cloth, the excess of which hung like a tail down her back and swayed every time she moved her head. Her constant turning around reminded me of a dog wagging its tail.

'Give her a shake!' she hissed at me. She kept poking her fist in the air, looking at me and grimacing. I thought the passenger behind the French woman would be the first to be disturbed, as she had laid her head back. The Jewish/Egyptian woman was getting aggressive, poking the air and peering at me.

To avoid her constant peering and gesturing, I closed my eyes and pretended to sleep, but mimicking sleep turned into reality. Left with only one third of my seat, I rested my head against the seat in front of me and didn't awaken until I found my right leg paralysed. I screamed lightly, 'Ow!' My right leg felt dead, completely detached from me, and I had no control over it. A few seconds later, I felt more pain. I had the feeling of being invaded by nasty biting ants devouring my leg from inside. I checked several times to see if my leg was alive. Had there been an emergency evacuation, I wouldn't have been able to save my life.

To avoid my right leg or any other body part going into

a coma again, I forced myself to stay awake. Pretending to remain still, I started pushing the French woman slightly and gently out of my seat. Bit by bit, I regained a part of my seat. That was enough to allow me to rest my head against the back of my own seat. I tried to keep myself awake, but in spite of my efforts, I fell asleep again, albeit in a different position this time.

At dawn, I awakened. We were still travelling and the sky had already shaken off the darkness of the night. Some people were squirming and stretching, but others were busy either smoking or lighting their cigarettes. Covered by a cloud of smoke, I felt nauseated. I had never felt or smelled anything like it. I turned, glanced around, and spied a very thin, gaunt man smoking a pipe from the corner of his mouth and held by his back teeth. He reminded me of the family dog, Dargan, grabbing a bone between his teeth and running away, which always meant no one should mess with him. What was erupting out of the man's mouth entirely drowned my head. I felt choked. *Hashish*? I wondered.

The coach seats were like a cluster of volcanoes emitting smoke, but outside everything looked peaceful and perfect. The sky was getting brighter by the second as the sun rose higher and higher. At the beginning, it looked like fresh, unpolluted blood, neither too red nor too pale. As the sun rose, the moon shied away.

The constant smoke disturbed me and kept me from enjoying the morning smile of nature. My wriggling woke the French woman. She suddenly opened her eyes and looked around quizzically as though she didn't know where she was or where she was going. She pulled her wallet out of her pocket and displayed a tiny lopsided mirror in the middle of it. She moved the mirror around, checking her hair and every part of her nose. She leaned down and grabbed a long, fat case from under her feet and put it on her lap. Her case was a mini laboratory, full of all kinds of make-up and colourful things. She proceeded to decorate her face beautifully, starting with her lips, making them a vibrant colour between red and maroon, which immediately changed her looks and age. To smooth the painting on her lips, she licked them like a cat. She pulled out a fluffy brush, like the one barbers used to soap clients' beards before shaving, only hers was slightly smaller and thinner. She dipped her delicate brush into a small jar, pulled out some yellow powder, and brushed her face with it. This was like Hollywood for me. I thought after a sleep, especially in the morning, the first thing to do was to wash one's face to get rid of the dust and the debris of the night, and the coach was particularly full of smoke and dust. I had seen cats using their own saliva to clean their faces and wondered if this woman was less intelligent and less clean than a cat. My jaw dropped when I saw her plucking hairs out of her nose.

Watching the French woman getting covered with pipe smoke didn't stop my worrying. Soon I would be in Fez and homeless. It was a great relief for me when the driver announced a stop.

'Taza!' he announced. 'We'll be stopped for precisely three-quarters of an hour,' he added. 'The coach is not going to wait for latecomers. We have to be in Fez on time,' he warned.

Some travellers shook their heads and others craned their

necks and looked around. A few well-to-do looking people grabbed their luggage and brought it down from the overhead racks. Everybody was happy to have a break from the rattling, nauseating coach. The French woman collected everything belonging to her as if it were the final stop. Obviously, she didn't trust anyone on the coach. Curiously, even when the coach was running, she checked all her belongings under her feet and above her head whenever she opened her eyes.

Shortly after the driver's announcement, the coach pulled up in the front of a few small huts on the outskirts of the town. Coffee and tea were served there, and several cars and passengers were scattered around, but there was no toilet. Passengers scuttled around like ants to relieve themselves, but there was no paper, no water – not even a hiding place. For me this was no drama, as I had never used paper or water, just small stones picked up at random from the ground to wipe my bum. I had learned from an early age to run as far away as I could to find a private spot where small stones were available and abundant. It wasn't dangerous during the daytime, but it could be lethal during the night. It was always possible to make a mistake, to pick up a snake or a dangerous spider instead of a stone. My cousin Jamila had picked up the head of a dangerous snake. She had been bitten, and her right hand and left leg had been paralysed for the rest of her life.

Most travellers were enjoying breakfast. An abundance of croissants, eggs, hot tea, hot coffee and milk was offered by the main café hut and street vendors.

'I want a coffee with milk and a croissant,' I said.

Moussa thought coffee with milk and a croissant was rather

extravagant, and the fact that I had thought of it made him somewhat jealous. 'Why not wait until Fez?' he asked.

Watching Moussa's face, I didn't want to give the impression that I had more money than I did or more than they had, so I passed on the croissant. But Samir was angry and thought Moussa's economising was unreasonable after a long night in a rattling coach.

'Avoid croissants,' Kamil butted in. 'Pick a *pain au chocolat*. A croissant is just a bubble of air. You need a bag full of them to settle your churning stomach.'

I didn't know the difference between a croissant and a *pain au chocolat*, but the aroma was appetising. A croissant appeared bigger and fatter than a *pain au chocolat*.

A street vendor threw himself in the middle of us and said, 'Help yourselves. Pastries, tea, coffee, boiled eggs with salt, pepper and cumin. No charge. All free.' Nobody believed him. We just looked at him in silence. 'Decide what you want. I will be back shortly,' he added.

He went away, selling his victuals to other travellers. We called a second street trader and asked prices. The first trader rushed at him and shouted, 'Don't take an order! Someone has already bought their breakfast. I'm just waiting for them to make up their minds.'

Puzzled, the second trader slunk away. We were equally bemused. 'Look! Take whatever you like! The French woman over there will pay your breakfasts. You can pick whatever you want from my tray. Help yourselves!' he emphasised.

I picked coffee with milk and a *petit pain au chocolat*, and the others did the same. We didn't trust the vendor, were frugal and prepared to pay, but he didn't ask for payment. He went straight to the French lady who had sat beside me in the coach. She paid the bill and waved to us.

We couldn't make sense of her generosity. Because I had sat beside her, Samir expected me to provide an explanation, but I had none.

The stop changed the travellers' moods; what a cup of tea or coffee and croissant could do! Travellers befriended each other, but there were still a few sad faces, although nobody bothered with them. I returned to my seat, and the French woman was already settled. I felt anxious and embarrassed; a woman, let alone a French woman, paying for a man wasn't in my tradition. Before I sat down, she muttered a few words, but I had no idea what those sounds meant.

Sitting beside her again on the jostling coach, looking at her, I didn't know if she was married or not, but I wished I were old enough or in a position to marry her. Her massive heart swallowed my tiny one, but my sweet dream was swiftly drowned by chaotic voices shouting, 'Bab Ftouh!' and people peering out of the windows.

9

We were greeted by a huge funnel of spiralling dust clouds rising high into the air, enveloping the coach and hiding the gate in a mass of grey. Shocked at what I was witnessing, I turned around to check on my new friends. Samir's face looked old, worn and depressed, with trembling lips. As if a snowball had smashed into his face, Moussa's mouth was wide open, in a desperate struggle to catch his breath. Watching Samir and Moussa drowning in shock and despair, Kamil threw out a lifeline – 'This is Bab Ftouh, boys!'

Anxiously staring through the window, I was gripped by a cold, icy feeling of disappointment. All we could see was a high, crumbling wall made with soil and sand, but full of holes. *This looks like a besieged town*, I thought.

The full horror of the scene caught me when I looked to my left – a high shrine surrounded by a massive graveyard in the middle of a hill. The shrine door was painted green, yet there was nothing peaceful about it, and it opened onto Bab Ftouh. *Was this some ancient ritualistic design or pure coincidence?* I wondered. Women lumbered from Bab Ftouh and went straight up to the shrine, while others descended from it and disappeared through the gate into a black hole – like ants, but there was no sense of rush or urgency.

Shrines and graveyards I had seen before, but I had never seen men, women and children wandering through them. Some were sitting on the gravestones and using them as tables for their picnics! From an early age, I was taught that a cemetery was a silent city of souls. Every person carried a seed of immortality under his armpit, and his seed was indestructible. Although it was detached from the body that was buried under the ground, the living seed preserved all its prime character-istics: life, feeling and memories. The seed would bloom at some point. It would begin like a mushroom in the form of a human being, but footless, armless and neckless with the head looking up to the sky. That was how resurrection had been explained to me and I believed it implicitly.

Disappearing behind the gate of Bab Ftouh and inside the old town, the medina, I didn't know what would happen next; certainly nothing was as expected, and the streets were not paved with marble. No palm trees lined the way, nor in fact were there any trees to hide the billowing dust. The coach squirmed through a narrow winding street, and the driver had to fight peddlers for every inch.

The road ended a few hundred metres away from the gate and in front of a dilapidated garage, which was small and narrow, but deep like a vault. Parked in front of the garage, the driver stood up and shouted, 'Get off! Bab Ftouh travellers!'

I stood quickly and glanced at the French woman, waved goodbye and wished I could speak French. She nodded with a gentle smile.

In the chaos, luggage had been lost or mixed up. 'My luggage is at the back!' yelled an angry traveller to the porter on the roof. 'Open your eyes! My bag is right beside you!' shrieked another. 'Mine isn't that colour!' screamed a woman. 'I know you have no brain!'

The porter became confused amidst the shouts and personal insults. We secured our luggage and turned to Kamil, a returning student, as our guru. Older and more experienced, he had been to the medina before, but seemed to be struck by amnesia and remembered nothing of his previous life here.

'Kamil,' I said, 'we need a roof over our heads.'

'Yes,' agreed Samir.

'*Funduqs* are the places to find a cheap room,' instructed Kamil.

'Do you know of any *funduqs* nearby?' I asked a porter passing by on his mule.

'Yes,' he said. With the possible exception of Kamil, we didn't know what *funduqs* looked like or even exactly what they were, only that they had cheap rooms for hire. 'Good *funduqs* are in the new French town,' the porter said. 'You will need to take a taxi there. They are expensive, though. They are for the Americans, the owners of the dollar! Most *funduqs* in Medina are no more than brothels.'

'We are not Americans,' I said, 'but we don't want to stay in a brothel either! What else do you suggest?'

'There isn't much left, son,' he said sympathetically. 'Ah,' he muttered to himself. 'I know of one or two places,' he said. 'Though they are far away, they are worth a try. But, there is one close by we should try first.'

I cheered with relief at our close escape from a brothel. I didn't, however, trust the porter straight away. 'How much do you charge?' I asked.

'Charge is according to the distance! Can't you see who I am?' he said wearily, looking at me. 'I am a black *Saharaui*. I charge the right price and people pay me for it. I wouldn't have done this job for forty years otherwise! This is my fifth mule. They all perished from hard work and overload. If this present mule dies, I will stop, but maybe I will die first! I am old and frail. If I'm first, my mule will be orphaned, left to starve.' He gently pulled the reins of his mule and loaded our luggage. '*Zid! Zid!* (Move on! Move on!)' The mule cocked its ear, head down and refused to move. Familiar with the pain, it scurried when it saw the whip twirling in the air.

Overwhelmed by the porter, we followed blindly. Despite the narrow, crowded street, he moved fast, very fast. The mule stumbled several times, but never fell. We scurried behind him like mad. At the corner of a dark, twisted tunnel, Moussa collided with a veiled woman who was waddling behind her husband. She stumbled and yelled.

'Barbarians should be kept out of Fez!' shouted her husband. Twice the size of Moussa, he lost his temper, lurched on him, grabbed and tore his shirt, then pushed him against the wall. Moussa gathered himself and punched the man straight on the nose. To everyone's horror, the man's nose became a fountain of blood. At the speed of light, Moussa lunged at him again, pushed him to the ground and trampled over him. The event and the speed at which it had happened terrified me. Words had ended in blood. Nobody butted in to help.

The wife shouted, 'Scum! Thugs!'

Kamil and I pulled Moussa off the man and sprinted to catch up with the porter, who had been waiting for the fight to finish. *God forbid I ever fight Moussa*, I thought to myself.

The porter took us to the nearest *funduq*. It was built in the middle of a poor, narrow, dark, busy street. A man emerged, his face a patchwork of varying pigmentation, with beady eyes staring out of the incongruous whole. He looked surprised, twitched and glanced at me, but looked disturbed by the sight of Moussa. Apprehensively, I peered inside the building. A clothesline dangled in front of each room. A few seconds later, two women emerged from the back and moved to the front door. Both of them were wearing short nightgowns, half-naked. I realised we had been taken to the wrong place and urged the porter to try somewhere else.

'Are you prepared to go farther away from here?' he asked.

'Yes,' I responded.

He took us straightaway to the other side gate of the town, Bab Guissa. Confused, we followed him down a dark alleyway. 'Here we are. This is another *funduq*,' he said.

Two men emerged, the owner and the caretaker. The snooty owner was unmistakeably a city dweller; he had light skin and was wearing traditional Fezzi clothes: the Fez hat with swishing tassel and yellow, clomping mules. His assistant was an Arab, a country man, rough like a cob, short, wide, and wrapped in a very heavy woollen *jellabah*.

We were raw enough to take anything, and the owner was desperate for cash. The *funduq* was a dilapidated complex. On the ground floor, it stabled between five and seven horses. Big piles of raw sheepskins covered practically two-thirds of the courtyard. A steaming stench, worse than a frog's puff, circulated through the air. There were two men sweating and toiling over the hot tanning vats. A blind woman and a crippled boy were busily involved in pulling the wool. There was a tiny toilet with a teeny hole in the middle, but no door. To keep people away, one had to make noises, whistle or sing. The *funduq* had a few rooms on the first floor. Some were rented to artisans, some to shoemakers, and the rest were for cursed tenants like us. Desperate, we hired the room.

'Follow me!' said the caretaker with a loud, booming voice. 'Here is the key.' He stomped down the stairs.

I opened the door tentatively, but Samir dived straight in; he jumped about and shouted, 'Look! Look!' Cockroaches were jumping and crawling everywhere. Samir grimaced and shook his head, indicating that he didn't want the room, and in actual fact neither did I. Looking at Samir, Moussa murmured, 'Well, what did you expect?'

What Samir had seen was just the tip of a filthy iceberg. I switched the light on, and the room immediately turned into a blaze of fire, the dancing flames made of what seemed to be thousands of copper-coloured cockroaches jumping about in the rubbish, which filled the room. Samir, in shock, kept moaning softly to himself. We deliberated leaving but it was getting late. It was either a filthy room or a night on the street, and however unpleasant the cockroaches were, we thought we would be a lot safer here than on the street where we had seen gangs roaming this part of town after dark.

I whispered to Samir in the hope of calming him, 'Let's

stay tonight and look for other places tomorrow. We can tidy and clean up the room.'

The room had been used as a dumping ground: hard boards, hundreds of sheets of paper of all kinds, odd pieces of leather and the remainder of a long-since eaten watermelon all littered the floor. As a team, we worked hard, throwing everything out, sparing nothing. The change in the room was unbelievable; the bare rectangle suddenly looked spacious, if still not clean, as we had no brushes, brooms, water or soap, let alone disinfectant.

Like refugees, each one of us occupied a corner of the now-barren room. Despite the conditions, we were pleased to be in Fez, and even happier not to be in the street. It was dark, and we were ravenously hungry. I ventured outside alone to buy two loaves of white bread and a handful of olives, dumped in salt and smelly garlic. I hurried back to the room with the shopping in my hands, but I found the bread had little taste and was not at all filling.

This was too much for Samir. He wept and ranted. I buried my face in an old manuscript on Arabic grammar and pretended to read.

Seconds later, we heard a thump on the door, and the caretaker's voice boomed out, 'Switch off the light! Switch off the light!'

'No!' I shouted, but nobody supported me.

Dawn burst with the cobblers' hammering. In a tiny room with no window adjacent to ours, several cobblers, sitting side by side, rubbing shoulders, shook the walls with hammers in their hands and anvils on the floor. It sounded like machine-gun fire. I got up, went out, and peered through their door.

Not happy with my staring, one spat and said, 'Push off!'

One of them shouted, 'He's our neighbour! Four of them!'

The first man retorted, 'Trash!'

Their hammering, however, was nothing in comparison to their gigantic radio – very tall, one metre long and volume turned up to its max. The shoemakers were tireless workers and never had a complete day off. After work at the end of the day, they rushed to the auction market to sell their mules, but often came back with them, many scorned, unsold.

Alternative accommodation proved to be impossible. Three weeks passed, and we had found neither a better *funduq* nor discovered how to register at the school, much less take the entrance exams. Those were still looming.

Disorientated in this town with which I had nothing in common, I went out to find the headquarters of the Scientific Assembly of the school, whose Board was composed exclusively of those who, after years of study, had obtained their degrees from Kairaouine University. They were arrogant, dismissive and politically dangerous, but also masters of their subjects. They also played an important part in Moroccan culture, its judiciary system and its political history. As academics, they were ruthless. I could expect no charity from these people, but had to prove I was worthy of being given a chance.

The office was on an unassuming corner of a noisy street, facing an open square filled with an army of silversmiths working their trade, feverishly hammering, looking demented, arms flying, engraving tea pots and trays. The noise permeated the surrounding area like an out-of-tune orchestra. While some artisans were working silver, others were dipping wool into large vats of dyes of different hues, then hanging the yarns over cords strung from tree to tree. Watching the artisans made me feel like a confident tourist rather than the lost boy I was.

Clusters of people were coming in and out of a narrow wooden door ornate with black metalwork. Pushing the door open, I was surprised by what I found. What I had seen from the street gave no indication of the secret jewels hidden there; the Scientific Assembly was a mini-palace hidden out of sight of the world beyond. Beautiful ceramic tiles glistening like a copper-red carpet stretched out before me.

'Walking barefoot on the tiles would have been preferable to having them spoiled and demeaned by my scruffy shoes,' I told Samir and Moussa later.

The walls were covered in complex mosaics that spiralled like coordinated rainbows up to the grand ceiling twenty feet above. The huge doors leading off the room were covered in leather and brass. Mosaic sinks were built into the wall and jutted out in each corridor like mini-fountains, each of which had two streams of water; one ran constantly and the other was controlled by a tap. For me, used to travelling many miles to a half-dry well for water, the sight of so many continually running streams was nothing short of miraculous.

I waited nervously to register and find out when I could sit my entrance exams. By midday, it became clear there were unfortunately no staff except the caretaker on site, neither professors nor secretaries, and only empty corridors stretching endlessly into the distance. I was not the only boy left waiting; hundreds of boys of all ages gathered in the hall day after day to register, but the assembly remained a lifeless shell. I went back to our room, optimistic that I would be able to register the next day. The following day, however, turned out to be no different from the one before.

I settled into a boring routine. Each morning, deafened by the hammering cobblers, nostrils choked by the invasion of dust sweeping in from newly fluffed wool and the over-whelming smell of tannic acid from the tanners below, I grate-fully left our little room and journeyed to the Scientific Assembly, a daily pilgrimage that I made from September to mid-October. Alas, the assembly hall was always empty. During this time our diet was very poor, just white bread and tea with sugar. We all suffered, for about ten days on average, from bleeding constipation.

Kamil was shocked to discover that Moussa, in the space of a few short weeks, had become a heavy smoker. Moussa and Samir became close pals, and I felt like an outsider. They often wouldn't return to the room until late in the evening. I joined them and bought a full packet of cigarettes, but to my surprise and secret relief, I felt nauseated, dizzy and ill after my second cigarette. By smoking, I had broken my covenant with my mother; I had promised nicotine would never pass my lips. Even though I knew I would never smoke another cigarette, I couldn't help but feel ashamed and guilty.

After weeks of wasted journeys, though still hopeful, I become frustrated, and Samir was deeply embittered and despondent over the situation. He cursed his father, his grandfather, his great-grandfather and his religion. I felt deeply indignant to hear him swearing at religion, but Samir's anger came in waves, wave after wave, like a tsunami.

One morning, back from my daily pilgrimage, I found Kamil profusely coughing blood. 'Why does blood come out every time I cough?' he asked me, bewildered.

'Is this the first time?' I asked.

'No,' he replied hoarsely.

'You might have injured either your stomach or throat,' I suggested. 'Have you eaten anything rough? A piece of prickly pear?'

'No,' he shook his head.

'Mrs Malani often gave me olive oil at home to treat a wide range of ailments,' I said. 'I wonder if it would be of any use for you. Let me go and buy some olive oil; that might soothe your stomach and cough.' I hurried to the closest shop, which resembled a pigeon-hole, and asked for two hundred and fifty millilitres of olive oil.

'Do you have a bottle or a container to put the oil in?' asked the shopkeeper.

'No,' I replied.

From a dirty corner, he picked up an empty bottle and poured the oil into it. The bottle had no lid, so he tore a piece of an old newspaper, wadded it up, and stuck it into the bottle.

Back in the room, I advised Kamil to sup it from the bottle. The oil soothed his cough.

Unless we start to cook, the same thing might befall me, I thought to myself. Determined, I went to the bazaar and bought a second-hand kerosene cooker, but the owner was crooked. He tricked me into paying twice. I argued with him, but he shook his fist at me.

'Look where I am and who I am! I am a Fezzi in Fez!' he shouted. 'And you! Look where you're from! You don't speak Darija!' I backed off, feeling conned, humiliated and insulted.

The vegetable market wasn't far, and I bought some potatoes, onions and half a kilo of camel mince which had been mixed with onions and coriander. I had never tasted camel mince before.

'You're mad!' exclaimed Moussa when I arrived with a basket. 'We can't pay for that! Take it back!'

Kamil was pleased, but didn't support me or shush his brother.

Samir, downcast, asked, 'Are we going to stay here forever?'

With no enthusiasm or interest from anyone, I found cooking a chore. To wash the potatoes, I had to go to the ground floor, past the tanners who always felt the need to impart their sarcasm and philosophical musings. 'Him and his potatoes!' called one of the pluckers derisively.

'Let's call him "Potato"!' one woman mocked, her face covered and peering through a narrow window in her veil.

All the pluckers sang together, 'Potato! Potato!'

I couldn't take any more, stopped in the middle and shouted, 'Slave! Do you know your master?' Like hens, they hunkered down to their work.

To add to my frustration, I had a real difficulty with the cooker; it kept switching off and going out. I sat beside it and pumped it constantly until a weak flame steadied. I fried the camel meat with the leftover olive oil and added the potatoes and onions. The aroma of cooking brought sudden excitement from Moussa and Samir, who rushed out to buy two loaves of bread to complement the meal. After weeks of only white bread, the hot meal tasted delicious, and Kamil felt much better, but was still coughing blood.

To our surprise, the landlord burst into our room that evening and announced, 'I have to increase the rent because you use a lot of water and don't switch the light off early, at nine o'clock.'

'We need the light,' I said. 'The *funduq* is too noisy during the day. We need to do some reading.'

Furious, the landlord looked at me, raised his hand and pointed his finger in my face, nearly poking my nose. 'Do your reading in the street, under the lamp-post. The light is free there!' he barked.

'Do you want us to drink less water as well?' I asked.

'Olive oil and water are both measured and sold by the litre. Neither is free,' he said. He looked at me again, fumed, and pierced me with his stare. 'You spend hours scraping a few potatoes under the water, the caretaker told me.'

'The potatoes are covered with soil, and need to be washed,' I answered.

'Peel them!' he retorted. He shrugged his shoulders and murmured, 'I never thought people could eat unpeeled potatoes. As far as I know, only pigs do.' He slammed the door and went away.

Still not registered at the school, I wondered if staying in the *funduq* was wise. The landlord hadn't specified the amount of increase and had left us to guess. Kamil was too weak to face a change, and it was nearly the end of October. The registration and exams might be posted at any time. *This is not a time for turmoil*, I thought. I suggested we accept the increase, but said, 'We must bargain with him.'

Kamil laughed aloud and said, 'Bargaining is impossible in Fez!'

'Why?' I asked.

'Bargaining is bluffing. You never know how much to offer, as the asking price is usually at least five hundred percent. Whatever you suggest, you will be conned. Conned.'

Kamil's words worried me and reminded me of what Maroine's father had said to me: 'Fez is a town of conners.' Trying to come to a decision, we debated until dawn. Had the landlord known that the light was on all night, we would have been evicted.

At eight o'clock in the morning, Kamil and I slipped out to the Scientific Assembly. We entered the building and felt like intruders; no one was around, just endless empty corridors. Posters were scattered on the walls. Kamil read the poster. 'The academic year starts Sunday the 1st of November and all registered and returning students must join their respective year and class'. The posters mentioned nothing about new arrivals. That terrified me.

I stayed aimlessly wandering around the building for the rest of the morning in the hope an official might suddenly appear from behind one of the beautiful, closed doors. It was twelve-thirty, and no official had so far ventured out of his room — assuming they were actually in their rooms. *Every office must have its own private bathroom. No one feels the need to venture out to relieve his bladder or bowels*, I thought. Around a quarter to one, a middle-aged man left his office to go home for lunch. He was short, plump and hooded, and moved energetically. Giddy with relief at seeing someone, I rushed up to him.

'I am new here,' I said. 'I have come from the north. I want to join the school and be registered. Is it possible?'

'Yes,' he answered with a firm, sharp voice. 'Come tomorrow.'

Excited, I sprinted back to the room, pushing through the crowds to tell Moussa and Samir the good news. Full of hope, Moussa, Samir and I went early the following morning to register. The main door, made with solid wood and a decorative iron cross in the middle, was closed. A big window, facing the street, opened late in the morning, and an old hooded man, with pen and brown paper, peeked out and yelled, 'Registration!'

Boys of all ages, from all towns and tribes, swarmed, scrambled and pushed each other to get to the window of hope. It was like a day of pilgrimage, a day of salvation, everyone pushing to reach the window to touch the Holy Stone. Moussa, Samir and I tried to stay together, but got separated. I tried several times to reach the window to give the officer my name and got thrown back. It felt like being caught in the current of the sea, impossible to get out of it. The wave carried me, and I didn't know where I was going to be dropped. It got to be almost mid-day, lunchtime, and the crowd was only getting thicker. Not giving up, I reached the window, but just as I was shouting my name, the officer gathered his papers and shut it.

The shutter was slammed closed, the magic window and

hope with it. The swelled crowd was left to look at each other. I searched for Samir and found him in an envious mood. He looked relieved when I told him I hadn't been luckier than he had.

On our way back to the room, we bought two round loaves of white bread, some sugar and a bunch of mint. That was our dinner for the day.

Our entire afternoon and evening were spent discussing how to reach the window and the officer. 'Just getting there earlier won't do,' I said. We engineered a trick that we thought would help us navigate through the determined crowd and reach the window. To be on the safe side, we decided to test it. We carried out the test in the room – two against one and one against two. Kamil was tolerant until Moussa knocked down our little table and broke all the glasses.

A yell filled the room. 'There's glass in my heel!' shouted Moussa.

'Try to walk!' coached Kamil.

Moussa tried, and the splinter dug in deeper. He yelled again, louder.

'Can I see your heel?' I asked. Passing my hand over it, I pulled a piece of glass from his heel. The blood spurted out. Moussa felt a sharp pain whenever he put his heel on the ground.

'Be brave! Be brave!' counselled Kamil.

'Speak for yourself!' retorted Moussa. The more he tried to walk, the more pain he felt. Moussa's problem made us forget our trick.

Just as I tried to find out if Moussa still had another piece of glass in his heel, the landlord shouted, 'Light off! Light off!' We switched the light off.

Before the cobblers started, I was awake. The office was supposed to open at ten o'clock, and I was there before seven. The streets were quiet and empty; all I could hear was the echo of my own footsteps. When I arrived, the swelling crowd of students was blocking the street.

At eleven, the window was still closed. Two policemen arrived; one was armed with a pistol; the other carried a baton and handcuffs. The armed policeman shouted, 'Order! Order!' and the crowd queued. He stood near the window with his colleague at the end of the queue. At eleven-fifteen, the window was still closed. The queue became purposeless, but that didn't stop it from getting longer and longer by the minute.

At lunchtime, the crowd dispersed. Moussa was simply disabled, so on our way back to the *funduq*, I bought a needle and tweezers (shepherd's tools). Neither Moussa nor Samir knew their purpose.

'Show me your heel,' I asked Moussa. It looked swollen and red. I recalled my father's horrible advice. As a little boy, playing around, a very heavy stone had fallen on my big toe. My father had looked at it, bleeding, and had advised me to urinate on it, which I had. My toenail became infected and subsequently fell off.

Gently, I pricked the sore spot with the needle and felt a small solid sliver. To free it, I delicately peeled the skin aside. As soon as I could see the splinter, I picked it out with tweezers.

'Here's the devil!' I exclaimed and felt like a surgeon,

holding the nasty piece of glass up for all to see. 'Try walking now,' I instructed.

Cautiously at first, the memory of pain fresh in his mind, Moussa put his foot on the floor, then gave it his full weight. A smile spread across his face as he gingerly paced the floor, then jumped, free of pain.

While I was having lunch, a teacup in my right hand, biting a piece of bread in my left, the landlord and his son burst into the room. 'This is your electricity bill,' said the son, as it was obvious his father couldn't read. The bill covered the electricity we had used after ten at night, but none of us understood the bill. To us, it was gibberish.

'You didn't tell us not to use the electricity after ten o'clock when we took the room,' I said. 'This restriction limits our only chance to pass our entrance exams.'

The plea didn't go down well with the father. He singled me out as a troublemaker. 'It's you who keeps the light on late. I wouldn't charge the others more if you leave.' He and his son swept away, and a strange silence filled the room.

Angry, I put down my tea and bread, put my shoes on and said, 'Let's go to be registered.' I expected Kamil, Moussa and Samir to support me against the landlord, but they didn't. I had no idea why. Leaving them behind, I headed to the registration window.

Two policemen were already standing near the door, and the window was open. To pretend I wasn't afraid of them, I asked what time it was. I was told the time and sat on the street below the window. In no time, the street was full and the policemen began organising the crowd into a queue. Being there first, and in time, didn't mean being first to be registered. The power of the crowd, like the waves of the sea, could easily displace anyone, but the policemen remembered me and called me to start the queue in front of the window. When the officer came to the window, he peeked out, looked at the crowd, shook his head, grabbed some brown paper and a pen.

'Your ID, boy,' he demanded.

'Here it is, sir,' I said, pulling it out of my pocket.

He looked at me, glanced at my photo and said, 'That's not you.' His voice was loud, and the policemen heard him. They both butted in to check my face and the photo. They looked puzzled.

It was an old photo, from when I was skin-headed to inhibit fleas; I was also wearing a little square hat, making my head look small and dark. Now I had very long hair, and my cheeks practically touched each other.

'Is there anyone in the crowd who knows you?' the policeman asked.

'Yes,' I said. 'Samir and Moussa.' I looked around, but Samir and Moussa hadn't arrived yet. The crowd started to shout.

The officer decided to register me, even though he was not sure I matched the ID photo. He wrote my name down and said, 'You are number ninety-two, exam hall number four. If you pass your exams, you will be assigned a year and class. Be there before eight-thirty in the morning next Wednesday, and bring your identity card with you,' he added. 'Next!' he shouted.

Not knowing how, I found myself pushed aside. The police

could hardly cope with the intensive shoving coming from the crowd toward the window. Despite the imposed queue, all order was lost when the crowd got near the window.

Moving away, I checked to see if Samir and Moussa had arrived. They were at the end of the queue. They must have seen the officer talking to me and the police interrogating me, but Samir pretended he hadn't.

'Did he register you?' asked Samir with an unhappy look.

'We saw him getting registered, didn't we?' answered Moussa.

I felt Samir was envious of me. He couldn't stomach how leaving the room half an hour earlier could give me such an advantage over him. I knew he could get jealous over a pencil, but still hoped he would be registered. Unwilling to listen to him, I left, saying, 'See you later.'

That afternoon, everything changed. Kamil was cleaning his glasses, and I was trying to read a manuscript that made no sense to me. We heard loud laughter and excited voices – Moussa and Samir rejoicing over being registered. 'I am number one hundred eleven,' said Samir to Moussa. 'You are seventy-seven, though you came after me. How come?'

I cheered to know that they were registered and was happy to see Samir in a good mood. The waiting time for exams was short, but extremely boring and taxing. Most of the time, Samir didn't know what to do with himself.

I waited anxiously for the exam day and rushed to the hall on Wednesday morning. I was acutely aware that I knew nothing, tried to remember times tables and a few practical rules of ritual, such as washing my face, cleansing my nose, dampening my hair, cleaning my ears, my feet and my privates. The queue was already formed, but orderly and subdued with no police needed this time. Glints of anxiety shone over the boys' faces, as if execution were waiting.

Professors were seated inside a massive hall, long and beautifully decorated with mosaics. The colour green was dominant on every wall to give a cool and fresh feeling whenever anyone stepped inside. The examiners were sitting in a row behind huge leather-covered desks. Outside the hall, two beefy middle-aged men acted as gatekeepers, shuttling people in and out freely and calling the examinees' numbers.

Only three girls were in the queue. Two of them were particularly talkative, joking and giggling as if nothing mattered. One of them was flaunting an expensive necklace, constantly flicking it. I hoped I would be in the same class with them if I managed to be admitted. In reality, there was no chance; boys and girls didn't share the same school. 'Ninety-two to desk three!' A sharp voice broke my fantasy.

The doorkeeper opened the door; I scrambled through the crowd and headed in a daze to desk three. Far from the door, behind a majestic, dark mahogany desk, sat Professor Allal. He was a tall man, broad and smartly dressed, in a navy suit with a silk tie. As I entered, he peered at me from behind his silver-rimmed glasses and followed me with his eyes, scrutinising every step, until I reached his desk. By the time I sat down, I felt he had already made up his mind.

'Where do you come from?' he asked, like a policeman rather than a genteel professor.

'I am from Kebdana,' I replied.

'What did you do there?' he asked.

A ripple of panic struck. *I can't tell him I was a shepherd!* I thought. *What will he think of me?* I stumbled about for an answer.

'Have you forgotten already?' the professor commented with a cold smile. Silence ensued, and he patiently waited for an answer.

'I was a shepherd,' I whispered.

The surprise showed in his face, but to my relief he then changed the subject. 'How is your maths?' He handed me what looked like an endless list of division and multiplication problems. 'Take your time; you have thirty minutes,' he said without a trace of irony.

While I was struggling with solutions, he chatted to his neighbouring professor at the table a few metres away. As his loud voice reverberated around the room with news of his son, it was a struggle for me not to be distracted.

'My son is in Paris,' he said. 'Last year he was in Polytechnic College, the most prestigious and famous college in France! He passed his exams, but now he has changed his mind and is doing medicine instead.' It was difficult for me not to feel jealous of this boy I had never met.

'Thirty minutes are up!' shouted the professor, becoming aware of my presence again. He broke off from his discourse, snatched my paper and peered down at me. Nodding and leaving, I had no idea what impression I had left behind.

Not having a second to gather my feelings or talk to anyone in the crowd, I heard a loud voice piercing the air. 'Ninety-two to desk thirteen!' It was a call from the second doorkeeper on behalf of Professor Farid. He motioned toward the door and went back to squat on his stool.

I knocked and stepped in. The room was beautiful; sunlight beamed through the huge windows which stretched to the ceiling elevated high above and bathed the entire room in a warm, golden glow. *I wish I were allowed to bring my blanket and sleep here in the middle of this room*, I thought to myself.

Professor Farid, lips stuck out, looked annoyed and gave the impression he did not appreciate his precious time being wasted. He had been reading a local gossip rag before I sat down and interrupted his reading. In complete contrast to Professor Allal, Professor Farid was dressed all in white: white shirt, white *kashaba* and white *jellabah*. Even his *babouches* were white! He would have looked like a snowball were it not for his head, which was swathed in a pink turban, a colour my mother had said was reserved for virginal girls. Professor Farid didn't scrutinise me as Professor Allal had; he barely lifted up his head to look at me.

'Sit down!' he told me in a harsh voice, but before my bottom could touch the seat, he handed me three pages of questions. The next half hour would be a blur forever in my memory.

It was lunchtime. Moussa, Samir and I were all supposed to meet at noon so we could go back to our room and, on our way, buy two round loaves of bread for lunch. Demented by Professor Farid and preoccupied with my next exam scheduled for two o'clock, I forgot to wait for them. By the time I realised my mistake, it was too late; I couldn't go back, have enough time for lunch and be at the exam hall before two o'clock. I prepared myself for Samir's and Moussa's wrath. *I'll try to explain the behaviour of Professor Farid, and that might calm them*, I thought.

Ashamed, I entered the *funduq* and blinked as my eyes adjusted to the darkness from the bright midday sunshine outside.

'How was it?' Samir shouted down from the first floor.

'Is Moussa here?' I shouted back.

'Yes, he's here.'

Thank goodness I didn't wait for them, I thought indignantly. As no one had bought bread, we had to content ourselves with what was left: unsweetened tea and unbuttered, stale bread.

I was very slow in chewing the bread and didn't want anyone to notice. I had developed a severe ulcer on my tongue, cracked and excruciatingly painful. Chewing was slow and laborious, and eating any spicy food was impossible. However, we were all short of bread and time.

We hurried to the exam hall in a panic and arrived early. Samir was taking pleasure in both worrying and exciting Moussa. I was half listening to their conversation when a booming voice cut through my thoughts; 'Ninety-two, room four, desk eleven!'

Professor Maliki was behind his desk and looked up earnestly at me as I entered. Unlike Professor Allal and Professor Farid, he looked young and rough, like a wild country horseman. He was a Sharia Law professor. With his hand outstretched, he indicated the chair.

I took the seat and waited for questions. 'Pick a question from the pot.' He slid a large pot filled with folded bits of paper across the desk. With trepidation, I reached forward, picked one, and stared at the scratches on the paper. 'Can't you read?' he snapped impatiently.

'No, sir,' I answered.

Snatching the paper out of my hand, he read, 'Do grandchildren have a share of their grandfather's estate if their father dies before their grandfather?'

'No,' I said. I couldn't have hoped for a better question than this! 'My uncle Hamid was killed in the Spanish Civil War, and died just a few days before my grandfather. He left eight sons and one daughter, and they were excluded from their grandfather's estate. For this reason, they had no land and, consequently, were destitute.'

'What do you think about that?' asked Professor Maliki.

'That is the law, sir. Maybe it needs to be changed.'

He raised his eyebrows and glared at me. 'Change the law!' he shrieked.

'Yes, sir.'

He smiled crookedly. Then with a frown, he grabbed the pot and asked me to pick a second question. He read it aloud. 'If a wealthy man dies and has one son and one daughter, how would you apportion his estate?'

'I would divide it into thirds. The son would get two-thirds and the daughter would get one-third.'

'Is this the law?'

'Yes, sir.'

He kept silent for a while as if something really bothered him, then presented the pot again, and asked me to pick another piece of folded paper. I stretched my arm, put my hand in the middle of the pot and my fingers fiddled with folded scraps of paper trying to find the easiest question.

'As you know, every Muslim has to tithe to the poor and the needy. What is the amount?' he asked.

'Ten per cent, sir.'

'Are the tithe and tax the same?'

'Yes and no, sir.'

'"Yes and no" is not an answer. Who is the collecting agent for taxes?'

'The government, sir.'

'What would happen if someone refused to pay the tax?'

'He would be put in prison, sir.'

'Who is the collecting agent for the tithe?'

'It is not the government, sir. It is self-policed.'

'What would happen if someone didn't pay the tithe?'

'He would go to hell.'

Professor Maliki exploded in laughter and other professors in the same room looked at him. Stepping out of room four, I bumped into Samir searching for room three. 'To your right,' I shouted.

By the end of the afternoon, my die was cast. I paced up and down, wondering what to do next. As I waited for Samir and Moussa, Samir came out first with a red face like an over-ripe tomato about to burst. 'Bastard!' he mumbled, his usual confidence and cynicism evaporated.

All finished and on our way to the *funduq* around six o'clock in the evening, we couldn't pass Moul Idrees shrine. The whole town seemed to have come out to enjoy a bizarre, erotic jostling. Men and women crowded the very narrow streets and went around endlessly, forward and backward. Women pretended to be pushed backwards, and men forwards so that women pushed their breasts out and men brushed against them. There was no age limit or moral boundary to this exercise.

Though having achieved nothing yet, we decided to surprise Kamil with a feast that night. We bought three-quarters of a kilo of camel mince mixed with onion, garlic and coriander.

To alleviate my anxiety, I asked Samir and Moussa over dinner, 'Would you like to escape the *funduq*'s stench and go outside the city tomorrow?'

'Good idea,' Moussa piped in.

'I'm not going anywhere,' grunted Samir, lips tightly zipped like a deaf mute.

That night, I didn't sleep a wink. *What am I going to do if I am rejected?* my mind simmered. In vain, I tried to convince myself not to worry for at least three days while waiting for the results.

Dawn stole the night. I felt motivated to get up, happy to hear life in the street, eager to leave the *funduq*, the narrow streets and not feel confined by the derelict, crumbling room. Unfortunately, when Moussa and I stepped outside the town, through Bab Guissa, we discovered that we could not play football there. It was sloping; the ground, uninviting and barren, was rocky and uneven with some aged olive trees here and there. A dotted shantytown didn't compare with Makran and Tassamat, where fresh air filled the lungs and wildlife inspired the mind.

'We should have gone to Bab Ftouh,' I said.

'Let's play the flute,' suggested Moussa.

Happily, we sat on soft soil under an olive tree. I tried to show Moussa how to place and move his fingers, how to blow, but his fingers were as stiff as steel and his whistling produced only a bizarre, windy sound.

Shaking and drying the flute, I was a few metres away from Moussa when a sharp yell pierced my ears. A tramp had crept up behind us and thrown a sharp stone, missile-like, which grazed Moussa's head.

I had no idea where he had come from, and had heard no footsteps. He certainly lodged within the area and had a hole within the shantytown one kilometre away. Maybe he had been hiding, sleeping behind or underneath one of the olive trees near where we sat.

Moussa's head was oozing blood from over his ear, and we were shocked and alarmed. We rushed toward the tramp to hit him as he raced toward us. We heard him mumbling, but couldn't make any sense of it. Very tall and wrapped in two or three coats, he looked huge. His legs were wrapped thickly with pieces of different-coloured cloth. His face was bearded as though he had never shaved; he had a big moustache shooting out like the horns of a wild bull, but dirty and greasy. Grubby and hairy, he looked faceless. Looking at this spectre, I pulled Moussa back. As the tramp swept the hair from his face, it suddenly looked familiar.

'This is my cousin, Ahmed!' I exclaimed under my breath.

Full of doubt and fearful of getting closer to him, I shouted, 'Are you Ahmed, son of Ben Kedar?' Moussa, armed with a heavy load of stones, was on the other side of me, and at the ready.

'Yes,' he said. 'Are you Jusef?'

'Yes, I am.'

Ahmed fell on the ground and cried like a saint. Moussa kept asking questions that I couldn't answer.

Ahmed got up, wiped his tears and asked me if his own father was still alive, what his brothers were doing and if his blonde sister had gotten married. In the middle of our conversation, he suddenly turned his back on me, picked up several bags, headed to the shantytown and disappeared in front of our eyes.

'What happened to your cousin?' Moussa asked.

'He came to Fez as a student, just like you and me.'

'And what then?'

'He failed his exams and couldn't face his family, who had looked upon him as a star and their future messiah to deliver them from poverty. He deserted them and has succumbed to his own engineered madness.'

'Are you going to be like your cousin if you fail your exams?' Moussa asked me with a laugh, wiping his bleeding brow.

Returning to the room, I happened on the landlord and the caretaker patrolling the front of the *funduq*. 'Mr Lazar, a ginger-haired man, has a message from your father!' shouted the caretaker.

'The man is expecting you!' added the landlord.

'Where?' I asked.

'Bab Ftouh,' he replied.

To meet this mysterious man, I would have to go to Bab Ftouh coach station very early the following morning. *Awkward time!* I thought. Examination results were expected that morning, but I couldn't ignore my father's call.

During dinner, we talked politics and its effect on us. Kamil wished he could be a journalist and expose corruption. 'Russia,' he said, 'is a gigantic animal, but the United States is a gigantic monster.'

'There is worse,' I told him. 'The worst is where I am, an abyss with no end or light.' Sadly, this was to be our last supper together as four.

In the light of dawn, before the caretaker had opened the main door, I was up and away. The streets were empty and quiet but for the howling, hungry feral cats creating a strange, eerie atmosphere. The more I hurried, the longer the streets stretched before me. Exhausted, I reached the station well before seven o'clock. There was no Mr Lazar. The first coach to the north was leaving at eleven-thirty; waiting until then wouldn't allow me to join Samir and Moussa to hear our exam fate.

I had never met Mr Lazar, and I wondered if it would be easy to recognise this rare bird – 'Lazar' meant 'redhead'. Before eleven-thirty, a redheaded man appeared. 'Are you Mr Lazar?' I asked politely.

'Yes,' he replied with a hoarse voice and long chin. A strange smell came out of his mouth each time he spoke.

'You have a message from my father, I understand.'

'I carry many messages. Who is your father?'

'Sarir,' I said.

'The blind one?' he asked.

'Yes, in one eye.'

He sat down on the ground, put his case on his lap, unlatched it, yanked a ten-dirham note out and handed it to me.

It was around midday when I left the coach station. Returning to the room, I met Samir, accompanied by Moussa and Kamil, emerging from the *funduq*. He had two cases in his hands. Samir's and Moussa's faces looked as if they were going to be slaughtered.

'What happened, Samir?' I asked.

'Nothing very serious. Moussa and I didn't get in. I have decided to leave now.'

Moussa added, 'I am leaving tomorrow.'

Kamil kept sombre and quiet. I didn't ask them about my own results, and I couldn't continue to the school and leave them, so we all accompanied Samir to Bab Ftouh to take the coach home. The next coach was going east, to Oujda, where I had first met them all.

Samir was resolute in action, but wounded in heart. We all waited for him until he took his seat beside the window on the coach. We watched the coach slowly move east, and Samir waved only twice before he hid his face in the crook of his arm. Samir's departure numbed me. The silence was heavy and total on our way back to the *funduq*. Moussa would have to sort himself out, and I had still to discover my fate. Whatever decision Moussa might make, he would have to discuss it with his brother, Kamil.

Inside our room, Moussa regained his power of speech. 'I'm going to buy a passport,' he said, 'and go to Germany. I am a *hafiz*. I thought I knew something. Obviously, I know nothing – that's my sin. If I had been aware, I wouldn't have come here.'

One of the basic rights of a child is schooling, yet this has been denied to us, I thought to myself.

Moussa's moaning threw me into deep despair. As a *hafiz*, I felt his pain, except mine went deeper. *Shepherding and all my years in the mosque have stolen the best of my youth*, I thought with regret.

The fact that Moussa and Samir had decided to go made me reluctant to rush and discover my lot. Yet I had to. Kamil offered his company; so did Moussa, surprisingly. My knees buckled when we reached the school. I could hardly breathe when I got close to the wall and stretched my neck to read the list very high up. My eyes watered and my heart changed its beat when I saw on the pass list, 'Jusef – Primary final, Division I'. Mesmerised, I turned toward Moussa, who kept patting me on the back, and we spontaneously exchanged brotherly hugs.

Moussa kept rereading the list, hoping to spot his name. Meanwhile, Kamil wouldn't stop nagging at us to go home. Just before six o'clock, staff rushed out of their offices, as if they had been chased by a troll.

At six o'clock, the two school caretakers switched off every decorative chandelier in the building and chased us out. The building turned dark and spooky. The tall buildings lining the narrow streets and the scarcity of streetlights added darkness to the sunset.

In the last few days, Moussa had become addicted to taking part in the erotic jostling near Moul Idrees shrine. Now he had lost his appetite for it, so we all hurried straight to the *funduq*, only stopping to buy one loaf and a half of bread. We had usually bought two, but now Samir had gone. We took our dinner earlier than usual, and the evening was full of talk and sorrow.

'I'm going to buy a passport,' Moussa repeated incessantly.

'To buy a passport, you need a mountain of money' I said.

'Some people sell their houses for it,' Kamil butted in.

'When you go to Germany, I would like to visit you. May I stay with you a few days?' I asked.

Moussa and I kept chatting for hours. Kamil didn't think our topics worth hearing any more. He tried to stay awake, but fell into a deep sleep like a coma.

Moussa's coach was to leave at five-thirty in the morning. We left early, at three o'clock, went through many twisted, narrow, dark streets, and felt a chill at every corner. We looked suspicious, but then, so did everybody else we met. Moussa's coach was on time. We had thought we were on the same path, but how naïve we had been.

10

At dawn on my first day of school, I woke up full of anticipation and wonder. Now that Moussa and Samir's hopes had been crushed, I headed alone to the school, which also happened to be a mosque. Bozaid, an Algerian student, had arrived before me. I looked at him and compared myself with him. He was tall and thin and his nervous character was apparent in his obvious uneasiness with himself. Whoever had cut his hair had made a mess of it. His voice, manner and outspokenness complemented his rough appearance.

'Where did you come from?' I asked him.

'Algeria,' he answered.

'Why did you come so far?' I asked.

'Do you want us all to perish, to die? My brothers have all joined the Liberation Army fighting French colonialism. I wanted to join them, but my father wanted to spare one of us. It happened to be me, the youngest.' His statement momentarily shocked me into silence.

While he was talking, a stout, impressive-looking professor came out of the student office. One hand was full of white papers, and the other held a silver pen. 'Primary final, follow me!' he shouted. He moved out of the office into the street and turned to the left; Bozaid, the other boys and I followed in a line until we reached the fountain embedded in the wall. Pedestrians stopped there to wash their hands or quench their thirst. The professor stopped, whisked a vial made from an animal's horn from his pocket, popped the cork, and spread a thin line of black snuff on the side of his fist. He unceremoniously snorted with first one nostril, then the other. He immediately launched into a frenzy of sneezing. Happy afterwards, he beamed at us over his shoulder to check whether we were still there behind him.

Following him, we humbly removed our shoes and entered the Kairaouine mosque, where the teaching took place. It looked dark and immense. Classes were on, and professors were shouting from their pulpits into the huge open space. Students of all ages were sitting on the floor, rubbing shoulders and looking up at their professors. The professor took Bozaid and me to class space B, showed us the group, ticked his paper and left, the other students trailing behind him in a row like ducklings.

Bozaid and I joined in and ensconced ourselves into the tightly knit group of students, all sitting cross-legged on the floor, the privileged on sheepskins. Our arrival disturbed no one. The professor, bobbing his head right and left, kept teaching and all the students were mesmerised by him. How to snatch wealth and punish perverts were my first lessons. It struck me as more like preaching than teaching.

'Americans don't wash their socks,' the professor said. 'They change them six times a day, and throw their dirty socks in the bin. Each person has at least two or three cars.'

I was stunned. To my frustration, the professor didn't teach in my mother tongue, Tarifit, or even in any Moroccan dialect. It was all in high, Classical Arabic. My concentration withered into a splitting headache. My heart skipped a beat when twelve o'clock struck, the official time for a two-hour lunch break. The mosque became empty, dark and silent. Tramps, looking for peace and tranquillity, replaced students, some to eat what they had gathered, and others to count the money they had collected.

The two-hour break allowed me to catch up. I scurried to the second-hand bookshop nearby and bought two small dictionaries, a few jotters, a couple of pencils, a single pen and an eraser. Carrying all that made me feel happy like a proper schoolboy, albeit one with an empty head. I had a quick lunch with Kamil, and was surprised to hear that he had applied for a job to become a primary school teacher.

A shivering fear struck. *I might be left here alone in this* funduq. *How will I pay the rent?* I wondered. Nevertheless, I was excited to start the second half of my first day at school.

Returning to school in the afternoon, I found Bozaid already there, nibbling dates from a big bag, biting on a long, thin piece of bread, and glancing at a newspaper spread out on the floor in front of him. He looked unhappy and lonely. A minute before two o'clock, space B was filled with students, swarming like honeybees. Just in time, Professor Haiani arrived with one hand full of books and the other holding his shoes.

He climbed the risers to the pulpit and announced, 'Today's lesson is "kill to live and live to kill".' *This is more preaching*, I thought to myself. The professor broke the rule. He taught us in Darija, not Classical Arabic. Bewitched, the students became excited.

'Before tackling this crucial topic, I want you to understand,' he said. 'Law, religion and morality are inextricably connected. Clinically splitting one from the other leads to the death of them all. This is an axiom you should always remember.'

In a flash, Bozaid stood up, put his hand in the air and said boldly, 'Sir, if a Frenchman kills an Algerian, is it kill to live or live to kill? What if an Algerian kills a Frenchman?'

Professor Haiani stopped teaching, closed his eyes and tilted his head back toward the ceiling. No words escaped from his mouth. We all looked at each other, wondering. Bozaid remained standing.

'Sit down,' said Professor Haiani, after too long a pause. 'Any more questions?' he asked.

Furious, Bozaid stood up and asked, 'What about my question?' The professor refused to answer.

The three-hour lessons were both confusing and tense, but fortunately also marked the end of the week, Wednesday. The main doors became bottlenecks with students running out. In the immense space, the shadows of ghosts could peer from behind every pillar and meet in any of the myriad of dark corners.

On the way back to the *funduq*, I wondered if it would help me to work with Faissal and Marnisi, who had sat beside me. There were other things also occupying my mind. *Could Kamil really hold a job as a primary school teacher in a rural area?* I wondered. My hope was that he would change his mind.

As I slipped into the room, Kamil asked, 'Do you know anything about hamsters?'

'A bit. Not very much. They are tiny animals, between rats and mice.'

'No, they're not,' Kamil said politely. 'Could you go with me to buy one tomorrow? I had one, but it died just before I came here. I really miss my hamster!'

'What do you miss? It's just a nasty mouse!'

'Could you go with me anyway?'

'A hamster in this room? Look — we are surrounded by hundreds of abandoned, homeless, hungry cats. We will be hounded by cats, and the hamster will be terrified. The hamster needs to be caged all the time, fed and watered.'

The absence of Moussa and Samir was already a problem. I wasn't certain that Kamil would survive here without Moussa, and was faced with the possibility of being left alone, so to keep him happy, I reluctantly agreed.

The thought of buying a hamster the next day, Thursday, made Kamil happy. He fell asleep over his jotters. I picked up a dictionary and concentrated on learning a few Arabic words. Forced to comply with the landlord's rule, I stopped at ten o'clock. The light went off, and in the darkness of the room, I rolled myself in my blanket and went to sleep like a dog.

Thursday was my first day off school, and I went out scavenging for second-hand books. Returning to the *funduq* at lunchtime, I found Kamil full of excitement. Moussa's corner had been turned into hamster-land. Before a hamster had even been bought, he had named it Kizzy. He wanted us to dedicate a quarter of the room to Kizzy.

'Kizzy needs a cage,' I argued.

'Yes, but also a playpen, and I would make sure it couldn't get out,' he said.

Kamil might have been clever and might soon be a teacher, but there was something about him I didn't understand. *Finding other accommodation is the only way for me to survive*, I decided.

Going with Kamil on Thursday afternoon to buy a hamster was an expedition. I was hit by the complexity of Fez's population. We left the old town and headed toward Malah, a Jewish ghetto, a society with no restrictions on women. Beautiful, portly women were walking about freely with no scarves or veils. The merchants struck me as entirely different from those in the old town; jewellery, clothes and stationery were the main wares. There was a completely different dynamism from the old town.

Beside the Jewish quarter was the French ghetto for the well-to-do. The area between the two ghettos was open, dusty and used as a bus station. Within this area, there was a big gambling stall with Indian music, deafening even to the already deaf, and a red light flashing every second. Traders came to the pitch to sell their goods and avoid heavy taxes. Bananas, oranges and grapes were sold far cheaper than in any shop in the town. Hot fried chickpeas and salted nuts were the favourite snacks of the shoppers. Pet lovers like Kamil had a number of choices: caged birds of all sizes and colours, caged hamsters as well as other animals.

The choice was easy for Kamil; he hated all animals except hamsters. A shrewd trader with two hamsters and several caged birds quickly caught his attention. Kamil fawned over two baby hamsters sleeping on top of each other in the corner, but he couldn't decide which one he wanted. To give himself time to decide, he bought a snack of fried chickpeas and moved around dreamily.

By this time, I had had enough of looking at the rodents. 'I'm going home, Kamil,' I announced.

'Yes,' he said, flustered. 'I'll buy the beige one!' Going back to the trader, he found the beige one had already been sold. Kamil took the news gravely, biting his wobbling bottom lip. With no choice left, he bought the white one. Happy after his initial disappointment, he cradled the cage close to his chest all the way back. Going back to the *funduq* with Kamil carrying the hamster, I felt embarrassed. I pretended that I didn't know him and wasn't with him whenever possible, but Kamil kept talking to me enthusiastically and ruining my disguise.

I spent the rest of the day tidying the room and cleaning my one shirt. Fortunately, I didn't have any underwear to wash or worry about.

Kamil soon happily settled into a daily routine with his hamster. I heard him many times in intimate dialogue with his pet, as if he were asking Kizzy questions or answering hers.

My second day in school began with Professor Allawi, who taught us maths. He was a very big man, very round and always happy. His one flaw was his habit of showering all those around him with saliva whenever he boomed out his explanations. He brought fruit and vegetables to explain mathematical concepts to us and cut an apple into many pieces to demonstrate fractions.

To make sure we could hear him and not miss any of the words coming out of his mouth, we all rushed in and fought to sit closest to the pulpit, facing him. Two boys in front of me quarrelled about space; they exchanged insults and elbowed each other, but that wasn't enough. They stood up to fight. One of them threw his *jellabah* off to fight unrestricted and, to our horror, he wore no trousers. All he had been wearing was his *jellabah* and a worn, torn shirt. Naked, he continued to fight for the best spot to face the teacher. *What a society!* I thought. *It can't even provide trousers for its most ambitious children!*

I I

It was holidays and Christmastime, but without Christ; Christmas meant nothing to me. All the students went home except Kamil and me. Kamil's hamster, Kizzy, drove me crazy. Dead during the day and alive during the night. I tried to keep her up during the day in the hope of a quiet night, but always failed.

The winter was harsh and wet; it poured more than the land could absorb. Local people had never seen weather like this, with such rain and clouds. The flooding and mountains of mud made streets impassable. The few tethered horses in the *funduq* were sunk in water and mud up to their knees. 'This is the second and the last flooding after Noah,' said the landlord. It was, however, a paradise for skiers; the Atlas Mountains were all covered with thick, powdery snow.

After New Year, exam results came back and were alarming. To stave off the calamity of failing, Faissal, Marnisi and I decided to meet each day after school in the mosque and work as a group. To revise, we picked a quiet corner far away from worshippers and sat on the freezing cold floor. Nothing was between our bums and the floor except a paper-thin rug made of jute, which provided neither heat nor comfort, nor did it stop the rising dampness.

Faissal, Marnisi and I hailed from different regions. Each of us carried heavy baggage: regional tradition, family background, humour, mood, accent, personal prejudice and temperament. Fruitless arguments started; competition and jealousy quickly bloomed, which wasted a lot of time. I suggested working more quickly and sticking rigidly to the school syllabus.

Marnisi agreed, but Faissal didn't. Full of idealism, he hated the West and all its products, even aspirin and penicillin. The West, according to him, justified their own thievery and crime. We spent hours debating our different views on stealing, adultery and the punishments for committing crimes. 'Cutting a thief's hand off for stealing doesn't fit the crime,' I argued.

Faissal was outraged at my comment and bellowed, 'Both the arm and leg should be cut off!' Marnisi showed real disgust.

Weeks later, all the students were surprised to be issued a card and number to attend a mobile clinic for x-ray screening. Six boys in my class tested positive for tuberculosis. Kamil, in a different class, was also positively diagnosed.

Kamil was ordered, as were the others, to not attend classes and to present himself to a specialised hospital for isolation and treatment. The hospital was the most hated in the town. It was a coffin before the grave. Kamil refused to go. For a few weeks, he did nothing except cuddle his hamster. Kizzy had lived in a cage, but now Kamil gave it full freedom to move around in the room, until one evening it ventured out. A hungry cat was waiting and snatched it away. Kamil and I watched what was happening, rushed out, chased the cat and I nearly killed myself tumbling down the stairs. The cat, like lightning, jumped on the roof with Kizzy still dangling from its mouth. Kamil blamed me for having an evil eye and never showing any affection or tenderness toward Kizzy. He went into a deep, strange bereavement. He refused to eat, to talk to me, to go out or wash himself. He became smelly, and the room with him.

A few days after the tragedy, at lunchtime, the *funduq* caretaker came up and gave a hard knock on the door. 'Kamil! Come down! Two French nuns are asking for you!' he shouted.

'That seems very odd,' I told Kamil. Curious, I went out first. Two middle-aged Catholic nuns in black cloaks stood beside each other. They were standing like statues, in complete silence, holding some envelopes like corpses in their hands. Kamil, peering down the stairs, came down hesitantly. The two French sisters didn't speak the Moroccan Darija, but they knew enough to get by.

'Are you Kamil?' asked one of the nuns.

'Yes,' Kamil answered.

'This is a letter ordering you to go to the hospital. You are very ill and a danger to yourself and your friend. You might die if you refuse treatment,' said the nun, while the other quietly looked on with a fixed smile on her face.

Kamil fell to the ground in a faint. For a moment, the sisters stood watching the scene, as did the caretaker. I had previously learned that a person or animal is only dead and ready for burial when the breathing stops. Kamil's chest was going up and down.

The two sisters left and the caretaker scurried off, leaving me behind with Kamil lying on the ground.

*   *   *

JANUARY LEFT US BEHIND, and February loosened its grip. The severe winter was showing decisive cracks; days were visibly longer and the sky noticeably clearer, but winter was not completely defeated. It felt cold. The spring holiday was in everybody's mind.

Kamil, frightened of a second visit from the nuns, decided to go home. 'Going home won't help,' I argued.

A resolute fatalist, he said, 'Everything is decided.'

Two days later, with a heavy heart, I accompanied him to the coach station. That same afternoon, I was supposed to meet Faissal and Marnisi, but emotionally upset and frightened about what would come next, I didn't. I went to the *funduq* straight from the coach station. When I opened the door, the room looked unusual, immensely big and with many shadowy corners. *The room is jinxed*, I thought to myself. *Everyone who has lived in this room has met his demise, including even innocent little Kizzy.* I had been taught in the past to recite verses from the Holy Koran whenever I felt in imminent danger, which I did immediately and aloud. I tried to trick myself into being a big brave boy, living as if the room were the same and nothing had changed, that Kamil and even Moussa and Samir were still in the room. A few hours later, the landlord rapped on the door.

'Kamil has left. The full rent is expected next week,' the landlord demanded. Now I found myself all alone in the *funduq* with no one to share the overwhelming burden of the rent.

I went to sleep but couldn't close my eyes, haunted by the fear of what might happen if I did. An object might fall from the ceiling or someone might stone me from any corner; every bizarre thing I had heard in my childhood and hadn't believed came alive in my mind. Even the small, crooked table looked sinister with the white strip of moonlight falling across it. To shut me up, my mother used to terrify me with the *Mo-Mo*, who would pull me out by my feet and gobble me up. No walls or doors could stop the *Mo-Mo*, an abhorrent beast that could go wherever it liked. The night dragged on and by the morning I felt physically aged by the ordeal.

At long last, morning arrived and the sun shone brightly all over the town. I left the room and felt a rush of happiness, a renewed love of life and relief at being out. I arrived at the school, where the first person I happened on was Bozaid, sitting cross-legged, surrounded by books and jotters, and eating Moroccan donuts. Before the lesson, Faissal and Marnisi arrived. They were furious with me.

'Where were you yesterday?' they asked. 'We waited and waited.'

'I was out of my mind. I have an accommodation problem,' I said. 'Kamil has left.'

*　　*　　*

UNABLE TO PAY THE rent, I had no choice but to join the homeless in the Mosque Rssif. I left the *funduq* and handed the keys to the caretaker, who looked at me carrying two sheepskins on my shoulder and several bags in my hands. He gave me a mean look and turned his back. He despised me as I did him. I looked like a tramp, but he looked and lived like a hyena.

On my way to my new home a dreadul image of my cousin

Ahmed clutched my mind. Without intending to, I had now outwardly become like him, a tramp.

The mosque was huge and open with towering ceilings that seemed to stretch to the heavens. It had no heating and with no warm carpets, only tiles, it was a very cold place to be at night. However, what it lacked in heat, it made up for in beauty; right in the middle of the mosque stood a magnificent mosaic fountain from which, day and night, huge streams of water soared into the air and smaller jets flowed all around as if dancing in watery precision.

After a struggle with the mosque's caretaker, I was allowed to sleep there, but during the day my belongings had to be out of sight so that respectable worshippers would not be deterred from worshipping there. The mosque was tidy during the day and a chaotic mess during the night. The students' presence was not to the liking of every worshipper; for some, we were cursed rats, and probably we were.

For peace and safety, I occupied a corner far from everybody and hid all my belongings in two bags. During school hours, I left them piled one on top of the other. At night, coming back late after revision with Faissal and Marnisi, I spread my two sheepskins and rolled up in my blanket. My pillow was my thin elbow. As the space was immense, drafts came from everywhere.

Though we were united in misery, the homeless, like jackals, scavenged whatever they could. Coming back from late revision one night, I found my blanket had been stolen. I felt a deep loss, plunged into panic and moved around, looking for it. Suddenly, a voice reverberated through the huge space.

'This is the third time you've passed me!' said an annoyed student.

'Give us peace!' grunted another.

'My blanket has been stolen,' I said. I spent a shiveringly cold night, despite layering every piece of clothing I had.

I didn't go to school the following morning, but to two letting agents. The first was not far away. The boss, well past middle-age, was clothed in a white *jellabah* and wore a tall red Fezzi hat with a tassel attached to the front.

'I am looking for a room to rent,' I said.

'How much are you willing to pay?' asked the man, perched on a high stool and looking down on me from above.

'What do you have and what is the cost?' I asked.

'I have rooms,' he said, 'but not for you. You are young. Bring your mother or sister to live with you so you will look like a family. That way, tenants won't think you are chasing after their wives.'

If only he knew! Despite being worried about missing more school, I left to look for another letting agent. It was about a kilometre away, in a street called Talaa, on a slope and paved with cobbles. The letting agent was in a cubby hole, one metre above the pavement. The owner was sitting cross-legged, facing a few keys on a board a metre away, and a young boy with bare feet outside the shop was relaying messages for him. Facing the man, I said, 'Peace be with you.' This was generally the way to start a conversation politely, but the agent glared at me as if I were a unicorn.

'I'm looking for accommodation. Do you have a room to rent?' I asked.

'Plenty,' he said, bobbing his head and looking at the keys on his board. 'My clients are rich and choosy.' He spent half an hour touting and praising himself. I nodded and pretended to agree, but the classes I was missing kept flashing into my head. 'I have a room,' the man said. 'It belongs to an important client who doesn't take just the first comer. Judging by your voice and appearance, you are the right tenant.' He picked a key, jabbed it at the boy and said, 'Quick! Quick! Show him the room!'

I followed the boy into a dark street, then into an even darker lane. He opened a door right on the street to a small tomb-like closet, whose walls were dripping water. Just across the threshold was a murky pool of water, over which was a rusted grate. Just beyond, leaning against the wall, was a ladder leading to a sleeping platform. 'Very nice accommodation,' the boy said. 'Don't miss it.'

My heart sank and I pulled back, as if I were about to be trapped. As I edged away, the boy grinned, 'Do you like it?'

I kept silent, still moving backward. The boy yelled louder, 'Say something! Say something, rat!'

So young and already so nasty. He's a seed of Fez. I pivoted and quickly ran to the main street, Talaa, then went back to join the afternoon classes at two o'clock. On my way, I happened on a narrow, small restaurant that had no seats in the front – only a few cement benches at the very back. *Harira* was the only food served, and all I could afford.

Professor Allawi was very snippy that afternoon. He picked Faissal to go forward to the blackboard to solve some easy problems. Faissal was confused, and the professor kept him there to humiliate him. 'Sit down. Sit down,' the professor said when Faissal's knees eventually buckled.

'To the board,' the professor motioned to me. I scribbled something. 'What you wrote is correct. Turn to the class and explain.'

Pleased with myself, I felt like an assistant professor, but was soon humiliated.

'Stop!' shouted Professor Allawi. 'Speak Arabic, not Tarifit!' he added. I couldn't turn my tongue into an Arabic one by magic; from that day, my class nicknamed me 'Riffy'. I lost my proper name and identity and embodied the entire north of Morocco.

All night, in the dim light of the mosque, I tucked myself into everything that I had and tried to sleep. Sounding like an orchestra in disarray, the collective snoring didn't wake sleeping students. No night passed without brawling, disputes, late arrivals and heavy knocks on the doors. It was a holy place, but human needs made it hell.

No two nights were alike. That night, loud knocking was heard on the main door. A distressed voice went with it. 'Let me in! Let me in! I'm cold!' No one, apart from the caretaker, had keys to the two huge main doors so nobody bothered to see who was knocking.

Like everybody else, I ignored the knocking and the voice in the hope they might stop, but they didn't. Disturbed by the voice and made uncomfortable by the cold, I stood up, crept to the door, and peered through the peephole. I thought I knew who was there, but wasn't absolutely certain. Far away from the main door was a large, high window locked by a deadbolt. I didn't believe I could reach it, but with my third jump, I was able to reach the sill and open the window. '*Aji, aji!* (Come here, come here!)' I whispered.

The boy came to the window, but it was far above the ground. I didn't want to give him my hand for fear of being pulled out, so I threw my belt out, held one end, and the boy caught the other. His knees were shivering, his fingers numb so that he could hardly hold the belt, but he reached the window and pulled himself up. I knew him by sight, but had never spoken to him. His name was Omar, in the same year, but a different class.

'I heard you lost something recently,' he said.

'My blanket,' I answered.

'I've got it,' he said.

If I'd known he had stolen my blanket, I would have left him outside. He handed it to me.

* * *

AFTER SEVERAL MORE WEEKS of misery, I asked Omar, 'Would you like to go with me to ask the rector for accommodation?'

He quickly agreed. One morning after classes, we rushed to the rector's office and asked to see him. 'What's the reason?' asked Mr Murzook, bold and thin, his secretary.

'Accommodation, sir,' I answered.

Mr Murzook ushered us into the rector's office, where the rector was sitting behind his majestic desk in a large, ornately decorated room. The light was filtering through beautiful vari-coloured stained-glass windows. We stood side by side feeling small and insignificant when Mr Murzook presented us and then stepped aside to listen and watch.

'Sir, we have been looking for accommodation since the beginning of the school year and have been unable to find any. Now we are squatting in the mosque,' I said. The rector didn't say a word, and Mr Murzook asked us to leave. We were simply ignored.

With life only getting worse, I suggested, 'Why don't we submit a petition to the rector?' Omar quickly bought the idea. We collected signatures from the homeless students and handed the petition to Mr Murzook.

He looked surprised and peered at me. I could read some irritation in his face. 'Listen, boys,' he said. 'I will give you some advice, but I want you to know who I am. Hopefully my words will be worth heeding.'

'I was a political activist for many years – the French police imprisoned me and put me in a psychiatric house with the most dangerously disturbed people. I was attacked and frightened. To chase the madmen away, I pretended to be worse than they. I shouted at them and chased them. Wisdom can save your life, but so can madness. I needed madness, but you now need wisdom. If the rector receives your petition, you will be classified as agitators. The cure is simple: he will expel you. I fear for you. I can pass this petition to the rector if you wish, or, I can wad it.'

'Can you give us any help?' I asked.

'We're aware of the problem,' he said.

Omar and I looked at each other, reddened and left. The other homeless students asked what had happened, and I lied.

'The petition has been sent to His Majesty, the King.' The lie bred hope.

*   *   *

IRONICALLY, THE LIE TURNED out to be truth, and the liar became a hero. At midnight in mid-March, the police awakened us. In a bellicose voice, waving his arms, the policeman said, 'His Majesty the King has mandated every homeless student be lodged.'

He took no questions, departed in a flurry and left everyone to guess. Before he disappeared, a squad of armed police burst in via the side door and a dozen civil servants jammed the main entrance. The process felt like deportation. A tall black policeman with heavily tinted glasses, a long moustache and wearing a dark navy suit with a white shirt and red tie acted as the commander-in-chief. All orders emanated from him and everybody bowed, including the police laden with pistols. Like a soldier, he advanced toward us.

'I want you in six groups,' he shouted, spreading his arms.

Confused, we pushed each other, everyone changing groups at least twice, but Omar and I stayed together. 'This has to do with our petition!' whispered Omar.

'Yes!' I whispered back.

Facing our group, the commander shouted, 'Your new home is Mr Tazzi's house, one and a half miles from here. The caretaker and an officer are expecting you there right now.'

The night was filled with fear and drama with no chance of sleep. Everyone was laden with bags; some had them on their backs, others in their hands. Getting to Tazzi's house was neither easy nor straightforward. We climbed a hill, almost vertical, then took the street to the left, then to the right, to the left again, then again to the right. It was a crisp, silent night and apart from us the street was deserted; the only noises to be heard were the gurgling of the spring that we passed and the voices of two men stoking the fire in the old bakery.

Tazzi's house was adjoined to another building, and both were at the end of a very narrow cul-de-sac. The door looked solid, made with heavy wood, and had ornate railings. We knocked and knocked like mad.

The caretaker, a middle-aged man blighted by alopecia, a tall Fezzi hat on his head, arrived with an assisting officer. The door opened and the world changed. Tazzi's house defied imagination: it was a mini-palace. I gazed at Omar, stroked my chin and nodded, bewildered. 'What's wrong?' Omar asked me.

'Look at what some people possess . . . and hide,' I answered.

The house, situated on the side of a hill, was built in a square with a huge courtyard in the centre, unlike anything I had ever seen. Mosaics caught the sun from every angle; the paths, the central area and even the fountain were made of the finest small shapes of bright blue, red and yellow woven together to create breathtaking reflective surfaces. The beauty of the mosaics were surpassed only by the three-tiered fountain that shot streams of water from three different levels and sent it cascading in perfect arches to land below with the most pleasant, relaxing sound. The trees, of differing heights, had been planted along the four walkways and provided a shady oasis. *If only I could sit under one of these trees and pass the time, I wouldn't have a care in the world,* I thought to myself.

The house consisted of three floors, the floors and walls were decorated with mosaic, and most of the rooms were humongous. Each large room could house between ten and fifteen boys. Two of the rooms were smaller; the smallest was occupied by the caretaker. I asked if Omar and I could take the second small room, which could take just four. Very tiny compared with the rest it was also darker and needed electricity both night and day. We opted for it because of its relative privacy. Omar's cousin Taji, and Rammani, from the southernmost part of Morocco, joined us.

Magnificent as it was, the house was cold, damp and had no toilet. It had a massive flat roof with some suntraps sheltered from the wind. We enjoyed it for a while, until the neighbours fiercely objected to our use of it. To escape the chill of unheated houses, women, like moles, emerged to sit and sunbathe on the roofs.

'No men should see or watch them. Roofs,' the neighbours said, 'are only for women.'

Extremely unhappy, the neighbours complained to the police, so a builder was immediately dispatched to block access to the roof. Recovering from the flu, desperate for sun and to escape the cold and dampness indoors, one student made a hole in the barrier to access the roof.

'Son of a whore! Come and meet me!' shouted a man from a neighbouring roof. The outraged man, who was short and stocky with a head like a melon sitting directly on his shoulders, burst into the house, axe in hand, and yelled, 'Where is he, that tall bastard?'

Hearing the shouting, we all rushed out to watch this man who was ready to kill. The caretaker, disturbed by the noise, ran out of his room and shouted, 'What are you doing here?'

'I am here looking for a bastard, the son of a whore!'

'What's the problem?' asked the caretaker.

'I saw that bastard on the roof. I want to quench my anger with his blood!'

The man threatened us all, yelling, 'I'll beat you one by one into a bloody pulp until I get the bastard. Then I'll tear him apart, limb from limb, and leave his remains to the hyenas!'

The caretaker grabbed the man's axe, picked him up by the scruff of the neck and ushered him forcefully out the door. The man kept shouting and swearing, 'I'll wait for that bastard outside! I'll get him!'

12

The full bloom of Spring arrived and cheered the depressed city. Nature tickled and reached its best; grass and flowers besieged the town. Like sheep, women went out in exodus to sit or lie on the grass, nibble snacks and feel the warmth of the sun. I joined the pilgrimage, picked a sunny spot, and no one chased me or claimed, 'Sun is only for women (*Liaalats*)!' During the spring holiday, wealthier professors abandoned the town and dispersed, looking to sample fresh air, milk and honey. For me, home was far away.

I revised from early morning to closure of the mosque in the evening. Revision was dull, hard, and food was constantly on my mind. The damp room, lack of natural light and lack of food hampered every effort to study. On the way from the mosque back to the room, I smelled *tagine*; I stopped, enjoyed the smell, and wondered who the lucky feasters were, boys or girls, and what they looked like.

Unhappy during the spring holiday, I celebrated its end, Sunday. It was also my day to cook. I shopped, cooked beans and waited for my roommates, Omar, Taji and Rammani, to arrive. They were late, and I kept checking on the simmering beans, adding water and reading as I cooked. A heavy knock made the door rattle. I threw my jotter down, opened the door and came face-to-face with the caretaker. Behind him stood a man, waiting to be introduced.

'Do you know this man?' the caretaker asked.

'Yes, Mr Lazar, come in.'

Mr Lazar stepped in slowly, took off his shoes and sat down. I made a pot of tea for him. Sitting cross-legged on the floor, leaning against the wall, Mr Lazar asked, 'What do you want to do next year?'

'School,' I answered. 'How is my father?' Mr Lazar pretended not to hear me. *Maybe he's hard of hearing, and the bubbling of the pot doesn't help*, I thought to myself.

Mr Lazar gazed at the ceiling, but there was nothing to see except cobwebs, then focused on the floor, on his worn-out shoes. 'He is dead.'

His words sent the walls and the whole room spinning around. The conversation stopped, and Omar came in. Not knowing how, I found myself in the street, my face wet with tears. I didn't feel like going back to the room, where my tears would be on show. I tried to be brave, but my mind was foggy.

Can my mother survive? I wondered. *What about Rabbia and Amina, with no school, no occupation, no job, and no husband? Salwa, Sanaa and Sakina are miserably married. They're raped in their own beds.* I forgot about the exams scheduled in a few days.

Coming back in the evening, I found Omar, Taji and Rammani waiting for me. Rammani put the kettle on and made the tea.

'There are plenty of beans,' Omar pointed out.

'I'm not really hungry,' I answered.

'Mr Lazar left letters for you,' said Omar.

We usually talked and joked at this time of night, but a heavy silence fell. In the early morning I awakened first, picked up my letters and went to the mosque. Its quietness and atmosphere were inspiring and therapeutic. I sat down and opened my letters. The first was small and white, with no return address, just my name. It was from my mother, written unclearly on scruffy paper, obviously by someone who knew the Arabic alphabet but not the Arabic language. Enclosed with the letter were fifteen dirhams in notes, five from my mother and ten from Mrs Malani, and the letter itself contained just a few disturbing words, 'Come home. We need you here. No one needs you in Fez.'

The second letter was from my Uncle Isaiah Ben Hamo, a converted Jew, now fanatically Muslim. He had seen my aunt, plump and beautiful, as a young girl and fallen in love with her. He had asked my grandfather if he could marry her and was refused unless he converted to Islam, which he did. The letter read, 'Don't waste your time in school. Come and take care of your family. Your mother and sisters could be raped at any time.'

The third letter came from Uncle Mimoun with a warrior's mentality. He hadn't written the letter himself, as he couldn't read or write, and it was in a jumble of Arabic, Tarifit and Spanish. 'Your mother and sisters are in danger of being raped. You risk finding yourself the uncle of children of fornication.'

School meant everything to me and nothing to them.

Deeply saddened and emotionally embattled, unable to

concentrate, I went back to the room. On my way, happening on an intersection where several doughnut merchants congregated, I spotted Bozaid carrying a dozen doughnuts, several books and reading a gossipy local newspaper. His voice rose like thunder, 'Is it too hard to say good morning?'

'I'm in a hurry! I forgot my book,' I apologised.

'You could share mine,' he offered.

'I like to scribble notes in my book,' I answered.

Walking and talking, I found myself inviting Bozaid to our room. Everybody was in, and it was Omar's turn to cook. The pot was ready for tea; all it needed was mint. I went out, bought a fragrant bouquet, and returned in an instant. Bozaid's doughnuts were shared, and everyone had a small glass of mint tea.

Looking at Bozaid leafing through the newspaper, I asked, 'What's the news?'

Bozaid folded the newspaper and passed it to me to read. I couldn't help seeing the front-page headline: 'French Army Kill Two Boys and One Girl'. On the same page, lower down, there was a second headline: 'Algerian Guerillas Destroy Two Bridges and Kill a French Colonial.'

'No one expects to be saddened in the early morning with such headlines, but this is how every day starts for me,' said Bozaid.

Rammani snatched the newspaper from me and said, 'How interesting this is!' Reading in silence, he suddenly said, 'This is "stop killing by killing".'

Bozaid, outraged, said, 'It's not the same.'

'I was thinking from a moral point of view,' said Rammani.

'So was I,' replied Bozaid, indignant.

Caught in in the middle of this heated argument, I changed the topic. 'Mr Murzook will give us the exam date...' I said.

Barely awake and appearing to suffer from a hangover, Taji shouted, 'The date? What exams?'

'Mock exams,' I reminded him.

'You've spoiled my morning,' Taji shouted back.

During the entire morning, my mind kept cogitating over my letters. I saw myself back home: shepherding a few sheep, riding a donkey, cultivating honeybees, and loosening the ground around fig trees. Uncle Ben Hamo had several daughters and would be delighted to be relieved of one of them. I wouldn't be the worst choice of husband for one of his daughters, since he had given his eldest daughter to a convicted murderer. Maybe I could buy a passport and get into the world of *hashish* — the market was open for the brave. Remaining at school required money I didn't have.

The time for class to start, eight o'clock, was getting closer, and for me, it couldn't come one minute too soon. 'It's time to go!' shouted Omar, and everybody jumped to put his soleless shoes on.

The street to the school was always noisy and crowded with schoolgirls. Bozaid, amazed and excited, thought he could steal a heart or two. Omar giggled at Bozaid's arrogance.

'We are to those girls what the untouchables are to Indians!' I scoffed at Bozaid.

Talking and almost racing each other, we arrived just in time, before Professor Allawi started his complicated lesson. Faissal and Marnisi knew my father had died. They both came and shook my hand. Embarrassed, I didn't want to be pitied.

Faissal took his seat, and to divert the attention from me, I asked him, 'What did you do on your holiday?'

'Revise,' he replied. 'What about you?'

'Revise.'

While we were talking, Professor Allawi and Mr Murzook appeared at the front of the class. As usual, Mr Murzook looked almost crushed with the heavy paper he was carrying. He looked quietly at the class and said, 'Mock exams start Wednesday and finish on Friday. The results will be announced the following Wednesday.'

Professor Allawi looked at him, smiled and said, 'More work for me!'

'The summer holiday isn't too far away,' said Mr Murzook.

'I have already booked my car on the ferry to Paris via Madrid,' replied Professor Allawi.

Mr Murzook left, and the lesson started. He went from geometry to algebra as if he were faced with geniuses.

The time before the mock exams passed in a wink, but while waiting for them and sitting them, I felt as if I had two heads – one where I studied and the other in the valley between Makran and Tassamat where I should be, home.

During those days, Taji made life hard for his cousin Omar and quarrelled with him constantly. He had a bullying attitude and brought up all the family problems and arguments. Every evening, Taji entertained us with talk of Omar's sisters' and brothers' problems, to Omar's disgust and embarrassment.

The Wednesday after exams was a nerve-wracking day. In the middle of the third lesson with Professor Himi, on the relationship between oxygen and breathing, the rector appeared in front of the class. He looked tired, heavily laden with paper and handed the pass and fail list to Professor Himi.

Professor Himi proceeded to read out the names in alphabetical order, and didn't use his gentle teaching voice. He pronounced each name with extreme clarity and strength. His voice reverberated throughout the mosque and one could almost hear him from the street. He announced the name, then 'passed' or 'failed'.

'Jusef, passed.'

The rector appeared again and announced five names. Mine was one of them. 'These five,' he said, 'have done very well and have won a financial award. Come to my office tomorrow with your ID to pick up your cash.'

Traumatised by my father's death, I was amazed I had even passed, let alone won an award. I went to pick it up on Thursday morning, but found the office closed. The rector had forgotten Thursday was a day off.

I never thought I could get money free! Thursday was a long day for me. I went to collect my award early Friday morning. I knocked on the rector's door, it slid open, and my mouth with it. Mountains of notes of all different sizes and colours, new and directly from the bank, were piled high on the rector's desk. He proudly nibbled from each pile and handed the cash, like alms, to me. I felt happy, but not proud.

Leaving the rector's office, I joined the class already in session. Every student knew where I had been, but not how much I had been given. My award didn't assuage my sense of guilt. *I am needed at home.*

13

I didn't usually wish my life away, but the few weeks left before final exams couldn't pass too soon. Omar and Rammani, terrified by their mediocre exam results, resorted to early morning yoga. Taji lost his cynicism and confidence. I rarely went out during this time, except to visit the public latrine half a mile away.

I was in the room alone one midday with the door closed and the light on, when a rough pounding shook the flimsy door. It opened, and a head peeked in.

'Stop! Stop!' I shouted, jumping up. *It's either a tramp or a thief*, I thought. A different head bobbed in, so I lurched to the door and jumped out to find Moussa and Samir standing side by side. With tears in my eyes, I hugged Moussa, then Samir. I wondered what had brought them here and how they had found me.

Via Mr Lazar, they had learned where I lived and had heard about my father's death. I couldn't have wished for any better surprise than seeing them. Both looked happier and healthier than the days when we had rotted in the *funduq*. I offered them tea and asked about Kamil.

'He's all right, but not as he should be,' answered Moussa.

Neither Moussa nor Samir wanted to discuss Kamil. *Something is wrong*, I thought, but couldn't imagine what it might be.

'Do you know what? I got an award!' I told Samir.

'Blood from a stone!' commented Samir.

It was Taji's rota. One o'clock ticked, but there was no Taji, and no food. Omar and Rammani arrived for lunch. I introduced them to Moussa and Samir, and they clicked immediately. Having two guests and nothing to eat was neither comfortable nor an honourable position for me. Thanks to my award, I invited everybody out for a meal in memory of my father.

As I hated Bab Ftouh, we all clambered to a nearby restaurant in Boujloud to have couscous. All young, but with no visible signs of youth, we sat around a low table. We spoke politics, religion, society and family. Omar and Rammani left in a hurry to resume their revision, but Moussa, Samir and I went to a nearby café. The weather was hot, and we sat on the terrace and watched the peddlers, some bustling and some shuffling.

'What have you been doing?' I asked Moussa.

'Nothing I haven't done before,' he replied with a smile on his face.

I looked at him and wondered. Moussa, who usually liked to tease, quickly realized he had lost me. 'Beyond obtaining a passport, nothing is obtainable in this land,' he said.

Samir and Moussa didn't say what their plan was for the night. I worried about where they might stay, as my room was far too small to house two extra boys, and I had no extra bedding. 'What are you up to tonight?' I asked Samir.

'Going home,' answered Moussa, sharply.

'How?' I asked.

'By lorry,' replied Samir. I was unaware there were lorry drivers with huge Mercedes carrying goods, such as potatoes and wheat, from the south to Nador. To add to their revenue, they stuffed people in the back of their lorries. *That's how I should get home*, I told myself.

The three of us headed to Bab Ftouh at half past nine in the evening. They wouldn't be able to leave until much later, as lorries had first to be filled with goods. Trafficking illegally, the drivers picked up people late in the evening. We went to a small café and ordered a pot of tea. Lamenting the cruel hand fate had dealt us, we waited for a smuggler to appear. When one showed up, Moussa and Samir headed to Nador, and I hurried back to my damp, dark, cramped room.

Living like a *Sufi* the following weeks, I continued my revision, my mind all the time full of bread, but my tummy, empty. On the eve of the exams, to fortify ourselves and raise our spirits, Omar and I purchased bread, oil and mint. To refresh our intelligence, we agreed to go to sleep early and that meant, for me, switching off the light. We all checked that we had our student IDs and the exam IDs. We knew no one would be allowed into the exam hall without them.

Dawn crept into the dark room. Unusually, we all awakened simultaneously and together prepared our breakfast of bread and tea. Omar and Rammani headed to the hall first, then Taji. I picked up my jacket dangling on the hook right above where I slept, checked again for my IDs and, to my horror, found they were missing. I frantically checked every piece of clothing I owned, my sleeping area and everything surrounding it. I found nothing, and the time for the exam was quickly nearing. With nowhere left to look, it was either stay or go. The exam hall was half an hour's walk from my room. Heart in my mouth and stomach churning, I took one last look at the empty room and left. I arrived just a few minutes before the main door was to be shut; two loud, rough men policed each side of the French door. In the hope of explaining my case quietly without making a scene, I approached one of them.

The man thundered, 'What?'

'I don't have my IDs for the exams,' I said.

'Go and bring them,' the man instructed, dismissively.

'I lost them,' I pleaded.

The sentry pretended not to hear. 'Unless you have your ID cards, we are not going to let you in!' the guard from the other side shouted.

Frozen, standing still, I watched the last of the very late students stepping in. Refusing to go away but not allowed to enter, I was spotted by Professor Allawi, who was just arriving. 'We know him! He's known!' shouted the professor. His words were my exam IDs.

Shaken to the bone from the start, I took my seat, pulled out a few pencils, a ruler, two pens, compass and protractor, and glanced about. Several nervous faces were scattered around, but I recognised none. The building was enormous, yet every room was being used. The bell rang to begin the National Exams, and my heart sank. The morning was pretty tough, and no one expected the afternoon to be better.

Back in my room during lunchtime, I told everybody I had lost my IDs. I was certain someone had lifted them, but who?

I remembered Omar had stolen my blanket, but that didn't mean he had taken my IDs. He kept quiet, and so did everybody else. For now, I decided not to trust any of them.

We returned to the exam hall after lunch and waited for the door to open. Omar complained of a splitting headache and his knees buckled, dropping him on the stairs. I sat beside him and spoke to him, but he didn't answer. He slowly closed his eyes and fell sideways onto my shoulder. I thought he was playing, and moved away. As I moved, he crumpled lifelessly onto the stairs.

'Don't fall asleep!' I yelled, then realized Omar had fainted. I didn't know what to do, and hoped some adult would come and help, but nobody twitched a finger. I fanned Omar while Taji talked to him. As if emerging from a spell, he slowly opened his eyes and sat up, dizzy, not knowing where he was. I put my arm under his, took him inside and handed him to one of those unsympathetic sentries. Omar's fainting triggered the rector's intervention.

Before the end of the afternoon, in the middle of the exam, a microphoned voice vibrated through the room and the building. 'Students, you are instructed not to leave until the rector has a word.' The rector, wearing heavy green glasses and surrounded by staff, appeared on the balcony. He looked down at us from above and shouted, 'Some students have fainted this afternoon because they are too frugal with food. Go and eat!'

It's not advice we need, it's food! I shouted to myself, indignantly.

* * *

WHILING THE TIME AWAY after the end of the exams and waiting to hear if I had passed or failed, I went out to buy a *jellabah* for my mother. She had never had one. But, buying a *jellabah* without a veil was like wearing underpants without trousers. A crooked trader tried to sell me a veil to go with the *jellabah*, but I couldn't see my mother, living on a high mountain, speaking to my uncles and cousins from behind a veil. They knew her and she had known them from birth. *A jellabah or veil would make my mother look like a clown*, I thought, and abandoned the idea. Now a widow, she had to face wolves and hyenas. Squabbles over gossip, a tiny piece of land, moving boundary stones or old inheritance never stopped.

After a feverish week of waiting, the moment of truth arrived. I went to the exam hall to hear my fate. The street and the stair where Omar had fainted were packed with students, some with their parents, others with siblings.

Within an instant of the door opening, those in the street pushed in, crushing each other; it felt as if the walls were closing in. The air became thin, and I could hear the heart beats of those close by.

The rector, like a prince surrounded by his aides and flanked on both sides by professors, emerged on the balcony of the first floor, his favourite place. With a vibrating and worrying tone, he read a short list. He stopped, took a long breath, and added, 'Tomorrow at eight-thirty sharp the oral starts.' He whispered to one of his aides and made a U-turn. It was quick and brutal.

The reality sounded unreal – the list was shockingly short. Over seventy per cent had failed! My name had been called, but none of my roommates'. Of those I knew, only Marnisi, Bozaid and Faissal had been called. The crowd was collectively struck dumb. Omar stood beside me, and Rammani slumped to the floor. With the help of Taji, I convinced Rammani to head back to our room.

We had all known exams would be tough, but never expected such a massacre. For most, years of schooling had ended painfully. My fate remained still uncertain; the oral exam would skim the cream.

In our room, I found Omar launching into a frenzied tantrum. He kicked, pounded and punched the walls, the table, the floor, the door, anything in his way. He cursed his father, his grandfather and hissed his needs had never been met. He had turned into a deranged *mahboul*. I was mesmerised by his kicks for a moment, but then, shocked, I yelled, 'Stop! Stop!', but nothing reached Omar's ears.

Holding his shoulders and looking into his red eyes, I whispered, 'You know what happened to my cousin Ahmed.' Omar had heard the story. In an instant, he calmed down, went to his mat and pulled the covers over his head.

It was my turn to cook that evening, and I asked Taji to swap, but he refused. I bought two loaves of bread and made tea.

The night was incredibly short, and the sun quickly rose hot and high, but never reached our room. Omar was up first, and I suspected he had never slept. He went out and didn't show up for breakfast. Rammani and Taji left after him, so I had breakfast alone. Still puzzled and anxious about my missing IDs, I carefully leafed through the books and papers lying on the floor. I opened one of Taji's books and, to my surprise and horror, found my IDs tucked inside. Feeling deeply betrayed, I wanted to take revenge. I picked up my IDs and put them safely in my pocket.

I went to the school which, just the morning before, had been besieged by students outside the door and packed with them inside. Laughter and voices had been heard from a distance away. Pedestrians had serpentined through the throngs. Now the street was quiet; the building itself like a ghost town. I entered and felt as if I were the only one inside. Then, I heard a vague whisper, but was unable to spot its source. I gave up looking, but the whispering continued. When I looked up, I spied Faissal waving from the balcony. He descended and greeted me with, 'Didn't you hear me?'

'Yes, but I didn't know where the whispering was coming from.'

'I was trying not to make too much noise,' he said. 'Two professors were chatting about their holidays. I hope I won't get either of them. By the way, we are on the same list. Your name comes after mine. This is a new list.'

Still whispering, I heard my name being called by Professor Drissi. As he stood waiting for me, he looked short and smart, as usual, and wrapped in an air of arrogance. 'Take a seat,' he said the instant I stepped into the classroom.

Watching him scribbling on his papers, I noticed how small his left hand was, and how small also, the watch on it. 'First question,' the professor said. 'Identify four positions where the grammar forces the tongue to flatten and touch the back of the lower front teeth.'

'It is not mentioned in the book, sir,' I answered, dazzled by the question.

He laughed. 'Page five,' he said.

I picked up the book, leafed to page five, and there stood the answer, in very large print.

'Question two: "She is the moon". Explain.'

'She is like the moon,' I said.

'You have watered down the poetry. What makes them alike?'

'Physically, nothing,' I answered.

'What, then?' he asked.

'The likeness resides in the poet's emotion, not in the physical resemblance between the woman and the moon,' I responded.

'How was the poet able to ignore the differences,' he asked, 'and liken a living being to a massive, dark stone? For me, it's almost an insult.'

'Maybe the poet was mad,' I said.

He laughed. 'You think his emotion was the source of his madness?'

'It could be,' I responded. 'The likeness is only in the poet's mind.'

'Even assuming he is mad,' he said, 'we all enjoy the poem. Why?'

'Because we are like him,' I said.

'By that you mean we are all mad, like him?'

'Not impossible,' I said.

'My wife likes the poem. I will tell her she is a bit mad.'

He scribbled something on his paper and asked me to leave.

Coming out of Professor Drissi's room, I felt like going home and thought to myself, *It's the same for everybody*. After a day and a half being grilled in my orals, I went to my room to wait for the results, but the atmosphere in the room was hell. Omar and I were no longer talking. I became suspicious and frightened of what he might do. Driven by bold and blind emotion, he might just set the room on fire.

Two days later, I went to hear my fate again. Faissal and Bozaid were already there, waiting. The rector came and stood on the first floor balcony with his entourage, but the audience, which had previously been several hundred, had been reduced to less than sixty. There were now more academics on the balcony than students on the ground.

Professor Bozian forced himself through the crowd towards me, 'You are first or second! A place at boarding school might be offered to you.'

Very happy I had passed, my mind immediately flew to the needs of my family. I suddenly longed to go home.

That afternoon, I packed everything that I owned, including my flute, which I had never had a chance to enjoy. Gazing at where I had slept, Omar, with a cracking in his voice, said, 'It looks like an empty grave now.'

I asked Taji calmly, 'What were my ID cards doing in your book?'

'You lost them,' he retorted.

'But I found them in your book,' I said.

'Which book?' Taji asked.

'Your dictionary,' I answered.

'I am not interested in your cards!' he shouted aggressively.

'I found them in your dictionary,' I repeated. 'They weren't on the floor. How did they find their way to the middle of your dictionary?'

'I never thought you would accuse me!' Taji responded. 'I swear I didn't put them there!'

I was angry and puzzled, but didn't know who to accuse. Nevertheless, whoever had taken my IDs had nearly ruined me. I picked up my belongings without looking back.

Leaving Omar, Taji and Rammani behind, I headed to Bab Ftouh to catch a lorry. While standing and talking, a gigantic man wearing a black leather jacket whispered, 'Where are you going?'

'Nador,' I answered quickly.

'Join the group,' he whispered, pointing to five men of mixed ages; some were sitting on the ground, looking tired and bored, while others were leaning against the wall as though waiting to be executed by an armed squad. One of them was very loud and doing all the talking in very crude language. I didn't take to the group and kept my distance, although, like them, I was waiting for the lorry.

A few moments before everyone lost hope, the lorry arrived, apparently from Meknes. It was an impressive Volvo, very long and with many wheels. It inspired admiration and confidence, but the lorry was already full, overloaded with grain.

With no joy, I joined the group. I wasn't sure I would be back to continue my schooling. I expected family problems at home and had no source of income. Leaving, I thought of Omar, Taji and Rammani. We had struggled for the whole year to make a future, but were all still lost.

It was midnight when the lorry driver and his co-driver shouted, 'Climb on! Climb on!' Everyone had paid, but was instructed, if asked by the police, to say it was a gift. I was the last to scramble on in the darkness of night.

14

Heading north to Nador, the lorry was a state-of-the-art Volvo, full of pulse, long, high and impressive. I eyed it enviously. *Life is where there's power*, I thought. With the other passengers, I was perched on the very top, like a dove on the branch of a cedar tree. Happy to be high up, inspired by the Volvo's speed, Tahar began to sing. He had a nice voice, and everyone was seduced by it. After some miles over the rough roads, it started to get cold. A sharp breeze was biting hard. Tahar stopped singing, hid his head from the wind, and so did I, but dodging the wind didn't stop the cold.

The road was busy and noisy with many lorries going up and down. Drivers flashing headlights at each other turned the road into a sky full of falling stars. I thought the flashing lights were a friendly night greeting between the kings of the road; in fact, they were a warning that the highway patrol was ahead.

Passing Taza, coming to an open space, the lorry stopped. *This is where the French lady paid for our breakfast*, I remembered. I wished she were here, but to be in darkness like this, looking for small stones to wipe my bum, I wouldn't wish even on Omar, who I thought had stolen my IDs and had certainly stolen my blanket.

The driver and the co-driver came and asked, 'Is all well?'

'It's too cold,' I said. Tahar supported me.

'The tarpaulin!' said the driver.

It didn't take long for them to pull the tarpaulin over us and cover the entire back of the lorry. I started to choke, but thought it was just me. A few minutes later, everybody was making gasping sounds. We pushed up on the tarpaulin and some air crept in, but it wasn't enough. We tried to keep still and put up with it, but it got worse. Tahar complained of a headache and vomited over me. The stench in the enclosed space made everyone retch.

I became desperate for air, gasped and gagged, and tried to get the attention of the driver by banging on the sides of the lorry. 'We can't breathe! Stop!' we yelled.

Hearing the shouts, the lorry slowed and ground to a halt. The driver and his helper rolled back the tarpaulin, and everyone drank in the fresh air, filling his lungs to the point of bursting. Tahar was limp, weak, and asked for water. We melted into the loose wheat while breathing in the precious air.

'You nearly suffocated us!' I complained to the driver.

'No,' said his assistant a few metres away. 'Pigs don't die,' he guffawed.

'We paid to be on the top of the lorry, but not under a tarpaulin,' I retorted, nervously.

As the lorry moved on, we endured the cold wind rather than lack of air. An hour later, we stopped again. The driver came to the back and said, 'We need the tarpaulin back on. The highway patrol is only a few miles away.'

'No tarpaulin!' we all shouted.

'I will come back to pick you up if you stay here until the patrol is gone,' yelled the driver.

I felt his real intention was to dump us on the road in the dark, in the middle of nowhere. We quickly bonded against his suggestion. Looking nervous, frustrated and irritated, the driver took a side road and stayed off the main road until dawn. We spent the night under the sky.

The lorry rejoined the main road just as the sun was rising enough to leave a haze. Feeling life coming back, I asked Tahar, 'What were you singing?'

'My own song,' he answered.

I thought I could sing much better than he. 'I play the flute,' I told him.

'Can you play now?' he asked me.

'I have no breath!' I answered.

We arrived safely in Nador, but felt worse than boars. With no immediate coach to Arkmane, I slept in the station and waited for the afternoon coach.

I bought a ticket and secured a seat, but beside a man who stank. Travelling east, sandwiched in a small seat, I looked out from the coach, where the Mediterranean Sea looked still, quiet and sky-blue. I wished I were on the other side, Spain or anywhere else in Europe. The bumpy road and rocking coach reminded me of playing my flute in the same coach on my first journey. I recalled the snake charmer tapping his snake beside me and terrifying the travellers. Now, I couldn't play. I wondered what had happened to me, what had changed me. I had become wary, too anxious, and suspicious of people, but still carried my flute like a talisman.

I arrived in Kariat Arkmane about eight o'clock, but life there died at four; I could see neither man nor donkey; just one policeman remained, patrolling the village and the prisoners confined to the low-ceilinged jailhouse.

My sister Zina (meaning 'beautiful') lived one and a half hours' walk from the village, and her two eldest children were older than I was. I decided to stay the night with her, though I anticipated her boys would tease me, as their father had taught them to do from an early age. I was very glad to spend the night with Zina, but more so to leave in the morning.

Before lunchtime, I was at home. Dargan, the family dog, black and handsome, jumped and ran around me until I bent down to pet him. Dargan's memory of me seemed to be strong as ever, as if I had never been absent. He bounded up the walkway in front of me, but I found the house empty when I arrived. The main door was open, anyone could get in, and the house was full of silence.

Not knowing in which field my mother was, I kept asking the dog. Dargan shot straight out the door, but soon he returned, dancing and bouncing in front of my mother as she walked toward the house.

Standing outside, I watched her put her hand to her brow to shield her eyes to get a better look at me. Her dim vision required glasses, but she had never had them.

'Wait!' I shouted, as she was carrying two bundles of wheat.

She stopped, dropped her parcels, and I ran to meet her in the middle of the field; she hugged me and I kissed her head. She looked at me as if trying to discern the exact changes in me, as if it weren't me, and I the same with her. She looked different: smaller, thinner and more wrinkled than I remembered. She leaned over to pick up a heavy bundle of wheat, and I saw her breasts, strikingly, very long, very thin and dangling. I felt sorry for her. I grabbed her bundles, and we walked back home together.

'Where are Amina and Rabbia?' I asked.

'Amina is somewhere in the mountain,' she answered. 'Rabbia is in a field cutting crops.'

Tired and hungry, Rabbia came home. She looked sad, wrinkled, shabbily dressed and not wanting to talk. I wished I could change her life. Impatiently, I went to find Amina, but my search failed. She wasn't where I thought she might be. There were several mountains and many valleys, and she could have been in any one of them. Having my flute with me, I played as loudly as I could. She must have recognised the flute and the tune, as peering into the very end of the valley, I saw a few sheep coming down toward me. As I kept looking, I saw my sister with a small stick in her hand as though she were a witch or living in Biblical times. She was chasing sheep and cows as fast as she could. We met in the middle of the valley and with an exchange of hugs, shepherded the animals home. Now coming from two different worlds, I from school and she from shepherding, I felt the difference between us, and we kept silent.

Dinner was ready when we arrived home. Mrs Malani joined the family for a jumbo couscous dinner. She looked at me again and again and said nothing. It was a reunion with an empty seat in the middle. My father was no longer there.

I gorged on couscous, enjoyed being with my family and

talking to Mrs Malani. I had left nine months before. Since then, the face of everything had changed. The summer had brought the best of nature: a variety of figs (black and white), peaches, apricots, but mainly prickly pear for those with big appetites and strong tummies to digest the seeds. It had been a prosperous summer; it had rained enough and in time. My family owned several small fields, scattered here and there; they had managed to plough them, but my mother, with no skills, no physical strength and no labourers, was now stuck. With the sun pouring its heat on the parched fields, the barley and wheat were wilting; soon they would become food for birds to pick and ants to carry.

The family's burden fell on me, and my mother wasted no time. She quickly handed me all the problems: crops to take care of, disputes with uncles and cousins, three of my sisters' marriages had become hell on earth, and she herself was tormented. I learned all that on my first night home.

The night was sweet but brief, and I woke up ready to go to the field. I picked the biggest, sharpest sickle and looked for four thimbles to protect my fingertips and enlarge my grasp, but there weren't any. Luckily, there were a few reeds scattered around, from which I made eight thimbles: four for me and four for Rabbia.

It was early dawn, and my mother was already dancing on her toes. 'Go to Tishibi,' she told me. 'The barley is crumbling,' she added. The field, Tishibi, was two hours' walk away. 'Do you want to ride the donkey?' she asked.

'No, leave it for Rabbia,' I responded, knowing how Rabbia hated walking.

'I hope she won't be too late. Otherwise, she will be fried,' my mother said.

The air was fresh, crisp, and my lungs felt full when I left in a rush. The sky was blue, and a slice of the sun was beginning to peek above the horizon. It looked bizarre and beautiful at the same time. I had to hurry to beat the oppressive power of the sun and wished I had a sombrero with a large brim.

On my way, I passed the beautiful complex, farm and factory, of a German capitalist rumoured to be an ex-Nazi. The factory with many acres of land was built halfway up a hill, fort-like, and was surrounded by a wall topped with broken glass so that no one would dare climb over. The factory had two connected swimming pools bordered with trees and grass. Passing by, I heard the gurgling of the water behind the wall. While shepherding on the neighbouring hill the previous summer, I had seen two naked girls playing and splashing in the pool, their father playing whack-a-mole with them, and I had wished I could be one of them.

Once I arrived, the barley field filled my eyes. It stretched forever and cutting it could only be a daunting task. I turned my back to the sun and started to cut the barley, but soon discovered how clumsy and unskilled I was. I grasped either too much or too little. The thimbles collided or simply fell off. I didn't know how to tie the barley into sheaves to keep the wind from blowing away everything I had cut. The higher the sun rose, the thirstier I grew.

One mile away, ten men were sickling barley, but they were too far away for me to copy their skill. *To cut and tie, that's what I need to learn*, I thought to myself. I trotted across the fields to the men and stood in front of two farmers while they were bent down.

'I will give you a job, if you are worth it,' the foreman teased. 'I will pay you one dirham per day,' he added, smirking.

'I own field thirteen across the way. I thought I might learn from you how to tie,' I said, smiling.

'He owns the field and doesn't know how to tie!' guffawed the foreman to the others.

'The man has a wife and doesn't know ...!' laughed another.

It was vulgar and personal. I swallowed the jokes and went back to my field, my skill no better than before. To my dismay, whatever I cut and piled was ferociously attacked by birds or stolen away by ants. Thousands, if not millions, of ants climbed over the stalks, energetically split away the seeds and carry them away. I toyed with them, disturbed their path, and delayed them, but they could not be deterred. Their speed, their precision and their vice-like grip amazed me. Some of them were light brown and others jet-black. The black ants, with big heads, long and sharp pincers, were to be feared. If they bit, their pincers got stuck in the skin. One of them crept over my legs, my thigh and reached my testicles. It bit and I jumped; the pain was quick and sharp.

'Yeoooooow!' I shouted.

I pulled my trousers down and yanked the black culprit off my privates. In my hand was half an ant, but the other half, the head and pincers, were lodged in my testicle. I scratched to remove the pincers, but they remained to torment me.

Rabbia and my mother arrived later in the day with water. My mother spoke in choppy phrases and looked emotionally and mentally absent. I thought she hadn't fathomed the scale of the job: sickling the stalks, tying them and taking them home, ten miles away, to be threshed and winnowed. She left in a hurry, and I asked Rabbia, 'Why is she so distracted?'

'There is a problem at home,' answered Rabbia.

Salwa had decided that day to take her eight children and leave her husband. She was beaten on a daily, if not hourly, basis, and despite her multiple injuries, my mother was against her leaving her husband.

I had thought, for many years, that all my sisters had wanted was a man, for I had hardly heard them talking about anything other than sex and men. Knowledge of the penis passed down from grandmother to mother, from mother to daughter, surpassed the best sexologist's. Rabbia was the exception. She didn't associate the penis, 'the dragon', with a husband. I had never heard her talking about the dragon's size, thickness and shape.

'A husband, for me, means the master of a slave,' she had told me. 'I would prefer to be slave to nature, the sun, rain, wind and stars, rather than be kissed by a pig, my skull disfigured with a head scarf, my face veiled.'

Rabbia and I stopped cutting the barley when we ran out of light. At sunset, night descended quickly, and the moon took over. Before leaving, we looked behind. 'We've made a dent in it,' said Rabbia. 'But it will take a week to harvest it all.'

'We don't have a week. There will be nothing to cut,' I said.

'The heat will crumble the stalks,' she agreed.

'Why don't we hire a few men to help us with the harvest?' I suggested.

'How would we pay them?' she asked.

'We could sell our two billy goats to pay for a couple of sicklers,' I said.

'Mother is sentimental about her billy goats,' she said. 'She argued fiercely with Father whenever he wanted to sell an animal. She has no farming sense. She preferred advance sale of the wheat at a rock-bottom price rather than see a billy goat going to the butcher. And you know what, whenever the drought hit, it took all the animals with it, so we were left with neither animals nor wheat. Mother loves her animals. Sadly, for her, they're all pets.'

Walking in the middle of the road, we had to give way to the German to pass. His white Mercedes left a huge tornado of dust. The road, made of compacted soil, was barely wide enough for a car. We had to dart off the road to escape the swirling dust.

Still walking, disturbed by the moon and a shooting star, Rabbia's legs started to fail her. She got slower and slower, and asked me to stop now and again. She was young in age but old in flesh.

As I expected, Salwa's brood, six boys and two girls, were at home when we arrived. The children shouted, cried, leap-frogged over each other, climbed the trees, jumped over the wall and ran all over the place. My mother, exhausted from kneading dough, looked sad and anxious. Rabbia disappeared the moment we entered the house. Amina was trying to bring the chaos to order among the shouting and scuffling boys with mayhem everywhere, but their mother was absent.

'Where is Salwa?' I asked my mother.

'Hiding,' she said.

'Hiding?' I asked.

'She left her husband . . . and has some nasty bruises,' she remarked.

Curious, I ran to find Salwa. I hadn't seen her for over nine months. My curiosity turned to horror when I saw her swollen head with old and new bruises all over, mainly on the face. With swollen eyes, bruised cheeks, she could hardly see from her right eye. She welcomed me as though she were in her own home. Acting as though her bruises were invisible, she asked me, 'How was your school year? Mother told me you did well.'

I felt that she tried to avoid the question I wanted to ask. *How can a man beat a woman, never mind his wife and the mother of his six boys and two girls?* Salwa's face said it all.

My mother continued kneading dough, and Rabbia refused to help. The children looked ecstatically happy at dinner and fell asleep one after another. Salwa grabbed their hands, I their feet, and we took them, swinging like ropes, to their corner.

I went to sleep, but the night turned out to be a turbulent one. I awakened in the early morning and heard my mother, Salwa and Rabbia moving around, whispering sadly. I jumped, as though a thief had broken in, but my mother quietly insisted I go back to sleep. 'What's the problem? What's the matter?' I asked.

'It's a woman's loss,' she said.

It was serious. Salwa had been between four and five months pregnant, and during the night, had given birth to a stillborn baby.

I was expecting them to bury the baby in the common cemetery, but it wasn't like that. I thought everybody should know about it, but they kept it secret. I saw them going out and digging a shallow hole on the boundary between us and our neighbour.

I was curious to see the stillborn baby and looked for it. Searching, I found a small package of bloodstained paper tied with cloth behind the door. I untied the cloth, the paper fell open, and the baby rolled out like a small dead rat. I put my hand on its head and felt the dark coldness. Trying to pry open its eyelids, I found them rigid. It had two very small, misshapen legs, and I noticed that it had been a boy.

I wrapped the shrunken body back into its makeshift shroud and moved it onto a high shelf, as we had two cats and two dogs, constantly hungry and hunting.

I watched my mother, Salwa and Rabbia taking the package away. They walked into the field and stopped at a stone that marked the boundary between two farmers' lands, where they had dug the hole. They were joined by several women and formed a circle with Salwa in the centre, then performed a precise ritual with their hands, palms facing each other and switching back and forth. I heard them repeat the phrase, '*Thwoh the lhadd* (This is the end)' nine times. In Tarifit, where one field stopped and another started was called 'the end' or 'the stop'. Burying a baby in such a spot and performing a verbal ceremony was believed to prevent any further miscarriages. In this way, Salwa would have no fear of another stillborn.

The baby was buried in a shallow grave on the boundary, 'the end'.

To prevent any more stillborn babies, Salwa had resorted to a superstitious ceremony. To dissolve her marriage, she asked me to journey to Sale to locate a famous sorcerer, Sfruy. I remembered that Lalla in Oujda had told me about him. When I refused to go, Salwa cried, wailed and chastised me.

She was married to her cousin and wanted to break the contract. She believed the sorcerer could destroy her husband's brain, and a divorce would be granted on the grounds of mental dysfunction. He would be pitied and she, excused.

I felt sorry for her. Apart from sex, there was no gravity between them. Salwa had never loved her husband, and he had never loved her either. They had despised each other before there was any idea of their getting married. Once the marriage was proposed, they hated each other even more.

Salwa's husband was very wide and short, with only a few short strands left on what was otherwise a completely bald head. My mother said, 'If only he had kept his hair, he wouldn't look so short.' Salwa had joked about his height, his ears and his hair since her teenage years.

Because Sanaa, her younger 'piglet' sister, had married first, Salwa lost her head. She wanted a man. My father exhausted all his abracadabra talismans, and they had all failed to bring a man for Salwa. My mother and father were convinced that a mysterious talisman had been composed by someone with significant power and a grudge against Salwa to keep suitors away. Every witch and witch doctor renowned in the region was contacted and paid well to dissolve this mysterious talisman, but still no man materialised. When marriage to

Salwa's prospective husband was broached, both my parents thought it was an opportunity not to be missed. That was how the tragedy of Salwa – and indeed, also her husband – was born. Both cried before and on the day of their wedding.

Salwa was able to find relief in a superstitious ceremony, in flying to Sale to ask Sfruy to drive her husband mad, but I wasn't. I sympathised with her; I shared her pain, her anger, and the loss of her child, but I wasn't able to drink from the same bowl of superstition. I criticised her and I lost her.

*   *   *

AS RABBIA AND I started on our fourth field, she fell ill. Her forehead was hot to the touch and she vomited frequently. I went and spoke to her several times, but she never opened her eyes or acknowledged my presence. With Rabbia ill, I was left alone to continue the sickling. I missed her presence and toughness in the field.

With Rabbia in bed, my mother was cornered. She agreed to sell her spectacular fighting billy goats. Amina was delighted with the news. 'Those two billy goats,' she said, 'never stop either fighting or running. It's torture to keep them safe.'

The abattoir was three hours' ride on a donkey; it opened each Wednesday at early dawn. Butchers came in a hurry to buy, slaughter, skin, butcher and sell the meat. The market was notoriously hectic, noisy, full of crooks and riff-raff. Curious visitors popped in to watch the fiery dynamism of selling and buying.

To sell the billies, I needed to reach the market at Kariat Arkmane before dawn. I awakened early; it was dark, and even the roosters were not yet crowing. I threw the saddle and saddlebags on the donkey and fed him with barley and water, knowing the day would be hard and long. My mother and Salwa tried to catch the billies, but it turned out to be too hard a job for just the two of them. I joined the chase and the billies were finally cornered and caught. I held them tightly against my chest and Salwa and my mother shackled their legs with a homemade rope. Each billy goat was stuffed in a saddlebag on either side of the donkey, and I rode the donkey, with my nephew Hussein behind, holding onto me. The goats never stopped kicking and bleating, and I checked on them constantly, as they could easily have been choked by the saddlebag rubbing against their throats.

Hussein was dozing, so I kept chatting to him for fear he might fall. It was still dark when we reached the vast dusty clearing called The Red Land. Out of the blue, one billy goat managed to loosen the knot and jump out of the saddlebag, causing the other goat to fall on the ground. We both jumped and ran after the escaped billy. We tried to corner him, but he defeated us and kept running away from the donkey and the other goat. After an hour of chasing in the dark desert, Hussein lost his breath and stopped, but I kept chasing the goat like a sheepdog until, turning, it came face-to-face with Hussein. He pounced on it and grabbed it. I took it back to where we had left the donkey and the other goat, but they were nowhere to be seen. I left Hussein with the goat and searched for the donkey. By that time, the sun was starting to rise. I found the saddlebag, but no donkey or goat. I moved farther and farther, then started to worry about Hussein, who was supposed to be under my protection. Carrying the saddlebag, I kept looking for the donkey.

Then, I spied it gnawing some straw left behind from cutting, as if it belonged there. Seeing me and guilty now, it darted away, but I caught it and lashed it, then took it back to where Hussein and the goat had been left. I left the donkey and goat with Hussein and went to search for the other goat; I looked and looked, but never saw it again.

I retied the rescued billy with my belt, and put it back in the saddlebag, balanced on the other side with stones. After a long while, we reached Hussein's home, where I left him. Continuing along my way, I was hit by a sharp pain in my head. To face my mother and sisters filled me with anxiety and dented my pride. This was my first big family responsibility since my father died, and I had failed.

I arrived at Arkmane late and exhausted. The donkey needed to be taken care of first. It might easily get lost, mixed in with all the other donkeys, or get involved in a fight over a jenny. To keep it safe and anchored, I laid the saddlebags on the ground, filled them with heavy stones and tied the donkey to them. The village was besieged with donkeys, thousands of them, and they all looked alike, either black or grey. I marked the spot, a shallow bridge, typical of primitive Spanish engineering.

The gatekeeper taxed me to enter with the billy on a leash. Feeling slightly nervous and naïve, I knew I'd have to be on my guard against clever, crooked dealers. Two middle-aged men ran up to me and asked, 'What have you been offered?'

'Nothing yet,' I said.

A ridiculous price was offered by one of them while his colleague kept palpitating the billy goat's neck, looking for defects. 'It is not fat,' he said. 'You should accept the offered price. It's good.' Again, he probed the goat's neck, its hind legs and added, 'Hm! Very little here!'

I resisted the offer, aware of their degrading technique, and for a while, the billy goat attracted no buyers. I just stood still and held the goat by a rope around its neck. Another buyer went past and shouted, 'What was the offered price?'

I told him. He shook his head, probed the neck of the goat, its hind legs, and said, 'Double price. Double price. Let it go. Let it go. Give me the rope!' He tried to snatch the rope from my hand, but I knew if I lost the rope, the deal was done and there was no title. I resisted his offer and held the leash tight around my arm.

As no other buyers appeared, I lost hope and wanted to get rid of the goat. I looked for the man who'd offered double, but he had slipped out of the market. I was lucky not to have done business with him, I was later told. He always offered a good price and promised to pay, but didn't. He would pass the animal to the butcher, collect his money and sneak out.

The market was thinning by the minute and I was still standing and holding the leash. The animal looked tired and almost ill. *I will never be able to sell it*, I thought to myself. *I can't take it back home. It will die.*

Fortunately, a butcher who had had a good morning's trade and had sold all his meat came in a hurry to buy more. 'What was the offered price, child?' he shouted.

'What is your offer?' I retorted.

With a good price, I was glad to clinch the deal. Receiving bloody cash on the spot, I relinquished the rope and watched the billy goat, once my mother's pet, on its way to be slaughtered.

The village Arkmane was a centre for gossip, playing cards, gambling, organising marriages and a murky spot for petty crime. Traders of all kinds – in barley, wheat, eggs, chickens, clothes, mousetraps, pigeon traps – spread their goods on the ground wherever they could and yelled loudly to sell their wares.

I needed to secure storage and went to Mr Hamoshy, who owned the shop at number twenty-one and was my half-aunt's husband. Mr Hamoshy had the reputation in the village of being full of himself, boasting about being handsome because of his red cheeks and being rich and wealthy because he rented a shop selling sugar, oil and salt. He had a maniacal interest in religious controversies, inviting self-professed scholars to his shop and trapping them with bizarre religious questions in the spirit of a Pharisee. He enticed them with tea to his shop only for them to be humiliated for his entertainment, as if they were rodents in a circus.

Scurrying, I burst into his shop. Mr Hamoshy was standing behind the counter pumping oil from a big barrel into a small bottle, drinking tea and talking to a group of religious zealots behind him, also sipping mint tea.

'Mr Hamoshy!' I called to him. He looked surprised that I knew his name and glared at me over the counter. Saying nothing, he kept staring.

'May I keep my shopping somewhere here?' I asked.

Mr Hamoshy only dealt with important men, and I didn't look like one.

'Who is your father?' he asked.

'I am the grandson of your father-in-law, Mr Hashi,' I said.

He looked surprised that I referred to my grandfather rather than my father. Distracted by his guests for a moment, he then turned back to me and said, 'Any spot there in the corner, behind the door. I recall you have used my shop as your address,' he added, 'and I have some letters here for you. They arrived ages ago, but don't worry, we read them and there is nothing important.'

'May I have them now?' I asked.

Hamoshy turned to the back counter, ferreted around underneath, but couldn't find them. 'They'll turn up by the time you finish your shopping,' he said.

While shopping, a big lorry full of fish arrived with two men perched on the top shouting, 'Sardines!' I joined the queue and bought two kilos. *A family feast*, I thought.

Returning to Mr Hamoshy's shop, I found him still talking to and entrapping his guests. 'Here are your letters. You see, things never get lost in my shop!'

There were two letters from Moussa and Samir. I went out, sat on a windowsill, and read Moussa and Samir's letters. They were not in Paris, as I had thought, but in Frankfurt. They both worked at the train station. Moussa wanted to be a train driver and Samir an electrician. *I will write back once I am at home*, I thought to myself, but soon realised I might not return to Arkmane for a while. I popped into several shops to search for writing paper and discovered such a thing did not exist in the village. Like many, I then picked up my shopping and headed home towards Makran and Tassamat, nature's awe-inspiring shrines.

The donkey hee-hawed the moment it reached the peak of the hill and saw the house on the opposite one. Salwa's children heard the braying and rushed out to meet me. I cheered them with hollow sweets, then they all fought over riding the already-tired donkey. At dinnertime, my mother washed and gutted the sardines; Salwa fried them while her children, all naked, enjoyed poking each other's bums.

Fried sardines dipped in flour and mashed garlic was a formidable feast. No one was full or had enough, but the sweetened mint tea was expected to compensate for the lack of solid food.

'I lost a billy,' I said at dinner.

My mother pursed her mouth and peered at me. Salwa scowled at me. In a tense and humiliating atmosphere, I left.

'He's not up to the task,' I heard Salwa say.

'You weren't there to witness the drama!' I shouted to her from the other room. 'You and Mother did a shabby job! You didn't shackle the billies properly, and you dare tell me I'm not up to the job!' I enjoyed the nonsense of Salwa's children, but not her sarcasm and snideness.

Though the night was short, morning arrived slowly, plodding like a turtle. With the money from selling the goat, Rabbia and I went to the sicklers' pick-up point. We arrived early and about twenty men, old and young, were sitting or standing around, waiting to be picked for work. At first, they scorned us. They didn't believe we had a job to offer, and, even if we did, that we could pay. I was ignored, and Rabbia became the centre of attention. Four men were needed, but all twenty competed aggressively to charm her. They pushed and spoke over each other. Rabbia forgot the task and enjoyed the excessive flirting.

When we picked the men and agreed on the wage, they requested to be fed and housed. Feeding wasn't a big problem, but it was impossible to offer accommodation to four men of dodgy character in a household made up of women and children. I refused. The deal collapsed and we headed to the field. While on our way, Rabbia dove into a moody silence. Tired from working, and impressed by the men, she wouldn't have minded filling the house with riff-raff.

'Haven't you hired any sicklers yet?' asked Salwa at the end of a long day.

'Not yet,' I replied.

'This was the reason we sold the two billy goats and deprived the females from mating?' Salwa retorted, belligerently.

'The sicklers wanted accommodation,' I replied, hoping she would understand.

'No sicklers, no goats . . .' she said as she scurried away.

I looked at Rabbia and realised how angry and tired she was, sweat trickling down her cheeks, her underarms wet. 'I need to go and see Salwa's husband tomorrow. He's a rough middle-aged man, and an accomplished farmer,' I told her.

I hurried to see Anzar first thing in the morning. I found him bored, not knowing what to do with himself, but his fate wasn't any different from other farmers when the summer harvesting was over. He was happy to see me, but looked anxious. 'Is everything okay?' he asked, his children on his mind, I thought.

'Yes,' I confirmed. 'I need to hire some sicklers. Feeding them isn't an issue, but accommodation is.'

'Do you really have money to pay?' he asked.

'Yes, I have enough,' I answered.

With Anzar's help and without the distraction of Rabbia, I hired enough workers and we sickled the fields.

When all the fields had been cut, the real hard labour began. I gathered and carried on my back, like a donkey, piles of barley and wheat, and stacked them to be threshed and winnowed. I fastened the cow and donkey together with a yoke, then stood in the middle of a small field, held the reins of the yoke, and kept them orbiting around me all day long.

Under the stomping hooves, the grain and stalks split, the dust floated everywhere and penetrated my nostrils, my ears, lodged under my arms and between my legs in the folds of my penis. There were moments when I felt crazy, itchy, and wished there were a sea or river to jump in and never surface again.

While I was rotating the cow and donkey, Rabbia kept shovelling the stalks back into the circle with a pitchfork, and never stopped singing:

> *Mother, you are hard, blind and deaf,*
> *My life was carelessly written*
> *Discovered in a talisman,*
> *Hanging on the tail of a dog.*

THRESHING WAS A JOB, but winnowing was a skill. I had to learn how to harness the east wind and winnow the threshed stalks and grain in the air with a pitchfork. The grain speckled the ground, the stalks were carried away by the wind and the chaff even farther. However, the east wind wasn't always present or blowing at the right strength. The west wind was useless. It would gust and die, and sometimes it collided with the east wind in useless wrestling. Rabbia and I spent hours and hours under the sun waiting to capture the east wind. Whenever we were blessed, I threw the stalks with gusto and Rabbia passed a huge and wide, heavy, prickly brush over the grain, for the east wind often failed to carry unthreshed stalks.

By the time we finished threshing and winnowing the grain, the summer began to wane. The sun started to lose its virility like an aged man, and the winds, like a mob, could be heard blowing the trees' branches, sounds that all farmers dreaded.

Farmers living in the high mountains and well versed in the ways of bees shivered when they saw the drones executed and expelled from the hive by their fellow bees. The massive execution was a measure of austerity and a sign of hard times to come.

In a seemingly confused hurry, summer tidied itself up, but no one was really happy to see it dying, despite the scorching heat. Before the summer breathed its final breath, I was free, with no specific job to do, but no money to go back to school. I avidly read every book I had. Rabbia, wanting to be a herbalist, started apprenticing to Mrs Malani.

15

'Do you think one of Mrs Zainab's sons would like to be a sharecropper?' I asked my mother early one morning.

'Her sons are not able, except maybe the middle one,' she said.

'If he could farm our land, we would provide the cow, the donkey, the plough, and the seed,' I suggested.

My mother looked happy and hopeful, but preoccupied. 'Sanaa wants to see me urgently. I want you to go with me.'

'Why?' I asked.

'I have an uneasy feeling. Her marriage is hell,' she replied. Clenching her teeth and without saying another word, she left the room.

I broke the day early and rushed to see Mrs Zainab and her son, Baja. Mrs Zainab lived with her five sons in a tiny one-room hut. It was not protected from the wind by garden walls or trees, or shaded in the summer. She and her children had been deprived from inheriting any land, for her husband had died before his father.

Mrs Zainab was happy to see me. She came out, gave me a welcoming smile, and was followed by an old, starved dog. I was struck by how tall she was and how skinny she looked, with painfully protruding cheekbones. Sadly, rumours around were that she had had an affair with the local *hafiz*, and for that reason, her women neighbours berated her.

'What's in your heart?' she asked me.

'I wonder if Baja would farm our land as a sharecropper?' I asked.

'He's here,' she said and beckoned him. I had never had any contact with him. All I knew of him was second-hand. He came out and in complete contrast to his mother, was short, looked subdued, his shoulders looked perpetually shrugged, and he was clothed in black. He looked shy, but had a piercing voice.

His mother explained, and he smiled. 'What would be my share in the crops?' he asked. (It was understood that most offers were one-fifth, and the best was one-quarter.)

'One-third,' I offered.

He and his mother looked at each other and simultaneously nodded their heads. 'You have my word,' promised Baja.

With Baja's words in my ears, I rushed home. 'Mother!' I shouted, finding her outside the house. 'Baja will work the fields for us!'

'If we have rain,' she said cynically. She looked distracted, not really listening to me. She had been stirred by Sanaa's messages. As the summer was on its last breath and winter was nipping, my mother couldn't put it off any longer. Frightened of what Sanaa might ask of her, she insisted I should go with her.

Like Salwa, Sanaa had many children, six girls and two boys, not counting those who had died. But, unlike Salwa, her marriage had not been arranged. She had fallen in love with her husband while crossing the mountain and had sung several songs for him:

> *Wherever you are, I want to be,*
> *Sharing the spoon, sipping the tea,*
> *Food of my soul, light of light,*
> *To be with you, no dark of night.*

UNFORTUNATELY, SANAA'S ROMANCE WAS short-lived. Her husband was tall, always smart, shrewd, a smooth talker, and Sanaa thought he was handsome. Sadly for her, he turned out to be a Casanova, but Sanaa wasn't a little creature ready to crawl into her shell and watch her husband have love affairs and a mistress a few doors down. She had hired every witch and sorcerer in the area surrounding the village, Zaio, to revive her husband's old romance with her, but they had all failed. She had paid many different witches to humiliate her husband by rendering him sexually impotent. The poor man had ingested many potions, and it was no wonder that he suffered from stomach disease, skin disorders and high blood pressure. Her husband was generous to himself and his friends, but frugal at home. Her limited allowance was sucked up by the witches.

Let down by witch doctors, she careened to vengeance. Not able to cool his carousing, she went for his brain.

'Come with me,' she beckoned me, a dinner plate in her hand, and out we went. I thought she wanted to visit one of her friends on the other side of the village, but she headed to the donkey park, where donkeys were tied against the trees or anchored to the soil with stones. I couldn't make sense of her destination. In the middle of the park, surrounded by donkeys, she yanked out a kitchen knife and began cutting donkeys' ears off. She had cut six ears before I fully realised the extent of her barbarism, cutting the donkeys' entire ears off, not just the tips for seasoning. I stopped her by grabbing her knife-wielding hand. Disgusted, I went to the small park, and she went home with a plate full of ears.

Coming back in the afternoon, I found two meat *tagine*s, cooked, seasoned and ready to be served. Sanaa's husband came and brought a visitor with him. She fed them with donkey-ear *tagine*. Her husband and his friend stuffed themselves and continued their evening discussion. I gave Sanaa a dirty look, but she wasn't bothered.

'I want his mind to match the donkey's brain,' she hissed. Sanaa had tried every Moroccan witch and witch doctor except Awisha, a Jewish witch and clairvoyant, domiciled in Melilla, a Spainish exclave on the northern coast of Morocco.

Sanaa knew about my desire to go back to school and my total lack of cash. 'I will buy you a shirt, a pair of trousers and your coach ticket if you are brave enough to go to Awisha,' she said.

At first, I refused. 'Awisha wouldn't help you,' I argued.

'Nothing is beyond Awisha!' she answered, naïvely convinced.

I had no idea who Awisha was, where she lived, or how to reach her. 'How can I find Awisha?' I asked.

'Easy. Go to Melilla, the place where Moroccans congregate, and use your tongue.'

'What does she look like?' I asked.

'I don't know.'

'How would I recognise her?'

'She will recognise you.'

'What will I tell her?' I asked.

'She will tell you,' Sanaa replied. She wasn't worried that to look for Awisha, I might get lost or arrested, have to stay two nights, sleeping who knew where, provided she could put a lid on her lover.

Because I couldn't scratch a penny from anyone to go back to school, I agreed to do the dirty job. I succumbed to my need, but the prospect of facing two borders, Moroccan and Spanish, gave me nightmares since I had no passport or even a proper identity card.

'Get up! Wake up! Get up! Don't miss the coach!' shouted Sanaa early the next morning.

With no food to start the day, I washed my hair with hand soap and took the earliest coach from Zaio to Nador. I paid the ticket collector, but didn't get my ticket. I thought the man would come back and give it to me, but he didn't. I reminded him, and he paid no heed, pretending to be busy fiddling with the large bag hanging around his neck like an albatross. Just before Nador, the coach changed ticket collectors. The new one asked passengers for tickets, which some had but others hadn't. Unfortunately, I hadn't. Those with no ticket were asked to pay from the coach's starting point, which created a riot. Luckier than some, I had two witnesses beside me who stood up for me. It was a ruthless and well-organised scam. I was happy to get off the coach.

I jumped on the next coach to Melilla and a world of difference hit me. The coach was packed with unveiled faces, young and old, speaking a mishmash of Spanish peppered with Tarifit. It ended its journey at the border, where Spanish and Moroccan police stood facing each other. The checkpoint was chaotic with no queue; passengers elbowed and jostled each other, and the atmosphere was unnerving. I followed the crowd, stuck closely to an old couple, and pretended to be their son. The old man showed his identity card, his wife moved forward, and I slipped by with her. The officer saw me and must certainly have thought I was an idiot, but my age was my saving grace.

In the 'no man's land' between the two sets of border guards, I found a job, though it was short-lived. Returning Moroccans who had arrived in Melilla from Europe were illiterate. I helped to fill out their entry cards, for fees that were surprisingly far superior to what my sister had promised me. The Spanish police saw me filling forms and didn't mind letting me go back and forth. I made their job easier and they thought I was there to make some money. It was ticking toward one o'clock, the police looked tired and relaxed, and in those instants of obscurity, I disappeared on a bus toward the centre of Melilla, where I had never been before.

Not knowing where to get off, I stayed on the bus until it reached its final destination and was the last to get off. It stopped in a beautiful square between the sea and the main street. It felt like paradise to me. The wide boulevard was lined with sidewalk cafés, swaying palm trees, and big shops selling rows and rows of watches: Prima, Omega, and the rest.

I heard the word 'Exchange!' and wondered what it meant.

I heard, 'Pesetas! Deutschmarks! Dollars!' Standing in the middle of the street, not knowing which direction to take, I saw rich as well as poor people and followed the poorest, looking African. I passed a terraced café where traders with piles and piles of money in front of them sat enjoying their coffee and cigarettes. Armed police patrolled the street, and the traders were unrestricted.

The attractive and ornate boulevard ended in a twisted fork, where I stood and hesitated again. I took the left, as more people were going that way. Not far along was a large, barren uncemented area with red soil agitated by dust swirling in the air and the smell of fried sardines. Two traders in front of massive piles of melons called, 'Hey! Taste and buy! Pick and taste!'

In front of a high pile of melons and amongst the whirling dust, I became lost in my thoughts. *What am I doing here?* I thought to myself. *What has brought me here? My needs or Sanaa's? We are both lost for different reasons.*

I spied two women, one far taller than the other, looking relaxed and happy, emerging from the boulevard, both carrying baskets and moving up a steep road full of wide potholes. From several metres away I shouted, 'Do you know where I can find Awisha?'

'The witch?' answered one of them.

'Yes,' I said.

'Follow me,' the older woman beckoned. A few metres up the hill, on the right side of the road, stood a row of dilapidated terraced houses. They all looked alike: low, with tiny doors and different shades of blue paint peeling off. The women stopped, spoke to each other, turned around to me, and said, 'Look! Cross the road. Number fourteen is Awisha's house.' *She must be very famous*, I thought to myself.

Crossing the road, I felt a wave of blood shooting through my head, then found myself at Awisha's door. I thumped on the door, and a woman opened it as if I were an expected guest.

'Come in,' she said, without asking who I was or what I wanted.

She struck me as dwarf-like, very short but very wide, and impressed me with a round, pinched face, full of energy. She was clothed completely in black with a scarf wrapped around her head, and the ends hanging down her back like a dog's tail.

'Follow,' she said. She took me to a seat in a small, dark closet with a low ceiling, no window, and just a thin candle spitting wax in a corner.

She sat opposite me, her knees rubbing against mine. 'I detect something important is troubling you, your family or someone you love. That is why I am here,' she said. 'I won't let you go from here before you see the light, and the tear is mended. Where have you come from?'

'Zaio,' I responded, 'but I live in Kebdana.'

'I know where it is,' she said.

'I am here on behalf of my sister Sanaa,' I explained. 'She has a marital problem with her husband and wants your magic power to bring her husband back to her, as he is a womaniser.'

Awisha scurried out of the closet and went into another closet, tiny and dark, adjacent to where I sat. There, on a little round table in the corner she lit two red beeswax candles. Then, she disappeared into the kitchen and returned with a big bowl of water that she put between the candles on the round table. Returning to me, she took me to the closet and asked me to sit beside her on a tiny, low chair around the small round table. Again, she sat too close to me; had she touched me, I would have taken her for a whore, and then I wouldn't have known what to do.

'Remind me of your sister's name. What is her husband's name?' she asked. She repeated the names after me. 'What does he do? How many children do they have?'

I got confused and started to count them on my fingers. I certainly gave the impression of being simple.

'For how long have they been married? Do they share a bedroom?'

'How would I know?' I answered.

I couldn't answer all her probing questions. She pulled two tall, thin cruets from a cabinet under the low table, one I thought was oil and the other vinegar. She poured a teaspoon of oil into the water. The oil broke into different sizes of drops, swirled around and floated on the top.

'Here he is.' She pointed with a wand at the floating drops and said, 'He is a womaniser,' and she pointed to the largest drop. 'Look at this. He has fallen in love with this big cow. Look at her! Look at her! Do you see her?'

'No,' I answered. I was looking to see a picture, to know who the woman was.

'She is following him wherever he goes and giving him no peace!' She then dropped a spoonful of vinegar into the water and asked me to watch. The vinegar sank down to the bottom and immediately dispersed. 'Sanaa is sinking. She is in a whirlpool between her husband and his lover. I will destroy this cow, bury her alive and restore the broken union between Sanaa and her husband.'

She led me back into the other room and handed me two balls of a black, foul-smelling, hardened mixture. Hesitating, I recoiled. Surprised by my fearful gesture, she gave me a piercing look, but smiled afterwards.

'What are those?' I asked.

'My might, my soul! Call it whatever you will!' she said. 'Stone and mortar need to be forced to hold each other before they support each other. Oil and vinegar are tasty when mixed, but they don't always stick together. There is a *bagra* (cow) coming between Sanaa and her husband. The *bagra* should die.'

Nervously, I picked up the balls and asked, 'How should I use them?'

'Nip a tiny piece and sink it in a pot of tea or coffee just for him to enjoy.'

I shivered. *Poison*, I thought. The fee was extortionate, more than Sanaa had predicted. I worried about how I would explain it to Sanaa so that she would believe me. Awisha took me to the door and gave me a dirty look. I left and she slammed the door behind me. I wondered why, as I had paid her in full.

I remembered the road and headed back to the melon market. I pulled the balls from my pocket, smashed them on the dusty ground and stamped on them, but they were very hard to crack. I jumped on them and ground them into the soil.

A middle-aged woman saw me and yelled, 'Sin! Sin! Don't stomp on food!'

'It's magic, not food!' I shouted back. She accepted my word and went away.

Quickly, the afternoon caught up with me. I hurried to the boulevard to catch the bus back to the Spanish border. Standing waiting, I wondered, *Will I make it home?* A sudden foreboding enveloped me, like a vulture circling above me and ready to nip. *There's something wrong with my trip here, something with Sanaa as well. Do I need to go through all this just to be able to pay for schoolbooks? Awisha has no magic for Sanaa, yet my sister needs to believe in something magic. I can't give her Awisha's balls to poison her husband.*

Still waiting for the bus, I spied what looked, from a distance, like a pig's dropping. I picked it up, tried to wad it in my hand, and it didn't crumble. It was a piece of burnt rubber. I wrapped it up and put it in my pocket.

The bus arrived and was only half full. Going out from Spanish Africa to Morocco was easier; no one bothered me. For the Spanish, I was one problem less. For Moroccans, I was worthless, carrying no goods.

Very little transport was available from Nador to Zaio so late in the afternoon. Travellers preferred early morning and avoided the spooky late afternoon. There were a few taxis, but they charged higher prices and didn't move until they were full. A taxi broker shouted, 'Berkan! Berkan!'

'A seat for Zaio?' I asked.

'Yes,' he responded, 'but full price,' even though Zaio was halfway to Berkan.

Leaving the town, the taxi was half-empty, but an arrangement had been made to pick up contraband on the outskirts. One smuggler was a distinctive, good-looking woman, full of energy and charm. She chatted all the way to me, and wanted to know what had taken me to Melilla. I told her the truth: magic and Awisha.

'Your sister should just do the same as her husband,' she told me.

She asked to be dropped several miles before reaching Zaio, in the vast desert of Sabra. It was completely dark, and no house or light was visible. Everyone wondered where she would go. She carried some blankets and a few loaves of bread. The driver dropped me in the middle of the village, in a eucalyptus grove, opposite a café.

* * *

SANAA SMILED AND LOOKED happy when she opened the door and realised it was me, late that night. She was in a hurry to hear what Awisha had said, had done, and what magic I had brought her.

'Things will get better and settled, Awisha said,' I lied.

'Is that all she said?' she asked.

'Your husband is harassed by a *bagra*,' I said.

'I knew that!' she exclaimed and clapped her hands. 'It's not his fault. But who is this *bagra*?' She tried to blame some women, but her mind couldn't settle on any particular one. 'I'll find out,' she assured herself. 'Anything else?'

'Yes. She gave me this magic.' I plucked the piece of burnt rubber from my pocket and handed it to her.

'What is it?'

'I don't know.' She looked at it in awe. 'A very small pinch should be burned from time to time,' I said.

Sanaa ran to the kitchen, pinched off a tiny piece and burned it. 'What a stench!' I exclaimed. The rubber released a horrific smell. Sanaa liked it, and the odour was so repulsive that it awakened her husband.

I was glad to leave; my mother and I walked about four hours through a valley, over the mountain, across several hills before reaching the long sloping valley that led home. My mother lost her breath several times and had to rest. I had never known she was asthmatic.

She collapsed the moment we arrived. I saw her breathing fast, with her mouth open and her tongue peeking out. I wondered if she were shuttling between life and death. My mother had been driven by compassion to make the journey to Sanaa, but Sanaa had tricked me; she never paid me.

* * *

THE TIME TO RESUME school was at my doorstep, but I was still at home. I had no money to travel, to buy clothes, books or for medical care. I had five brothers-in-law, three of whom were teachers; the other two were in Frankfurt. They had never offered a penny when I first went to school, and I wouldn't go to them cap in hand.

Not hesitating, I found myself pounding on Uncle Mimoun's door. Luckily, he was at home, surprised to see me, and invited me in. He had a guestroom and, in the middle, a massive radio and battery to match with an antenna strung through the window to the outside, a flag of wealth. When Mimount heard I was there, she joined us, but her presence made it embarrassing for me to explain the motive for my visit.

'Can I borrow some money from you?' I asked Uncle Mimoun. A long, deep silence followed. I didn't know what was bubbling in his head.

'How and when would you repay me?'

'I don't know.'

I left with no idea what he was thinking, but, nevertheless, any hope was much better than none.

Later on, Uncle Mimoun popped in unexpectedly. He came with Mimount and his rifle on his shoulder to show who he was. He would have carried a cannon if he could, or were allowed. Mimount was gracious and chatty. No dinner was offered, just tea with barley bread, but no butter. The snack was nearly over, and still I had no idea if Uncle Mimoun would lend me any money or not.

After the meal, while everybody was in a good mood, Uncle Mimoun thrust his hand in his breast pocket and handed me thirty dirhams. Neither my mother nor sisters knew the reason for it. 'This is the price for your flute that your uncle destroyed,' said Mimount. 'He's always felt guily about it,' she added. Uncle Mimoun and Mimount went home, and I was asked to explain the mysterious thirty dirhams.

16

The night before leaving for school, I talked with Rabbia. She was deeply unhappy with herself and her life, and with our parents for giving birth to her.

'How is your herbalist career progressing with Mrs Malani?' I asked, hoping to change her mood.

'Mrs Malani uses a variety of herbs and some are very delicate, but now everything is dry and dead. She loves to walk the mountains and survey the hills.'

'What about your soul stitching?' I asked.

'I despise people; I look at their skin, their eyes, their lips and their tongues. Rarely do I see harmony. Usually it's a fountain of hatred, doubt, sex, abuse and crime.'

I packed a small case with a few books and clothes, and trudged the deserted gravel road in the early morning to Moulay-Rachid, two hours away. I left worried that Rabbia might kill someone or herself. Extremely thirsty, I could see only dust and desert around and ahead. At Moulay-Rachid, I took a siesta under a eucalyptus tree and waited for the coach coming from the east, heading north to Nador. The first coach was full. The second came and was full, but the aisles were free. I paid for a seat, but didn't get one.

From Nador, I took the night coach to Fez, a long, lonely journey. Arriving at Bab Ftouh evoked an old anxiety; a feeling of insecurity grabbed me. I threw my luggage on my back and headed to Tazzi's house. I passed the door of the Rssif Mosque, and remembered the nights I had spent there, wrapped in cold air. I reached the house and made a beeline to my tiny old room, where Rammani, Taji, Omar and I had spent our last days together. The light was on, but the door had a new lock. I knew my old friends wouldn't be here. Others would be.

I waited until the caretaker came. The new caretaker was an old man with a white beard who looked religious and wore a tall Fezzi hat. After checking my ID, he said, 'You are sharing the room with two people. Wait until they come to let you in.'

More space, I thought to myself. I squatted near the door and waited for them. Nabil came first and opened the door for me. The first thing I saw were posters of half-naked men and women all over the walls. The two best corners were already taken. I had to content myself with the end of the room, close to the door and exposed to the draft.

I looked at Nabil and noticed that he was tall, older than me, but one year below me in school. Mounir arrived next and was surprised to find me laying my bedding out. He was also older than me, but short and lumbering. I felt uneasy with Nabil and later, he made life miserable for me. Both Nabil and Mounir refused to share the cooking, which made the room cramped and smelly.

Coming back from school, I found Nabil with a very young boy, naked, in his corner. I chased the boy out of the room, but he was starving and Nabil had paid him, so I found him in the room again the next day. I felt the room was dirty.

I asked to change my accommodation and reported Nabil's abuse to the caretaker, who didn't care, was rude and graphic in his reply. 'I can't put a lock on a boy's ass or castrate the abuser!' he said.

I was very lucky to get a spot in another house, Dial House. With two boys, I shared yet another exceptionally narrow, long room with a partition halfway up the wall, allowing only a façade of privacy. I began to run out of money and prepared myself to go home, as there was no job I could do; my only other choice was depravity.

I couldn't contain my joy when I was told in class that I had a boarding space in the new dormitory. I spent the night packing my books and left my blanket and sheepskins behind for unlucky Mahamad, who was not accepted as a boarder based on his marks and only lasted two more months before giving up and going home.

From Boujloud, I took a taxi. The driver dropped me at the amazing French wooden door, ornate in a Middle-Age style, with a forbidding and constantly manned barrier. A smaller side door was craftily inserted within the massive entrance. The moment my foot crossed the threshold, I heard a shout. 'Hey! Where are you going?' demanded a huge, burly man rushing to ward me off. 'Do you have any papers?' he asked.

Pulling my papers out of my jacket pocket, I showed him my ID.

He didn't look at them. He was illiterate and with his index finger, pointed to the bursar's office, which was at the very end of the school and at the top of several flights of steps. The school, a complex, was new and whitewashed. Outside the bursary door, a thin black man, looking bored to tears, was squatting on a small chair behind a tiny table and waiting for orders.

'Get in!' he motioned to me. The room was large, its walls were painted white and it looked chic. Spontaneously, I crossed to a young man who looked extremely pleased with himself, and yet not entirely at ease. Facing him, a girl was pounding on a typewriter sounding like a drum roll. The young man jeered at me with contempt, ticked my name on his roll and threw my school ID back at me. While scribbling, he flirted with the fashionable young typist, who looked like a whore. They spoke French and gestured to each other to express what their words failed to convey. I understood nothing of what was passing in front of me. French, like Greek and Latin, was for the intelligent, Arabic for the slow and awkward, and I was counted as one of them. To check there was no name-swapping, he passed me to a second man in authority in an even bigger room. The man was obese and his left ear was twisted as small as a pea. He wrote my name on his final checklist and shouted, 'Pavilion Eleven! Take any empty bed. The bedding will be provided later.'

On my way to Pavilion Eleven, strolling between the buildings, I felt as if I had moved from the Middle Ages to modern life. The school had been a French army barracks, entirely secured by a high mud wall. Massive classrooms had been built in parallel buildings. On the other side of the campus were several dormitory pavilions, behind which was a huge refectory with accommodation for the kitchen staff. At the very back, far from it all, on a sloping hill overlooking the campus, two luxurious houses were built, one for the bursar and one for the rector. The school and the houses were worlds apart.

While I was finding my bearings, looking like an intruder, I met a moustached sixth-year prefect who pointed the way to Pavilion Eleven. Coming face-to-face with the pavilion, I spotted Bozaid coming out, using crutches. I was happy and excited to see him. At first, I thought he might have injured himself, but getting closer, realised he had no leg and had the trouser leg folded up and pinned.

'What happened?' I asked.

Leaning on one of his crutches, Bozaid stopped and wiped his eyes. Watching in shock, I stood frozen beside him.

'During the summer, I joined the Algerian Liberation Army,' he explained. 'We infiltrated a complicated protected zone beyond Oujda and Saidia. We cut through the electrified barbed wire, which created a massive spark, drawing French fire. Waiting until the guns were silent, we moved deeper into French-Algerian territory. Unfortunately, several metres away from the wire, the French army had laid land mines. We combed the land slowly, but somehow, I stepped on a mine and my leg was torn to pieces. The mission was aborted. I was pulled back and rushed to the hospital. No bones were left to stand on, so they amputated my leg above the knee. I woke up with no leg.'

Frozen in horror, I listened to his story until the prefect jostled us to move inside for dinner. The refectory was impressive, long and wide, with large glass windows covering two-thirds of the walls. Tables were designed to accommodate six chairs, all made with wood and steel, military style. Four boys were already around the table finishing their soup. It wasn't easy for Bozaid to sit. He was still learning how to use his crutches, as well as how to live with one leg missing. The shock and sadness crossed my body like a muscle spasm each time I watched Bozaid struggle. He had been as strong as a lion and as agile as a squirrel, but now needed help to sit down.

It was reassuring, somehow, for me to sit at the same table with someone I already knew. Controlled smiles and low voices were the tempo of the table. The moment dinner was over, each prefect took his charges to the assigned revision class. Bozaid was given an exceptional privilege, a key to the dormitory. I followed him, and inch by inch we reached the dormitory pavilion, which looked like a large, long hangar with twenty-four bunk beds inside, most of them occupied. Some were tidy, and some just barely. At the far end, there was one empty bed on the lower bunk, beside the window. I sat on it and threw my belongings on the floor beside it. Puffing on a cigarette, Bozaid was at the other end, near a window, on the lower bunk.

'New arrival!' shouted a man, papers flying in his hands, who burst into the dormitory. A second man behind him carried blankets and sheets. I showed my ID and after much ticking of paper, I received two sheets, two blankets and a round, long pillow, property for which I became fully responsible. Beside my bed stood a tall steel locker allocated to me, but buying a padlock was my duty.

It passed in a blink of an eye. If I awakened and found myself behind goats and sheep, I would be convinced I had dreamed a fantasy I wished were true.

While I was trying to make my bed, cuddling my sheets and blankets, Bozaid was babbling like a burst pipe. His smoke clouded the room, and he raised his voice each time he thought I had missed one of his words. He felt the need to talk.

'Be aware,' he shouted, with an ironic tone in his voice. 'The light goes off at ten o'clock. The queue for the toilets is very long. You might pee in your trousers.'

He hadn't lied. Twenty students burst into the dormitory. Books, bags and jotters were chaotically thrown on beds; lockers were slammed in anger and frustration. There was no listener, and yet everyone talked. Like a stampede, a massive rush to the bathroom began. Two single sinks, not enough to keep up with the sudden flood of thirsty boys, lined the wall. I heard verbal skirmishes, saw shoving, and those were the norm of the night.

Toilets were where most vicious fights erupted. Bullies often tried to eject other boys from the showers or push them from the sinks. Bullies were not fighters, but cowards; they never stood up to a real fight, but they bullied. Often, they picked the wrong victims. Boys with quiet demeanour often turned out to be fierce and nasty fighters.

At lightning speed, we were all in bed and quiet; the light turned off. A thin beam of light pierced the window and darted in and around the darkness, giving me a fright. I sat up in bed and peered around, but no one else was bothered. It was the prefect's final check to make sure no light was on, to save energy. This was my first night ever sleeping on a mattress or in a bed, and I found it amazingly comfortable.

Up early, I was the first in the shower room. There was no competition, no queue and no hot water either, but I ventured into the shower. The icy water, hitting my neck and head, took my breath away.

Dormitories shut their doors at seven in the morning. Like a herd, we rushed to the refectory door a few metres away.

Breakfast was cold: French baguettes, butter, jam and coffee. At the table, Bozaid was mute, cold like a stone. He brought with him a small transistor radio that he was fiddling with, but was not allowed to listen to; waves of frustration crashed on his face.

From the refectory, we shuffled down to the new, modern buildings, all bungalow-shaped and sun-facing. I expected to be in the same class, but boarding school brought a different selection of boys, and of all those I knew I found only Faissal. Happy to see him, I asked, 'Where is your seat?'

'At the very front,' he pointed.

'Who is beside you?' I asked.

'You,' he said with a twisted smile. 'No one wants to sit beside me.' I took the seat beside him and dropped my bag on the desk.

Looking around the class, I found myself mingling with the sons of successful traders, judges and teachers. Milodi, Jalil and Gabran were not the only bigheaded boys in my class. Shami, the shortest boy, with thick, black eyebrows, constantly brought the local tabloid to class. He was highly motivated and fanatically dogmatic. He loved to invent city gossip involving sex, thievery, scandal or incest. I hated his enthusiasm for dirty stories, and he disliked my criticism, but we sat in the same class and learned the same lessons.

I enjoyed every class except Professor Sculli's religion class. I was naïve, and he nearly ended my education. Short, stout, blond, balding and blind, he taught enthusiastically and used his bellicose voice to subdue the hyperactive and fascinate the lazy. His voice rang out whenever he heard a squeak of a chair or table. He never sat down; he swung from right to left until the end of the lesson. From time to time, he checked with his left hand that he hadn't stepped too far astray from his desk. I was unlucky that morning, and he was in a bad mood.

On the subject of Mecca, I asked, 'If it is a matter of congress, could it be held in the United States of America?'

He leaped off the riser and lurched in my direction. 'Where is he? Where is he?' he yelled.

He reached me, threw my jotter on the floor, pulled me by my ear and pushed me. 'This is your last day!' he growled.

I never believed a professor would act like that and hate America that much. I was terrified, and Faissal started to giggle, but the class was shocked and lapsed into complete silence, as expulsion meant the end of schooling. Five minutes later, I was handed to the rector like a criminal. I protested vigorously, but the rector gave me no ear. With both his hands, he pushed me in the chest until I stumbled backward. I was out of the office and out of the class, ostracised into the walled garden of the school. I couldn't believe what had happened to me.

At lunchtime, when the refectory opened, everybody in my class and dormitory knew that I had been expelled. I went to the refectory, but felt like an intruder. *Where will I spend the night?* I worried.

The afternoon came, and classes started at two o'clock. I didn't know what to do. *Should I go to class? That might make things worse. It might look like defiance*, I thought. I headed to the office, but the rector wasn't there, so I waited. At four o'clock, the rector rushed into his office, blindly ignoring me standing outside.

On the same afternoon, Faissal told me later, Professor Zakiri, young and newly qualified, brought the class' homework, corrected and graded. 'Jusef!' he called, 'number one in class. Come forward and read your essay aloud.'

'He's been expelled,' the boys chorused. He read my essay to the class himself.

While I was standing at the rector's office door, Professor Zakiri entered and disappeared into the rector's office. Fifteen minutes later, I was called in.

'Join your class tomorrow morning, but you are expelled from boarding for two weeks. Go and clear out your belongings from the dormitory,' said the rector.

'I have nowhere to go,' I said.

'Go and search,' he replied.

I went back to the dormitory, packed up my belongings and found myself on the street in front of the school with nowhere to go. With no bedding, I headed to the *funduq* where I had lived with Moussa, Samir and Kamil, hoping to find a room for two weeks, but it had been engulfed by fire. Wandering up the street, dragging my bag, I happened upon another *funduq* that had a spare room on the first floor.

Two weeks were filled with sleepless nights, the groans of the endless stream of whores and their patrons, abundant cockroaches, and most difficult of all, a diet of bread and water.

Emaciated, I returned to the dormitory. Traumatised, I rarely ventured out of the school the rest of the year. Boys were free to relax in the town on Friday afternoons, but I hid myself in the reading room and read my books. On rare occasions, Bozaid and I went to a café in Boujloud. We sat, read newspapers, discussed politics and watched men, women, children, donkeys and sometimes mules passing by.

I remember the last time we went to the café, Bozaid was depressed. He disappeared before the first sprouts of spring, and those I asked had no news of him.

Frozen in class but not in time, I awakened one day to find it was already June. The school year had reached its end. The weather was hot and the exam schedule was brought to every class. I couldn't expect to be boarded the following year if I were to fail my exams.

On the nineteenth of June, coming out of the revision room on my way to the refectory for lunch, I was handed a scrunched-up letter from home by the prefect counting students at the refectory door. It was extraordinary the letter had even arrived, with an incomplete address and indiscernible writing. I hadn't received or expected any letters for the whole year. Looking at it, my heart shivered. I shoved it in my pocket until lunch was over. Out of the refectory, away from the boys, I opened the letter and read, 'Your mother has been sick in bed for three months.'

By this time, I had sat two-thirds of my exams, but the

more difficult and important ones were still to come; Professor Sculli's subject was one, and I knew he hated me. He had expressed more than once his dismay that I was still in the school.

The moment I finished my exams, I went to the rector and asked to leave.

'Won't you wait to see your exam results?' asked the rector.

'I would like to, sir, but my mother is ill and I'm needed at home,' I answered.

'Very well.'

The night before I left, I asked Faissal, 'Would you write to me?'

'Shall I tell you all the results?' he asked.

'Of course,' I replied.

In a hurry, I packed. From jinxed Bab Ftouh, I took the night coach. As it moved north, so did the moon across the sky. A strange transcendence absorbed me, as if I had no legs, no arms, no body, just a mind perching here and there, home, school, moon, anxiety.

17

Back home, I did not recognise my mother. She looked threadbare-thin, frail, pale, and just waiting to shut her eyes and leave. She couldn't stand up. I put my hands under her arms and tried to lift her, but she kept falling like a newborn calf, long legs but no power, and no dignity either.

'Has Mrs Malani been here recently?' I asked Amina, who was standing, watching and wondering.

'Yes, she's been here every day,' she said. 'She's tried everything, but produced no magic.'

Worn out, Rabbia and Amina were ready to see our mother be called home where she could find peace and leave the pain behind. The drought was devastating, the fields produced nothing, and it was not worth picking the sparse amount of grain amidst the nettles. Only the fields at the foot of Makran and Tassamat produced some barley, yet they required a lot of work, much of it fruitless.

Baja and I toiled like father and son. Sickling, threshing and winnowing produced very little to take home and only a little hay to bale.

One hot day, Baja stood up straight, looked at the sky and the mountain, and yelled at me. 'Jusef,' he said, 'I quit.'

Stunned, I didn't know what to say. 'What's next then?' I asked him.

'I wish I knew,' he said.

At the foot of Tassamat, in the middle of the field, under the burning sun, he shook my hand and said, 'Goodbye', a nauseating word. Baja went east to his home, and I south to my dying mother. After ten months of work, Baja went home with nothing to show for it. *I will be in the same position if I've failed my exams.*

Whenever my mother needed to relieve herself, Rabbia called me. We each held her under one arm, helped her onto the pot in the corner of the room, but she never managed to sit and was rarely able to crap. Rabbia would wipe her bottom while I held her around the waist.

I had wanted to take my mother to the doctor from the day I arrived, but had faced many barriers, not least of which was financial. While there was a wizard or a witch in practically every house nearby, there were no doctors, never mind a hospital, in the whole region. Nador, the nearest town, was over a hundred miles away on dirt roads. Hiring a taxi from Nador to our house would cost a king's ransom, and most taxis didn't go that far anyway, refusing to travel the country roads.

All Wednesday night, Rabbia and I discussed what to do about mother. At dawn on Thursday morning, I went to my brother-in-law Himich, a few miles away. I knocked at the door and awakened a fierce dog which refused to retreat or stop barking. Opening the door, Himich looked shocked to see me. He must have thought my mother had died, but soon realised from my gentle, faked smile that wasn't the case.

'I need your help,' I asked him.

'To do what?' he asked.

'To take Mother to the doctor.'

'Doctor?' he said. 'Let God finish His job!'

How was it possible for my father to hand his daughter to a man with such thoughts? How was it possible for my beautiful sister to spread her legs for a man like this? I wondered.

I made a beeline to catch the coach to Nador, and it was a long walk, two hours with my legs stretched to the max. I waited four hours for the coach coming from Oujda. Numb from the journey, I found myself finally in the middle of the town surrounded by expensive Mercedes of differing sizes, colours and models. With no order, the drivers all yelled, 'Taxi free! Taxi free!'

'I want to bring a sick woman from the mountains, Makran and Tassamat,' I said to one. He slithered away. While standing and wondering what to do next, a taxi driver sitting in his car and playing with the steering wheel, called me.

'I will take you,' he said. 'Three hundred dirhams.' I jumped in the taxi and sat beside him. 'People living near Makran and Tassamat don't hire taxis,' he remarked.

'You're right,' I replied.

He drove fast and got extremely angry when we reached the dirt road. He became even angrier when he had to drive across the field. We arrived at home, but my mother could not sit up, and he was worried she might soil his Mercedes. Rabbia and I carefully wrapped her and laid her on the back seat, with Amina and Rabbia at each end. After driving a few miles, the driver became curious and talkative. The beauty and innocence of mountain girls contrasted with the seasoned thieves and sophisticated prostitutes he knew in the city. The contrast between Rabbia and Amina, one blonde and one brunette, puzzled him.

'Are those girls sisters?' he asked me.

'Yes,' I answered.

* * *

DOCTOR MEHDI WAS A living god in the town, was well known and highly regarded. His surgery was in a typically small, Spanish, terraced house. It was packed with sick men, women and children, with a queue of patients lying against the wall outside. His receptionist was a Spanish girl called Señorita. She was beefy, small and stocky, but not overly so, beautiful, fresh and clean with a beet-red face. Because she spoke only Spanish, I couldn't explain to her how ill my mother was. The most I could get was a ticket with the number twenty-nine. Seeing me stuck, a Moroccan woman, a maid, butted in and translated, 'The doctor might see you later this afternoon, but, if not, tomorrow.'

I cringed when I heard 'tomorrow'. *Where am I going to take my mother tonight?* I wondered. *No hotel would rent a room to someone as sick as she was.* A wave of panic washed over me.

'What is your ticket number?' I asked a man sitting uncomfortably on a wobbly, bare wooden chair.

'Nine,' he answered.

'Would you like to sell it?' I asked.

He looked at me as if I were out of my mind. 'It's not a

passport,' he said with a smile. 'I have been here since dawn. I am a miner,' he said. 'To be here, I have lost my day's wage.'

I paid him and handed him my ticket number twenty-nine, but the deal created a riot in the reception room. 'I am before them!' shouted a woman to the receptionist. 'They bribed you with eggs and chickens!' she shouted.

'No!' I intervened in her defence. 'I bought this man's ticket. My mother won't last until tomorrow!'

The woman continued to heap personal insults on Señorita, as she knew the Spanish girl didn't understand Tarifit.

My mother was a puzzling case to the doctor. He failed to diagnose her illness, but prescribed two injections a day for three weeks. I was shocked when the pharmacist told me I needed a nurse to administer the injection.

The doctor knows we are in a land of witches and wizards, not nurses. I had heard Mr Yamani, an old nurse, was extremely arrogant and charged for just moving his fingers. He had taught Uncle Mimoun how to administer injections when his son Mohamed had fallen ill. Uncle Mimoun had bought a vial of penicillin and had injected him with it. Within one hour, he had died.

I remembered Mohamed's death. I had been shepherding on a high hill when I heard women yelling and lamenting, going in and out of Uncle Mimoun's house.

With no other choice, I went to Mr Yamani, who lived on a steep slope, and whose house was protected by four fierce, hungry dogs. I couldn't get near it. I waited until a boy came out and saw me waving. The child ran inside and the entire family emerged. Mr Yamani was first, and the rest appeared to be either his sisters or wives. His arrogance showed from the start. He peered at my open shirt and sandals, covered in dust, with a look of contempt.

'What has brought you here, boy?' he asked.

'Uncle Mimoun told me you are a qualified nurse,' I answered.

'Of course I am,' he answered. 'I learned from masters, Spanish doctors and nurses, and served the best army in the world, General Franco's unit.'

It was getting late, dusk was creeping, and my mother was getting worse by the hour. Frustrated, I waited until he finished his glowing self-appraisal.

'My mother is very ill and needs injections. Could you help?'

'No,' he answered. 'You live too far away, but I could teach you as I taught your Uncle Mimoun. I still have some syringes that I stole from the Spanish army, and, if you wish, you could buy a few.' This turned out to be more complicated than I had anticipated, but I agreed to pay and be taught.

Mr Yamani arrived at our house the following morning at eleven and I received him like a king. I took care of his mule, which was black, beautiful and showed all the energy of youth. I tied it to a carob tree and provided it with a cauldron of water and a bowl of barley.

After a big meal of chicken *tagine* and tea, I asked Mr Yamani to see my mother in her room. Ready, he pulled out a small pan, filled it with alcohol, threw all his tools in it and lit the fire. After all the liquid was evaporated, he picked everything up with a flimsy tong and gave my mother an injection. He expected me to remember and do as he had done.

I tried to remember visually every movement of his hand, but I couldn't shake off the memory of Uncle Mimoun who had killed his son, Mohamed.

'It's time for my injection,' shouted my mother the following morning.

Remembering Mr Yamini's lesson, I gave my mother an injection. Despite two injections per day for two weeks, my mother showed no progress. If anything, she was worse, but for my sisters, life went on as if she weren't ill.

Sanaa and Rabbia mounted the family donkey and, like two idiots, headed to see Thamrabt, a powerful witch, who refused no one. Sanaa recounted the visit, her eyes shining with enthusiasm.

Sanaa and Rabbia sat quietly side by side, and Thamrabt sat cross-legged, facing them, a long, narrow table between them. On the table was a clear glass of water. Thamrabt's head was covered with a loose, white silk scarf. Underneath it, her black hair shone like a wet raven's feathers. Her hands were busy counting a string of ninety-nine beads. The room was exceptionally big, with windows on each side and a door at each end, one leading into the garden and the other into the house. At odds with local custom, the walls were completely bare, with no mirrors, pictures or wardrobe; it was like a mosque. The floor was tiled, with a Persian rug in the middle of it.

Thamrabt didn't ask Sanaa or Rabbia their names or even what their problems were. 'I will share this glass of water with you,' she told them. She stretched her long, left hand, lifted the glass of water and passed it to Sanaa, who happened to be sitting across to her right. 'Take a sip,' she said.

Sanaa sipped several times and felt nothing. She put the glass back on the table. Thamrabt picked up the glass and sipped from it. Immediately, she yelled, put her left hand behind her back and shouted, 'My back hurts me!' At the same time, Sanaa felt a burning heat, like fire, passing through her bones.

Hearing Thamrabt's words, Sanaa exploded in tears. Thamrabt handed her a small bottle of dark brown water to sip when she felt depressed. 'This is all I am allowed to give you now.'

Thamrabt picked up the same glass and handed it to Rabbia. 'Have a sip,' she said.

Rabbia did as Sanaa had. She put the glass back, and Thamrabt picked it up and finished the rest of it. Rabbia felt nothing, nor did Thamrabt for a while.

After a threatening silence, Thamrabt lifted her eyes, looked at Rabbia, smirked peevishly and cried, 'Rabbia! Rabbia! You want my soul! For the life of me, as long as I live, you will not get it! Get out! Get out of my house!'

After the visit to Thamrabt, Rabbia sank into depression and left me alone to wash and care for our mother. In this climate of poverty and despair and unable to work our land, I resorted to a cursed and primitive practice called 'temporary swap', where the landlord passed the land to the user, and the user paid a fixed amount to the landlord. Until the landlord paid back the exact amount, the land was in the user's hand. If after a certain number of years passed and the landlord hadn't repaid the money, the swap became a sale. I swapped two fields with Mr Mashtro in the presence of three witnesses, members of the bingo club. With the swap, my mother got some money to bridge the winter, if she survived.

Thinking she would not recover, my mother became obsessed with her mortality and embarked on finding husbands for Rabbia and Amina. For me, she wanted her niece, Samira, a beautiful girl of medium height with big, brown eyes, a straight nose, and olive skin. She was good-tempered, kind and had a soft voice.

My mother spoke to my ear, but not to my mind. She had no clue how life was in school, and Samira was not in my heart. My mother wanted me to settle close by, but she didn't realise how unhappy that would make me.

Back from the market one day when summer was waning, finding my mother on the mend, I went to her bed on the floor and whispered, 'Mother, it's time for me to go back to school,' but I felt that wasn't what she wanted to hear.

18

Arriving at the school gates, I felt a swell of joy, but also a tinge of angst. *I'm in the right place. I know I am*, I told myself resolutely. Still, my mind dragged me five hundred miles away to my mother, Rabbia and Amina lost between rocks, dreams and poverty.

Dinner time came and I was seated at a new table in the vast dining hall. It was packed with noisy, excitable boys reuniting after the long summer, but looking around, I didn't recognise one single face. New students had arrived, and a lot of the old guard had simply been swept aside, their places unceremoniously filled with newcomers.

Faissal and I were joined at our table by Abdu, a boy I had never seen before, but who spoke Tarifit. No sooner had he sat down than he breathlessly spilled his news. 'Do you know, the school will be hit by a strike? The school will be closed!' he announced excitedly.

'What?' I exclaimed, shocked. 'Why? We just got here!'

I never managed to get more of an answer as, hearing the thumping and the raucous voices, a prefect quickly dispersed us. Abdu struck me as a mysterious, bold and brazen boy.

Professor Drissi, a stern man with an uncompromising

outlook, soon found my nonconformist thinking to be particularly troublesome. In class, to straighten me out, he prescribed an essential list of approved books to read, analyse and report upon. Professor Drissi was confident that, navigating through this vast library of literature containing selected authors from North Africa and the Middle East to Islamabad and Kabul, I would soon join him on the straight path. Unbeknown to him, however, my focus was engaged elsewhere.

At a very early age, whilst a refugee in Algeria, I had seen a foreign family for the first time, an Italian family, a father, mother and their four children, all sitting around, not on the floor, but at a table. The children had scrunched small pieces of paper and thrown them at each other, laughing. I had stood transfixed, staring at their colourful clothes, their smart shoes and the fun they had playing their game. I had wished I could be one of them. Later, as a shepherd in the Rif mountain foothills, I had encountered French men holding their wives' hands; the women, poised and captivating, exuded an air of self-confidence like royalty. It was all a far cry from what I had seen around my village and in my own family.

I felt boxed in a crippling culture with which I couldn't identify and trapped by a local language barely recognisable in the wider world, a handicap that felt almost physical in its burden. I yearned to escape, like an unhatched chick, to break free from the constraints encasing me to my reality. But the ties were strong; how could I do it? The only solution I could see was to learn the French language, prestigious and known internationally, to give me the tool to break free from my bounds, to finally crack the shell and soar. Determined, I went to the Catholic convent run by two Franciscan Fathers and begged them to register me for the evening French lessons.

Professor Drissi went berserk when he was told that I had gone to a Catholic convent and registered for evening classes. He detained me after class, warned and reprimanded me. *You hypocrite!* I thought but didn't dare say. *Your children go to a French mission school where Arabic is not only not taught, but despised!*

French classes started at seven o'clock and were held in an old traditional house in a quiet part of the old *medina*. Teachers, all French, were volunteers and included professors, doctors, accountants and nurses.

I enjoyed the lessons and to my delight, found myself progressing well under their tutorage, but it was not without a cost: I had to miss my evening meal. Missing my dinner three times a week in the middle of winter was hard to endure, and the hunger made the long nights in the unheated dormitory more arduous. Tired, hungry and weak, my loud, painful stomach rumblings gave me away wherever I went.

Oujdi was in the same dormitory as I and sneaked whatever bread was leftover from dinner for me, but he couldn't get the days straight. As we sat at different tables, he often forgot, and when he did remember, I had often been at dinner and didn't really need any leftover bread, however well intentioned it was.

To get to the evening class building, I had to cross three big, empty lots and a large cemetery. Leaving the school at six-thirty was not such a big problem, but coming back certainly was, especially during the winter when the evenings were menacingly dark. The lots were unlit, and dishevelled tramps and beggars slunk out of dark corners as my footfalls startled them. I walked through on high alert, always ready to run, and circumvented anyone who crossed my path, but crossing the cemetery was a different and altogether stranger story.

The cemetery was not a quiet or revered place, but a safe haven for sexual activity. I saw and heard people engaging in sexual encounters despite the gentle darkness of the night. It wasn't unusual for me to see a couple busily engaged while two or three other men waited at their feet. Yet passing through the cemetery, I felt safer than anywhere else on my journey, for everybody was busy.

One afternoon in June, I found the school had posted the timetable for the final year exams. I was shocked. *It's too soon! It feels like I've only been here a few weeks!* Dread and panic overwhelmed me; from then on, sleep proved to be practically unattainable. Professor Drissi was still expecting regular reports from readings covering hundreds of years of Islamic literature. Yet to my dismay, not one single book was relevant for the exams. Then there were the French classes; they took up three evenings a week, and with significant work to take home on the other evenings, I seriously contemplated whether it would be best to drop them altogether. *If I do*, I thought to myself, *how will I be able to tear the blanket from over my head?* Upon completing my exams, I left in a hurry for home before knowing the results and whether or not I would be able to return.

19

At home, I found everything off-colour and changed. My mother, completely grey, had degenerated, her legs and arms were no longer under her control, but she managed to move now and again with the help of a stick. Amina had grown taller and older, with the look of a woman. I expected to see Rabbia, but there was no sign of her.

'Mother, where is Rabbia?' I asked.

'She's in her house,' she replied.

'Is she married?' I exclaimed in surprise.

'Yes, but her husband is in prison.'

I didn't know Rabbia had married, and I had never met her husband or heard his name, Zgooda, mentioned. Naïvely, I had believed she disliked men.

'What's he in prison for?' I asked.

'Ask Rabbia,' my mother replied. I understood my mother disliked him.

Rabbia came and asked me to go with her to see her husband. 'I haven't seen him since he was locked up six months ago,' she said.

'I can't go now,' I said. 'The harvest . . .' The harvest was worse than meagre, and I worked alone in the field, sickling, threshing and winnowing. Despite my mother's objections, I went with Rabbia to Nador to see her husband in prison. Rabbia barely recognised him. He looked as if he'd been in a concentration camp.

'Zgooda, this is my brother, Jusef,' she said, taking his hand.

He looked at me through hazy eyes, and I could tell he hadn't had a good night's sleep in months. I wondered what he had done to deserve that.

As if reading my thoughts, Zgooda said, 'I was convicted of stealing and selling a donkey. I found the beast astray, starving to death, and took it to the market to be saved and sold it for peanuts . . .'

Rabbia butted in and said, 'The judge didn't understand the well-being of humans, let alone that of the donkey.'

'The judge asked me, "Would you drive a car away and sell it if you found it abandoned?" "No, my Lord," I said, "Cars don't starve. Cars are registered. The owner is identified. Donkeys are not numbered, and hundreds and hundreds are abandoned, because of old age, weakness, or simply illness,"' Zgooda said. 'But the judge thought I was hot-headed, arrogant, and needed straightening in prison.'

Saddened by his story of injustice and Rabbia's disconsolate state, I turned to face the wall in the corner of the tiny room to give them a moment of privacy before we were ejected from the visiting area by a burly, unsympathetic guard. Rabbia was silent on the return journey, and I had no way to cheer her.

Upon finishing the harvest, I went to the factory nearby to look for a job. There was none, and I returned the following morning. Again, there was none. Tired of looking for jobs that didn't exist, I succumbed to my mother's nagging to go with her to see my uncle miles away.

I later found my mother hadn't been honest with me. While I had been working in the field, she had been preparing a visit to her brother and had never expressed to him her secret motive: she was determined to commit me to Samira, her niece. For her, love was a matter of legend and myth.

Though slightly paralysed, my mother made the best of her looks that she could, trying not to look old. She wore a white Indian-like sari covering the lower and upper parts of her body, and always split with a silk belt. She took a particular interest in her eyes and eyelashes. To line her eyes, she bought very dark blue stone, which she pulverised with extreme care. For her face, she used olive oil. To clean her teeth, she rubbed them with charcoal. Afterwards, she chewed bark, which reddened her mouth, gums, tongue and lips. Watching her, I wondered if she were looking for a lover or a new husband.

We left at two in the afternoon and arrived at twilight. Two fierce dogs met us. Samira and her mother, Jamila, usually emerged at the first bark of their dogs – curious to see who was there and happy to receive a visitor, but now there was no sign of either. I challenged the dogs and edged closer to the window, which I peppered with small stones. Peeved, Jamila peeked out of the window.

My mother had known Jamila, her brother's first wife, for many years. Though three wives had come after her, she bore no grudge against them, but rather felt sorry for them. Jamila was small in size, but had an attractive face, placid voice and generous nature. We soon realised Jamila was unhappy and noticed also the absence of Samira as we were ushered into the guest room and left wondering.

'Where is Samira?' my mother asked when Jamila returned with tea, expecting Samira to come and sit beside me.

Jamila didn't answer, and I felt a real unease. My mother and Jamila looked at each other in dismay.

Jamila sighed and said, 'Unknown to us, she got pregnant. We only realised when she ballooned to twice her size. Horrified, dishonoured and ashamed, my sons hunted the boy living just across the valley, and swore they'd kill him. Fearing for his life, he ran and hid in the mountains. His mother agreed to enter into a dishonourable wedding. I fought it, but I lost.

'The boy's mother didn't want her son to get married to a non-virgin and took revenge. She humiliated Samira on her wedding day. Instead of carrying Samira on a horse from our house to hers, she put her on a jenny with a red cloth on it. Imagine all the people watching and talking about it! On her arrival, instead of entering through the main door, she was carried over the wall, and many men, unrelated to us, were called in to participate in the operation to keep her from falling. Instead of passing through to her husband's room by the door, she was pushed through the window. In the end, she fainted.

'The following morning, there were no fireworks to celebrate her virginity, and there was no white flag to show her blood. There was no blood to show, to test or smell.'

My mother slumped with depression. She had come with a devious plot to marry me to Samira, and the plot had failed, by the grace of God. Our visit was not enjoyable and shorter than my mother had expected. I was relieved to come home and look for a job again.

I was bored and wanted to do something to make money, but how difficult it was! I decided to go back to the factory and offer myself for day work. I arrived at the gate and waited. Job seekers like me came here and waited for Mr Pepe, the manager of the factory, to open the gate and pick. If the gate remained closed until eleven, the jobless understood there was no job. The choice was either to go home or to join the bingo club.

The manager came, opened the gate, and recognised me, as I had been there before. 'Are you a student?' he asked.

'Yes, I am.'

'Wait,' he said. He kept me waiting until ten o'clock, then he came and took me to a large pile of shredded yucca leaves and handed me a pitchfork. He asked me to heave the leaves into the air to dry them, then move them to another pile.

At first, it was fun; then it became a real chore. My hands blistered quickly, then popped, and my nostrils filled with dust. A nasty old man called Abdo-Kader, the one in charge, kept shouting at me every time I paused. He was extremely short, ugly and bearded, and his soul wasn't much better.

'Is that all you can do today?' he called to me every ten minutes.

I was pushing a wheelbarrow, moving between two piles, when I heard hellacious screaming from inside the factory, where over one hundred men, women and children were working. I heard the wailing and the cries, 'She's caught! She's caught!' I heard men yelling, 'Papee! Papee!', as he was the only engineer who knew what to do. Hundreds of workers, terrified women and girls yelling, ran out of the factory.

It was Fadila, a big girl in her twenties, who had been feeding a huge grinding machine. She got her fingers caught under the press and was sucked in. Before Papee could shut off the machine, her entire body was minced. Blood, pieces of flesh and bones were splattered everywhere, on the floor, the machines and the walls. Papee shouted, 'Everybody go home!'

The pieces of Fadila were buried in the late afternoon. Shocked and terrified, several skilled men and women chose to stay at home the following morning. They couldn't return and face the juggernaut that had shredded Fadila. With so many absentees, the main production lines couldn't start.

Papee couldn't find anyone to replace Fadila. Manically mumbling and furiously frustrated, he repeatedly pounded the palm of one hand with his fist. As he passed me by, checking on everybody, I jumped on him. 'I could do Fadila's job,' I said.

He stopped and looked at me as if he had seen me for the first time. '*Mañana*,' he said, and moved on.

During that day, I thought of nothing but Fadila. She had been tall, beefy and bubbly, with big breasts. They may have been too heavy for her, but then, I didn't have to carry them. I had just watched them.

The following morning was the same. The most qualified workers stayed home. At around ten o'clock, Papee came, handed me an apron and took me to the press. First, I saw blood on the wheel. The cleaner had mopped the floor, but hadn't touched the wheel. As the wheel moved, the skin started to drop off. I shivered. Again, I thought of Fadila and her breasts, but my feelings were different now.

Though I had endured a horrible job which had given me nightmares, I stopped only when it was time to return to boarding school, and I had earned only enough to pay for the coach and a few loaves.

20

Leaving behind the juggernaut that had shredded Fadila, I felt as if I were on holiday when I reached the school, but soon I was struck by a disquieting change. I was now lodged in Pavilion Six, closer to the rector's house and the bursar. This was a promotion, with only twelve beds in my dormitory, albeit the space was small. There was less fighting over the toilet and showers. For boys with stubble enough to shave, mirrors stretched from wall to wall. Pavilion Six provided a panoramic view, though mainly of the school grounds, and enjoyed open space all around, dotted with a constellation of trees. For the promotion, a price was attached: the rector and the bursar could hear any goings in or out and could peer into the dormitory.

Because I was the first in Pavilion Six, I had my pick of the beds. I chose one near the door and in front of a massive window. By the time I had unpacked my belongings into the steel locker, the siren broke the silence. The refectory was only two-thirds full; new arrivals were trickling in. The new prefects clambered to learn the names of their charges and exercise their authority. Faissal and Abdu were sitting side by side, but there was no free seat beside them.

While we were finishing our dessert of shrivelled, dried figs, the bursar, bald and fat, jumped on a large, high table in front of a window and welcomed us with a catalogue of warnings in his hand. The official speech over, dinner finished, Faissal, Abdu and I found ourselves outside the main door. Heading slowly toward my dormitory, Faissal and Abdu threw themselves on my bed and we talked late into the evening. Abdu looked comfortable, yet waves of sadness covered his face and changed his colour.

'Is something bothering you?' I asked him. 'How was your holiday?'

Abdu turned toward Faissal and kept silent. I didn't want to press him any further. Later, Abdu's anger erupted like a red tongue of a volcano. 'I have a biological father, but not a loving one,' he said.

'What have you done?' I asked, not expecting anything dramatic.

'Nothing! My mother and my father's second wife were roaring at each other, and my father's second wife, young and strong, raced toward my mother like a bull. As I stopped her, she fell on the ground and got a few self-inflicted surface scratches. I had pushed her, she told my father. Being the monster he is, he renounced me. Dead or alive, I am not his son, he said. I don't know how long I will stay here, but I will do my best to get my baccalaureate and go into the military.'

Listening to Abdu lamenting, Faissal butted in, 'My father has two wives, but they live in different houses. They would have to travel to fight. Your father should have locked them in different houses as well.'

'My mother and my father's second wife would swim the river to fight with each other,' sneered Abdu.

I wondered to myself, *why does a man need two wives?* Then I remembered my religious lessons. *A man needs another wife ready when one wife is having her period.*

Faissal boasted about reading seven books during the summer holiday, and that they were all hard and difficult to understand. 'What were the books about?' I asked curiously.

'They were about religion,' replied Faissal.

'About religion? Wouldn't one book be enough?' I asked.

'Certainly one too many!' Abdu added.

While we were still talking, the prefect popped in and glared at me; I returned his glare with contempt.

'We're not new here,' I said, rolling my eyes. 'How did that snitch get the job? It wasn't advertised. Why does he get a room all to himself with all the tea and coffee he wants, a good wage, and many other advantages?' I asked. 'He doesn't have leadership qualities or academic skills, but the bursar needed a snitch, I guess.'

My first lesson was English, taught by Mr Green who was from Chicago and a member of the Peace Corps. His introduction was like preaching in an empty cathedral, and it was as clear as a bell that he was a do-gooder but a bad teacher. To make it worse, he hadn't prepared anything, no papers or handouts, and he was given the most difficult, ambitious and clever class. 'What a teacher! What a teacher! What a teacher!' we echoed around the class after he left.

We stormed into the rector's office and demanded a different teacher. Not wanting the incident to start a precedent, the rector resorted to expulsion threats. He called me to his office in the afternoon and told me, 'You are mad! You're on the watch list!'

He has no idea what goes on in the classroom. All we want is a good teacher, I thought.

A week later, Mr Green returned to hold class again, but there was no one to teach. We had boycotted his class. He was replaced by a tough Scottish teacher from Glasgow. Fascinated by his accent, we at first thought Scots were inhabitants of Texas.

* * *

AFTER THE TRIMESTER EXAMS, Abdu hadn't seen his half-brother, Bo-jaama, a day student, for two weeks. 'Let's go and see him,' he said to me. With two other students, Bo-jaama rented a room in the Jewish ghetto from a rabbi who occupied the ground floor.

We pounded on the door; the rabbi's wife came out and looked furious. 'Could we go upstairs?' I asked.

'Reason?' she asked, suspiciously focusing on me.

'My brother Bo-jaama lives here,' Abdu replied.

'Up you go!' she said, and up we went. Bo-jaama's door was ajar, maybe to let some air in, as the room was small like a coffin and had no window. Sadly, Bo-jaama was lying ill inside on the floor. He looked extremely pale, with no energy even to talk.

'Are you all right?' I asked.

'No, I'm not,' he replied weakly.

'You have been ill for two weeks, you missed school, exams,

and you didn't try to contact your brother?' I asked. Bo-jaama gave no answer. 'You could have asked your landlord to call an ambulance for you,' I added.

'They saw me dizzy and holding onto the wall, but they never bothered.'

Abdu, taken aback, didn't know what to do. He kept muttering to himself and pacing. 'Let's call the ambulance,' I suggested.

We went to the post office and waited a long time before we could make a phone call. We called the ambulance, but it refused to come. It was nearly five o'clock, the post office was closing, and we had to be back at the school before seven. Abdu went back to his brother, and I went to the police to ask their help getting an ambulance. The police called it, and it came soon after. Semi-conscious, Bo-jaama was taken to the hospital.

We expected Bo-jaama to be out of the hospital within three or four days at the very most, but he wasn't. Though there was no sign of him at school, the first visit we made was on Friday, three weeks after his hospital admission. Abdu and I scrambled to the hospital to find him. Unrecognisable, he was far worse than when he had been brought in and was lying in a huge dormitory in the midst of many. He was mentally alert but physically very weak. Before we left him, he asked if we could visit again and requested some food, but it was against hospital regulations to bring in food to patients.

A week later, I bought a tiny loaf, two oranges, and went with Abdu to see his brother. Entering the dormitory, we spied a visitor sitting on Bo-jaama's bedside. Upon closer scrutiny, we saw a small, white man in his forties, holding Bo-jaama's hand. As he saw us nearing, he kissed Bo-jaama on the lips, then departed hurriedly in the other direction.

Abdu, jaw dropped, raced toward his brother and demanded, 'Who was he?'

'My . . . friend,' Bo-jaama returned sheepishly.

Abdu was shocked; he had never suspected his brother was homosexual and was lost for words. He bolted out and left me to finish the visit.

When I saw Abdu later that afternoon before dinner, he burst into a tirade. 'Bo-jaama is the shame on the flag of my family. What am I going to tell my father?'

'That Bo-jaama is very ill and in the hospital. The rest is up to Bo-jaama,' I answered.

After dinner, Faissal and I went straight to the library. 'What did you do this afternoon?' Faissal asked.

'Nothing great,' I answered, not wanting to elaborate about Abdu's brother. 'And you?'

'I went to the New Town and spent my whole afternoon strolling up and down. I saw our chemistry teacher. He has many children, and his daughters are beautiful,' said Faissal. 'He's a biased marker.'

'That will not be the case in the baccalaureate,' I said. 'The marking is done by external examiners.'

'That's what's good about the baccalaureate,' replied Faissal.

'There are different types of baccalaureates, do you know? A prestigious one requires French,' I said.

'I wouldn't invest my time learning French,' he said.

Just as I had been dying to leave the Koranic school and shepherding, I was thirsty to learn the French language, intellectual oxygen.

*   *   *

I WENT TO THE Franciscan cultural centre in Batha, a chic boulevard, and asked Father Antoine, 'Would it be possible to find someone to teach me French, but with no fee?'

Pessimistic, he promised nothing. Two weeks later, he surprised me. 'Mademoiselle Michelle will give you her free Friday afternoon and teach you French. She has just arrived from Bordeaux. She can't make it today, but next Friday,' he added with a short, half-smile.

There were plenty of French books around, plenty of newspapers for those who could read, including the famous French newspaper, *Le Monde*, which I glanced at but couldn't read. I left, downhearted that I would have to wait a week, and joined the street, packed with veiled women milling about, and men in groups trailing behind them. Two young boys, going down a lane, were shouting the deepest insults they could hurl on each other.

'You're a son of a bitch!' said one.

'You're a son of a whore!' retorted the other.

'May God curse you!'

'May God cut off your legs and arms and let you live!'

As I passed them, I thought, *That's the depravity of the city!* Before time to return to school, I met Faissal wandering around. 'Let me buy you a tea before we go,' I offered.

'Yes!' replied Faissal. He had never refused mint tea, and

he also loved to have a fuss made over him. He didn't like French people and hated priests, who could do nothing right in his eyes. Heading back to school, we arrived in time for dinner, avoiding trouble. We didn't go into our pavilion, but stayed outside arguing loudly until Abdu and Oujdi joined us. The argument ended in a huff, as Faissal was an absolutist, right versus wrong.

The school siren was a relief. Abdu and I joined the queue and inched at a snail's pace toward the refectory. 'Did you see your brother today?' I asked Abdu.

'No, I didn't.'

'Bo-jaama was very hungry last time we saw him,' I said, thinking that Abdu's anger might have receded. Each time Bo-jaama's name was mentioned, Abdu's cheeks set like stone into a heavy frown. He obviously didn't want me to talk about his brother.

Dinner was macaroni with cheese, white bread and, as a dessert, one small orange each. The service was very slow that night. Roaring voices and shouts came out from the kitchen; there had been a bloody fight. A worker had stabbed the chef, whose assistant had retaliated. In the midst of the hubbub, the ambulance arrived and rushed them away.

For the entire week, my mind teetered between Bo-jaama's illness and Michelle. I couldn't wait to meet her. I had no idea how old she was or what she looked like. Friday was a religious day; for me, it became Michelle's day in the Franciscan House.

Michelle was anything but what I had imagined. When I met her, she struck me as a beauty contestant: personality and charm were hers in abundance. She fixed the hours, and I was always on time, waiting in the library for her. Her Citroën 2 CV (or *Deux-Chevaux*), with its distinctive noise, could be heard from the library.

Reading, dictation and pronunciation were the meat of the lesson, which took the full afternoon. Michelle disliked the Parisian style of life and its arrogance, but, 'if one were learning French, one might just as well speak like Parisians,' she told me. Emphasis was on the pronunciation of 'r' to avoid picking up the Marseille accent.

Michelle was twenty-seven years old and engaged to a French student living in France, and for her, one year in Fez meant making a fortune. She taught French in an affluent girls' school, but she disliked some girls, the *filles à papa*. 'They are arrogant and spoiled,' she told me. 'Whenever parents are called in to see me, first and foremost, I have to listen to who they are, how important they are, and who they know. "My brother is a Minister", one said. "I have access to the palace", said another, and so it goes.'

Michelle was fascinated by the Moroccan social fabric and asked me, 'Why can a man end a marriage with just words and why should he pay a dowry for a bride?'

'It's the price for virginity,' I told her.

'Do you believe in that?' she asked me.

'Yes, I do,' I answered.

'I don't accept that,' she said.

'If you had lived here as long I have, you would understand it,' I said. I tried to explain the paradox of the dowry. 'It's a gift, as well as payment for the hymen.' But I refrained from telling her that two of my nieces had been married and divorced before dawn, as their husbands had declared they were not virgins. They had handed back the dowry and their parents had had to repay the wedding expenses. As for divorce by words alone, I recited the Bible to her, 'The power of life and death is in the power of the tongue.'

'Do you read the Bible?' she asked me.

'No, I collect proverbs,' I answered.

The next time we met, she gave me a Bible.

*   *   *

WITH THE SPROUTING OF the spring flowers and trees, the school shut its gate for holidays. Most boys flocked home, but a small bunch stayed. With fewer students, the nights felt quieter and, during the day, the school was empty and spooky.

With more free time, Oujdi asked me if I would like to go to the New Town the following Friday.

'I'm going to see someone in the hospital,' I replied.

Intrigued, he insisted on accompanying me. Oujdi knew nothing about Bo-jaama; he didn't know Abdu had a brother who was homosexual and in the hospital. He thought the hospital would be a place full of beautiful nurses, and hoped he might talk to some of them. He liked the nurses' uniform, their white, short skirts and bare legs.

After lunch on Friday, Oujdi and I rushed to the hospital. On our way, I bought a few oranges, as Bo-jaama would be disappointed if we arrived empty-handed. The hospital gate was manned by a burly security guard: broad-shouldered, bold, stocky and full of authority. In his narrow hut, he enjoyed sipping his tea and listening to local music on a small radio close to his chest. The moment the gate opened, visitors stampeded in.

Some knew where to go, but most didn't. Oujdi and I followed the visitor tide to the main hospital door. 'It's to the left,' I said, remembering my last visit weeks ago. Confused, Oujdi and I went into the big ward where Bo-jaama had been lying. The excitement with which Oujdi had come evaporated as soon as he entered the patients' dismal ward, where twenty or more men were lying on beds in two long, narrow rows. We looked around, but found no sign of Bo-jaama, just many other patients, some sleeping and others with eyes open, watching who was coming in and hoping someone would say 'hello' to them. Not finding Bo-jaama, I thought he might have recovered and gone home.

Outside the ward, we came across a male nurse. He was very tall, had moderately black skin and was half bald. Wearing thick glasses, he stirred right and left while walking down the corridor, as though losing his balance. He looked around thirty and was holding medicine in his hand. I scurried and stood right in front of him, as if trying to ambush him. 'Sir, could you help?' I asked.

He hesitated, skirted me, and kept moving on, his eyes glued to the label on the medicine in his hand. I motioned to Oujdi to follow the nurse, who finally stopped and looked at the oranges in my hand. 'What's the matter?' he asked.

'We're looking for Bo-jaama,' I replied. The name didn't ring a bell. 'He was in this big ward weeks ago,' I pointed out.

'Weeks ago, weeks ago, weeks ago,' repeated the nurse, shaking his head. Suddenly, the name Bo-jaama jogged his memory. 'Follow me,' he said, striding off on long legs. Oujdi had to jog to keep up with him.

The hospital was a real labyrinth. He took us far away from where we had been. Without a word, he pointed to a new door and a different ward. He looked at us and said, 'He is very ill.'

He disappeared, and dazed, I whispered, 'Thank you.'

Bo-jaama's ward, several steps down, was accessed via a dark, narrow corridor. There was Bo-jaama, lying in bed number three, facing the door and in the midst of about twelve other men who were just as ill as he. They were all covered with blankets, just faces popping out like mushrooms. It was impossible to distinguish who was young or old; all were unshaven. Bo-jaama had a patchy beard and looked one thousand years old. Like many, he was expecting no one.

'*Assalamo, Assalamo,*' I repeated while standing at his bedside. No reply. This wasn't what Oujdi had expected, and he looked overwhelmingly shocked.

When Bo-jaama opened his eyes, he seemed confused. Oujdi, standing beside me, confused him even more. He looked Oujdi up and down several times, but didn't ask who he was.

Bo-jaama gained some strength and consciousness, recognised me and tried to prop himself up against his headboard, but he failed. Last time, Bo-jaama had asked for food, but not this time. He noticed the oranges at his bedside and gave them a slow smile, exposing green teeth, unbrushed for a long time. I was certain Bo-jaama didn't know which month, day or year it was. I didn't want to mention school, but there was no other topic to talk about.

Oujdi kept silent all the time and looked perplexed when Bo-jaama asked, 'Where is my brother Abdu?'

'He wanted to come, but he has exams. He sends his regards,' I lied, trying to comfort Bo-jaama.

Before we realised it, the bell rang and visitors were swept out. 'See you soon,' I mumbled, not really knowing what to say.

From the look of it, Oujdi's desire to be cheered by a semi-naked nurse had been dashed. 'What's Bo-jaama's illness?' he asked.

'I don't know. I'm not a doctor yet,' I replied. 'Whatever they're doing for him isn't working, by the look of it. A hot pot of mint tea would probably work better.'

After the visit, we lost our inclination to go to the New Town. We didn't even try to find a café to sit in to while away the time. We headed straight to the school library to leave behind the spectre of Bo-jaama's ward. Oujdi hid himself in a book he wasn't supposed to read.

Abdu plodded in late to the refectory and nearly missed dinner. He took a seat beside Faissal and me and looked exhausted.

'Where have you been?' I asked.

'In New Town,' he replied.

He looked shocked when I told him Oujdi and I had seen Bo-jaama. He nearly fainted.

'Does Oujdi know that Bo-jaama is homosexual?' he asked me outside the refectory.

'No, he doesn't,' I replied.

'Does he know that Bo-jaama is my brother?'

'Yes, Bo-jaama told him. Bo-jaama is very ill, do you know?'

Abdu blinked his eyes and showed no emotion. Because I wished I had a brother, I was shocked, but then began to think.

'Hospitals have plenty of doctors and nurses, yet people are ill and die. Schools are stuffed with teachers, yet people can't read or write. Streets are full of police, yet crimes are rampant. Tribunals are full of judges, yet people are still seeking and waiting for justice, and some are misjudged,' I told Abdu. 'Evil is not the opposite of good. There is only one evil and one good, and they are one apple; they both reside in the flesh. They are the flesh itself. It is like that, it has always been like that, and it always will be like that.'

Back inside the dormitory, it was quiet, except for Oujdi's abrasive snoring. No one dared wake him, but everyone wished someone would. I lifted his book, freed his nose, and he immediately lifted his head up.

'I was dreaming,' he said. 'Having a nightmare!'

'What was your dream?' I asked with a smile.

'I dreamed I was riding a broken bicycle and chased by two Scottish women. They were headless! I pedalled as fast as I could, but I went nowhere, and they caught me.'

'How did two Scottish women appear in your dream?' I asked him.

'You took me to the hospital with you,' he answered. 'The half-naked nurses I dreamed of turned into rough, tough Scottish women!'

During this spring holiday, the prefects didn't care where we sat at dinnertime. There were so few of us anyway, and soon it became a habit for Oujdi, Faissal, Abdu and me to sit at the same table. But the table gathered the people with the most contradictory views. The debates turned into shouting and table-thumping. Prefects, worried, succumbed to eaves-dropping.

'I can't understand why, when two countries are rubbing shoulders, one is poor and the other rich!' shouted Oujdi.

'I can,' I told him. 'This is how my sister's donkey died. It was stung by a swarm of wasps while tied to a hook in the field. My sister saw it jumping, kicking in the air, trying to break the rope to free itself, and she thought it was happy-dancing. The donkey was restricted by its leg; you and I by the language typed into our brains.'

Our discussion was halted by the sixth-year prefect shouting, 'Out! Out!'

*   *   *

THE SPRING SUN REVIVED the spirits, hearts and minds of men and beasts. I remembered cows stampeding, sheep and goats jumping and running, sexually excited, but I had felt nothing like that during this spring holiday. It came and went like the melting of a snowflake on the skin. Whenever my heart jumped, my mind opened a new chapter that I had to read and think about. Friday was the last day. *Bo-jaama expects me and I must visit him*, I thought to myself. I also knew I must work flat out the following weeks for exams, then go home.

'Would you like to visit Bo-jaama?' I asked Oujdi at lunch-time.

'No,' he replied with a grimace. He had been put off by the shocking scenery of the hospital: men, women, young and old, either lying, weak and pale, in bed, or the fit ones wandering around in striped pyjamas, not much different from those worn in prison.

I went to see Bo-jaama on my own. On my way to the hospital, I bought three big, good-looking oranges. It was about three o'clock when I arrived. I went straight to ward three, where Bo-jaama had been bedded. The ward's French doors were open wide, but there were few visitors. The ward was uninviting, and the patients were unshaven, looking jaundiced and deeply depressed. Searching for Bo-jaama on the left, I couldn't find him. Going back to the main door and looking right, I didn't find him there either. Searching frantically, darting around the room while some patients were watching me, I thought, *Bo-jaama is not here. He has either changed wards or gone home.*

As I emerged from the basement, I saw the Sister, a mature woman with grey hair, holding a pile of paper in her arms, her pockets stuffed with medicine. Her look and walk inspired confidence. As she was walking fast, I sprinted to catch up with her. 'Sister, Sister,' I pleaded. She looked, but didn't stop. She wore tinted glasses and I wasn't sure if she had noticed me. 'Sister!' I called again, now beside her. 'Could you help? In which ward is Bo-jaama?' I asked, while she was still walking.

Abruptly, she stopped, turned to face me, peered straight into my eyes and said, 'Is he your brother?'

'No,' I replied.

She gave the impression of confusion and wondering. 'Come to my office,' she said in a grave voice.

I followed her to her office, situated at the very end of the corridor and, once in, she asked me to take a seat. No one had ever asked me politely to 'take a seat' as she did. 'I will be back in a few minutes,' she said.

I didn't know where she had gone, but she came back in the promised time. She didn't sit behind her desk as the rector had. She sat beside me, close to me – too close. 'What is your name?' she asked. 'Where did you come from?' The Sister was as pleasant as she could be, but her face alternated between relaxed and tense, happy and sad.

'My name is Jusef. I'm from the north,' I uttered, lips pursed. 'Bo-jaama is my friend's brother. We go to the same school,' I added.

Like a bullet, the truth emerged from her lips. 'Bo-jaama is dead,' she said. 'Nobody was beside him when he died; the nurse discovered him at ten o'clock in the morning. We don't know the exact time he passed away. We kept him in the mortuary for three days, but no one claimed him, so the council took over and buried him. As far as we know, he was buried in the nearest cemetery,' she continued.

Listening to her, I felt my chest tighten and the room change position. The Sister pulled a bundle of keys from her pocket and yanked a tiny one. With it, she opened a drawer in a small cabinet. She pulled out two pages, looked at them patiently, and came back to sit where she had been, beside me.

'Bo-jaama left a will,' she said. 'He left you his watch and a gold ring. I have some papers for you to sign, then the watch and the ring will be your property.'

It was too much for me to take in. Just as the Sister was fiddling with papers, a tall young black doctor came in. 'Madame Omlil had high blood pressure last night,' he said.

'Go and test her again,' she told him. 'If it is any higher than yesterday, instruct the nurse to medicate her and make sure the nurse carries out your instructions.'

The doctor wasted no time and waltzed out of the room. I was struck by his dark black skin and long white teeth.

'Sign this paper for me,' the Sister asked me, but my French was not good enough to understand medical or legal jargon. Fearful, I refused to sign.

'I don't need Bo-jaama's watch or ring,' I said. 'I have a watch. Look!' I showed her the watch on my wrist.

The Sister realised how nervous I was. 'It's a gift,' she said. 'You can do whatever you want with it.'

I thought I would never be able to dig myself out of the hospital, but the Sister shook my hand and showed me the door. I scrambled for a while to find the main door and went straight back to school, hoping against hope to see Abdu. Back earlier than planned, I went to the library, not to read, because my mind was spiralling wildly, but to hide and collect my feelings. My presence in the library, however, didn't please the librarian.

'Where are your friends?' the librarian, thin as a pencil, asked me.

'Some are in the *medina* and others in the New Town,' I replied.

'Why aren't you with them?' he said.

He wants the entire library to himself, I thought. *Librarians are a strange kettle of fish. They know where books are, but never what's inside,* I thought to myself. With no one to shush but me, sitting and fiddling with books and papers, the librarian spent all his time looking out the window, yawning. To take a break and kill his boredom, he patrolled empty aisles.

By six-thirty, the library was shut. Like lemmings, boys flooded to the toilet room. I searched for Abdu, but there was no sign of him. Oujdi appeared with a big smile on his face, trying to absorb a French poem by heart.

While we congregated in small groups, jittering and waiting for the refectory doors to open, I kept searching for Abdu. The siren sounded, and Abdu appeared, trudging. I held back and waited for him; we were the last to the table. Sitting at the same table, Faissal looked morose, but no one bothered with him. Oujdi was in a manic mood, and no one could stop him talking or make sense of what he said.

After dinner, Abdu reached into his bag and threw on the table two balls of yarn and two knitting needles. That brought Faissal out of his mood. Abdu started to knit, but he kept dropping stitches. I demonstrated how to keep from dropping them by blocking the stitches with one finger, as I had knitted my own hat while shepherding.

'Where did you get the yarn?' I asked him.

'From a wool shop owned by an old but attractive French woman with grey hair. "Do you know how to knit?" she asked me. "No," I replied. She showed me how to knit and gave me two needles and two balls of yarn.'

I wondered who this generous woman was and remembered the French woman who had paid for our breakfast.

Before Abdu had finished his story and demonstration, the bursar came in and saw our dining table turned into a knitting workshop. Abdu stepped out, and I trailed behind him.

He went far down the slope ahead of me. I caught up with him, and we slowly ambled down to the library. Abdu's legs moved heavily, as he was certainly exhausted.

'Abdu,' I said in a soft, sad voice, 'it pains me to tell you Bo-jaama has died.'

Abdu didn't doubt me and didn't ask any questions. He stopped and squeezed his head between his hands.

'Let us move,' I said. Abdu moved on, but took refuge against a tree and wept quietly to himself. Standing behind him, I felt powerless. It felt as though the tree had hugged Abdu forever and time had stopped. 'It is the will of God,' I said, tapping Abdu's shoulder.

'It is also the will of man,' replied Abdu in a strange voice.

Abdu had no choice but to travel home to inform his father and stepmother. But first, the school needed to know and he needed permission. The office was closed. We went to the chief prefect, not to get permission, as he was not credited with such authority, but to inform him.

Days later, Abdu arrived with his father and his stepmother. Although I wasn't introduced to them immediately, I could see they were a provincial couple. His parents looked like Adam and Eve dropped into a twentieth-century city. Abdu's father was exceptionally tall and thin, his wife two-thirds his height. He had a beard with two contrasting colours, black and white, that competed for visibility. A very long turban first choked his head, then what was left of it covered his ears and was used as a scarf. His shoes were made-to-measure with straw, supported by tyre rubber. His wife looked half his age and was strikingly beautiful, with no veil, no headscarf, and no *jellabah* either. She wore a long dress, tightly tied at the waist with a masculine belt. Her youth and beauty couldn't hide her distress. Everything was dazzling for her. She wanted to know about her son's life and death, but neither she nor her husband spoke French, Spanish, Arabic or even Moroccan Darija – just Tarifit.

Bo-jaama's parents relied solely on Abdu; they believed he could tell them when and where his brother had passed away, and would certainly know in which cemetery Bo-jaama had been buried. Abdu knew nothing of all that, and what he knew of Bo-jaama's private life, he couldn't reveal to his parents. He told me he felt squeezed between an unjustified guilt and duty to his father and his stepmother. He had to take care of his father and the wife he had never liked, yet his baccalaureate exams were only a few weeks away; he felt terrified and had already missed two important tutorial revisions and even the mock exams.

Abdu rushed to the rector and begged to resit the mock exams. It was the first time that the rector had heard about Bo-jaama's death, but, unsympathetic, he told Abdu to clear off.

When Abdu took his parents to the hospital, no papers relating to Bo-jaama's admission or his death could be found. His parents were pushed and rattled between doors and corridors and left feeling exhausted and overwhelmed.

Abdu's stepmother, intelligent but wrapped in tradition, murmured loudly, 'Is Bo-jaama really dead? Has he ever been here? If he is dead, who killed him and why?'

'She is an embarrassment. She and my father should hurry home,' mumbled Abdu. He asked me to give him the name of the ward sister, as with her name in his hand, his stepmother would get some of the information she was seeking.

Abdu's hopes, however, were dashed. I hadn't taken the name of the sister; it had never come to my mind that such a need would occur. But I remembered her distinctly.

It was Friday morning. A refreshing breeze poured through the windows and got lost in the dormitory. I was looking forward to my French lesson that afternoon with Michelle.

Abdu was on the brink of a mental breakdown. 'Nothing can get into my head; I can't pull anything out of it either. All the lessons are gibberish. The more a professor repeats, the more deaf and dull I get,' he told me over lunch.

'There will be no sunrise if you mess up your baccalaureate,' I told him.

Listening to me made Abdu even more agitated. An avalanche of resentment toward his stepmother engulfed him – even more than Bo-jaama's private life had shocked him. Hoping to put the lid on Abdu's emotional lava, I offered to go with him and his parents to the hospital.

Friday lunch was expected to be better than on the other weekdays, to be tasty and certainly filling, but that day the spaghetti was watery with a few pieces of cheese floating here and there. On the plate, it looked like a high and fatty hill, but its height didn't quench the hunger. Abdu and I didn't stay for the dessert, though we saw it coming, a trolley full of small oranges, one for each boy.

Abdu's parents were waiting for him and surprised to see me, as Abdu had never mentioned my name. Abdu's mother addressed me as 'My son', a sign of respect, affection and the difference in our ages. All the way to the hospital, Abdu dodged his parents.

'How are the crops this summer?' I asked Abdu's father, to make conversation.

'We are plagued by the wrath of drought with wind and dust,' he replied. 'We would have perished but for my eldest son, who is now working in a Roman country.' (He meant Europe.)

I knew Abdu's parents had already spent two nights in a *funduq* nearby. Abdu's stepmother couldn't sleep. 'My legs are prey to fierce and mysterious insects,' she told me. 'My legs are covered with itchy, red bites.'

It didn't take long to reach the hospital. Visitors didn't look particularly happy to be there; their faces said it all. The door and corridors were familiar to me, and we went straight to the ward sister's office. The door was closed, so no one dared to knock. While waiting, Abdu's father could hardly stand up. He leaned against the wall and, from time to time, cushioned his back with his hands. Abdu was silent, and I worried I might miss my French lesson or keep Michelle waiting. It took a while before a young nurse came and opened the door; there was no one inside. Before I was able to ask her for help, she was already away.

'Coming here would make the healthy unhealthy,' said

Abdu's father, peering at the nurse. A while later, a male nurse came, opened the door and sat down. Abdu and I forced our way in, and the nurse immediately understood our frustration. By a stroke of luck, the black doctor with the white teeth entered and nodded to me.

'Doctor, where could I find the nurse who was here just last Friday?' I asked.

'She is no longer here,' he said. 'She's in Jerusalem.'

'These are Bo-jaama's parents. He died here. They want to know more about how he died,' I explained.

'Speaking from memory, I saw Bo-jaama twice. He didn't respond to the penicillin. That's all I could confirm,' said the doctor.

'Where did you come from?' he asked me, avoiding more questions.

'From the North,' I responded. 'And you, Doctor?'

'From Senegal, Dakar.'

That was all the information Bo-jaama's parents could get. From the hospital, I led them to the cemetery nearby. Bo-jaama's mother wanted to know where her son's grave was, but nobody knew. There was an abundance of fresh new graves to choose from. Bo-jaama's mother looked at them all, cried and grieved at each grave as if they all belonged to her son.

Bo-jaama's father spoke very little. His wife was his spokesman; he appeared overwhelmed by the cemetery. 'It's a city under the city,' he sighed.

Bo-jaama's mother succumbed to the reality; Bo-jaama was dead. 'He is here, somewhere, but no one knows where,' she said, tears flowing. A few hundred yards away, a voice filled the air; a man, unbearded, sat on a cemented grave and recited the Holy Koran. Bo-jaama's mother saw the man moving from grave to grave, reciting. She understood that he had been hired to sanctify the dead, and decided to hire him to do the same for Bo-jaama.

Abdu thought it was a waste of money. Against his wish, I beckoned the man to Bo-jaama's mother, and having no bargaining spirit, she unfolded her second belt, yanked out a few coins, and without counting, filled the man's hand.

'Which grave is yours?' asked the man, graciously. His question prompted more tears from her eyes.

'Sit anywhere you like,' she said. 'He will hear you.'

The man was confused. 'Do all those graves belong to her? Was her family hit by a plague?' I heard him mutter to himself. He sat between two fresh uncemented graves, closed his eyes and began quietly reciting the Holy Koran. The reciting didn't last any more than ten minutes.

Watching Bo-jaama's mother weeping, I remembered with sadness Miloda buried in Algeria on the top of a hill, and now no one would know which one. She would be dust and part of Algerian soil.

There was not much time left for me to tarry. I thought Bo-jaama's mother should have his watch and ring. I would have preferred to hand them to her in a private place, but thought I might never see her again.

'*Lalla*,' I said. 'I have two mementos that belonged to Bo-jaama.' I thrust my hand into my pocket and pulled out the watch and ring.

She looked at them, and the ring puzzled her. Her cheeks

wet, she fondled both and looked intently at the ring. 'He was getting engaged!' she said. 'This is the ring that he bought for his fiancée, the girl he loved, but his journey was cut short. I wish I knew this girl. I would go and hand it to her.' As it happened, I knew that Bo-jaama had stolen the ring from his brother Abdu, who had stolen it from a Jewish jeweller when he and I had gone into the Jewish quarter for a stroll.

I left Abdu to take care of his parents and rushed to my French lesson. Michelle was in the Franciscan library, reading a road map, facing a wide, open window, when I arrived a bit late that day. On the table in front of her was a pile of photos of all kinds: landscape, flowers, trees, donkeys, young boys and girls, and women carrying heavy jugs on their heads. She had shown the photos to Father Paul and was waiting for me to see them.

'Are you a photographer?' I asked.

'I did all that with my little Kodak,' she said, proudly. As if I didn't believe her, she yanked it out of her bag and held it up. 'I had a fabulous holiday! If my fiancé would agree, Marrakesh would be the spot for our honeymoon, but he's allergic to the sun; it makes his skin crack and ooze blood.'

Michelle was a real chatterbox and very bubbly that afternoon. I had left Abdu's mother and rushed in order not to miss my French lesson. Michelle, however, had come to say goodbye.

'I won't be able to see you next Friday, or for the next few weeks. I'll be busy. Organising my wedding takes all my time. My parents are expecting me on Saturday and my wedding is on Sunday,' she said.

Father Antoine walked in while she was laughing. 'Are you inviting Jusef to your wedding?' he asked.

'No,' she said. 'But, I am inviting him to stay with my parents for two or three weeks. My father will teach him how to make wine. He is the best wine producer in Bordeaux.'

The telephone rang next door, and Father Antoine disappeared. 'I will give you a lift to Bordeaux if you wish,' she offered. For me, this was a dream beyond hope, but I didn't have two coins to rub together. Michelle had provided me with a living window into a sophisticated mind and culture, plus the French language. The end of French lessons meant the end of the vision.

Returning to school, heavy-hearted, I took refuge under a small tree almost my height and waited for the siren to ring. Faissal and Oujdi joined me under the tree. We talked over each other like bees.

Leaving the refectory after dinner, I went straight to my room, sat down and watched some magnificent eucalyptus trees through the window. While I was still struggling with the day's events, Abdu popped in. 'I am misplaced,' he said, 'in space and time. I am called to be a *Sufi*.'

'Anyone but you, Abdu! You have attempted rape, remember? You broke into the house of the woman you'd stalked and put your hand on her husband in bed!' I exclaimed.

Unhappy, he breathed in, filled his lungs with air, and breathed out a worrying sadness. 'I thought you would take me seriously,' he said, 'or at least listen to me.' I was preoccupied with how to map out my summer to find work to survive the following year.

It was late June. The days for us to hear our fate had arrived. The deputy rector came, files in hand, opened the classroom door, exchanged nods with the professor, and bellowed one of two words for each student from the depths of his lungs: 'pass' or 'fail'.

I couldn't believe my ears when I heard the magic word for me – 'pass'! My boarding scholarship would be renewed. The deputy rector had stunned the class with joy and sorrow and went to the next class to do the same.

In the days that followed, Abdu begged me to embark on a strange behaviour that deeply disturbed me – 'the *Sufi* life'. He destroyed his shoes, walked barefoot, and asked me to do the same. He bought a heavy, black second-hand coat, which was meant to cover him entirely. The excessive heat in Fez didn't bother him. His hair and beard were left to grow as long as they could and go wherever they fell. Tall and thin, he was getting thinner every day. He ate less and less.

His madness evoked fear, and I felt sometimes like running away from him, yet his tongue always indicated an intelligent brain at work. He puzzled me and reminded me of my cousin, Ahmed; Abdu was intelligent and Ahmed was stupid, yet they shared something.

Abdu did succeed in getting his baccalaureate and a place to study Sharia Law was waiting for him, but he didn't want to be a lawyer, judge, professor, farmer, landlord or businessman. He felt trapped in his own flesh, 'an incoherent mosaic of colour', he told me.

'Your flesh that you hate is the same flesh that allows you

to fly!' I told him. 'For the sake of a simple life, you have entered into a far more complex one!'

Abdu had hoped to see me become a *Sufi* like him so he would have a companion with whom to disappear either into the desert or the mountain, but I disappointed him. Before leaving, looking completely bizarre, he came to tell me goodbye. 'What are you going to do for your holiday?' he asked me.

'My mother is old, hard of hearing, her sight is failing, and arthritis is crippling her. She needs me, and so does my unmarried sister, Amina. I shall look for a husband for her before she's raped and becomes damaged goods forever.'

21

Heading north, I took the night coach to Nador and left the dirty city of Fez behind. The coach was big, long, solid and equipped with a diesel engine, giving the travellers a lot of noise to put up with and fumes to breathe in.

The night was long and tiring. I peered continuously through the window during the night and through the dawn. Carcasses here and there made me dread to think of what I might find at home. Nearing Nador, the welcoming sun rose bit by bit, and bored passengers watched it turn the sky orange and pink, but soon it rose higher and became a bother. Everybody dodged to seek a refuge from it, as the windows had no shades.

Dropped in the middle of Nador on a street with deafening noise and crushing crowds, I rushed to the taxi station. Travellers wishing to reach remote villages and countryside had assembled here and there to fill a taxi and share travelling costs. It was a lottery; a group might be already formed, just waiting for the last lucky rider, or one might be the first to arrive, hope and wait, but all in vain. At the taxi station, I found myself alone. I stood waiting and watching the taxi drivers playing cards.

Hours passed, and with nostrils full of dust, I was grilled under the sun. No one showed up to share a taxi with me, and the city fired its familiar gun: one o'clock. Desperate, I went to the coach station. *I will take the coach to the village, Arkmane, and from there to my sister Farhana's, five miles away, to spend the night.* I rerouted myself. There was a snag in my mind, however. *It won't be a sweet night in my sister's house. Her husband, though a hafiz, is a despicable man. He's full of sarcasm and nasty comments. I could match him, but for the sake of my sister, I will play the oaf. If I spend the night at my sister's, I must get up and leave before he starts barking.*

The coach connecting Nador and Arkmane left at four in the afternoon, and it would have been easier to buy a ticket to hell than one for this coach. Tickets were sold, resold and sold again, yet to buy a ticket, there were some bonuses to be paid first: bow, be polite and discreet. A station cleaner, a hard-talking, embittered old man, playing with a broomstick rather than cleaning with it, sold me a second-hand ticket. The coach was full, seat boundaries counted for nothing, and the roof was packed with bags, bottles of olive oil and animals of all sorts: chickens, rams and goats. They were all cuffed, subdued, and subject to the sun, wind, and whirlwinds filled with dust.

The aged coach was overloaded, crowded, and the animals were tortured, but everybody was happy, cracking jokes and passing sweets. The coach was wracked with chaotic movement and shouting. Unexpected stops were requested. 'Stop! Stop! You have gone too far!' a passenger shouted. 'You stopped too soon! Go a bit farther!' shouted another.

Whenever there was a stop, I wondered where the people were going, as there was no road or visible path. From time to time, a honking Volvo or Mercedes with people leaning out the windows and waving, would overtake the coach. For them, the coach was just a small dot full of troglodytes, but for me inside, the little dot was like a space shuttle in the sky.

Those for whom the village Arkmane was the final stop were never happy. The coach was too slow. 'I wish I had my donkey!' someone shouted loudly, all the way from the back, to insult the driver.

The coach arrived in the village as the sun was setting, leaving behind broad streaks of pink and red in the sky. Nothing was obvious to the eye in the village except the prison. Looking at it, I remembered what my father had said years ago, 'Those in power stripped us of our wealth and built us a prison. Yes. A prison.'

Before the engine was switched off, travellers were elbowing each other, some already on the roof identifying their goods, others grabbing their luggage. They all headed to the mountain with their backs to the sea, as though a terrible tide were chasing them. I saw a man put his goat around his neck and walk as fast, straight, and comfortably as the rest. As the sun hid, darkness crept in. I dared to wonder, *What if my sister is not at home? It's been over nine months since I've seen or heard of her. Where would I spend the night?*

I found myself alone on a dusty path and the beating of my heart got heavier, but I still kept walking until I reached a main intersection with many paths, each leading to different family ghettos.

Trying to figure out where my sister Farhana's house was, I got lost in the darkness. Each house was walled with stacked stones, prickly pear trees and aloe vera; in my mind, her house was the last, but which one? Packs of fierce dogs, growling and barking, came from every side. I stopped, and they encircled me. Any move made them fiercely aggressive. The abundance of stones allowed me to pick some and, in the dark, throw them in every direction. One dog managed to grab my trousers and tear off a piece. I picked up some more stones, hit the dog on the head; he yelped and abandoned the fight. The pack followed him. *I wish I hadn't come here*, I mused. Farhana's house had a huge tree at the front and though I remembered the tree, I couldn't see it.

I skirted a second pack of dogs and walked on rough soil and stone until the massive tree emerged from the darkness, only a few metres away from Farhana's main door.

Farhana herself had never had a dog. She always complained, 'Dogs wake me up! I could never get a full night's sleep! Dogs invite each other to bark! They create an unnerving symphony!'

Farhana looked shocked when she opened the door and came face-to-face with me. She feared I had come to tell her bad news, that our mother had died. 'This is an unusual visit,' she said. 'I was on my last leg, about to jump into bed. I'm just waiting for my husband to come home from a wedding. He's late as usual.'

Waiting up for her husband and her son to come home, she dug deeply and probably unconsciously into her youth and marriage, but I knew nothing of that. She had married between the ages of eleven and twelve, before I was born, and her husband had been four times her age.

'I am thin,' she complained. 'My husband wants me to be fat, with big breasts and a huge bum! Can you buy a tablet to inflate my buttocks?'

'Your buttocks are already big,' I told her, hoping to dissuade her. I wondered how large she wanted them to be.

'Not big enough, compared to many,' she answered.

I felt sorry for her, but, *she's being selfish*, I thought to myself. *Where would I find a drug to enlarge buttocks?*

Dawn couldn't come too soon.

* * *

AT HOME, IT WAS Amina who answered the door. The two dogs didn't bark, and the donkey near the front door was tied by the leg to an iron tether. Amina came in a rush, but didn't open the door immediately.

'Who is there?' she asked.

'It's me,' I replied.

'Who is there?' she asked again.

Her voice is funny, isn't it? I thought to myself.

When her doubts were dispelled and her hesitation overcome, she opened the door; an exchange of hugs opened the gate to tears.

'Let's go and see Mother,' I said, hoping to distract her.

'Mother is dead,' she wailed, her face behind her hands. Amina couldn't bring herself to explain anything. Her mouth was flooded with murmured words. She tried to talk, to explain, but everything came at once, her throat choked with sobs.

I ran to my mother's room, where she had often sat and prayed, saying her rosary over and over. There was no sign of her except what she had worn, the small precious rug she had loved and used for praying, and the rosary beads hanging on the wall. The room was not large, but it felt like an immense space with no boundary.

Amina went to the big room and stood right in the middle of the door, like a statue.

'Can we go to the cemetery?' I asked.

'Yes,' she replied.

The small but fast-growing local cemetery would have been a beautiful spot if only it were not a cemetery. The soil was red, the space open, with scattered trees here and there, but it inspired fear and horror even to drivers passing by. No names were written, or markers to distinguish who was buried there; everyone had to remember the spot where his own lay under the ground. Within a short time, they were all mixed up and confused. My mother had been laid beside my father. 'This is where she wanted to be, as though they were still alive, side by side,' I said.

After I got used to the new reality and conditions, with just Amina and me living in the house, I went to see Uncle Mimoun. 'You have really grown up since I saw you last!' Mimount exclaimed, pulling back and glancing up and down at me. 'What a pity your mother isn't here!' Her words fell on me like a hammer.

'A pot of tea?' asked Uncle Mimoun, trying to zip her lips.

Arriving with tea and her daughter, Kadija, trailing behind her, Mimount sat down to finish making the tea, adding mint and sugar. Extremely nervous, not knowing what Uncle Mimoun's reaction would be, I shot him a question, 'Would you lend me some money?'

Shocked, Uncle Mimoun turned to look at his wife, who was equally mesmerised. 'What do you want to do with it?'

'Trade currency,' I replied.

'What is that?' Mimount asked. She had no clue.

'A dangerous trade!' said Uncle Mimoun.

'Don't worry,' I replied.

'Trading in black market currency can be lucrative, but lethal. Some traders are well-organised and in the midst of criminals, well-armed and ruthless. You want to work among them, to compete with them and the banks? Don't forget the Spanish police are badly paid and expect to be bribed. Once you have competed with banks(only God knows who owns them), and with the traders, from the big sharks to the small piranha, very little will be left,' Uncle Mimoun warned me.

'That's why I want to start with a good deposit,' I said.

'You are naïve,' said Uncle Mimoun. I went home empty-handed, just as I had come. Amina and I cooked potatoes and chatted the whole night.

I noticed what my mother's absence had done to Amina. Being alone and isolated had made her jump at the faintest sound of a bird or rustle of the trees. The only guardian angels were the two dogs, Dargan and Dina. The poor dogs, fed only a few spoons of husks and prickly pears, left droppings every-where. I thought Rabbia and her husband would have offered Amina love and support, but they hadn't.

'Despicable!' said Amina, when I mentioned Rabbia's

husband. 'He came to see me just one week after Mother died. He said he wanted to know how I was doing and give me a hand. Rabbia had asked him to do so, he said, because she was worried about me. What a kindness, I thought. That made me happy and cheerful. There was quite a big pile of rubbish just behind the main door. He removed it, and the place looked cleaner and tidier. After that, there wasn't really very much to do, but he was hanging around and constantly behind me. I felt suspicious, but thought it was just my imagination. I was inside the small room, and he came in and got so close to me that I was sandwiched between him and the wall. He suddenly kissed me on my lips and began fondling my breasts with both hands. I pushed him with all my strength and yelled, "Rabbia! Rabbia!" He backed off like a beaten dog.'

Listening to Amina, anger and deep sorrow gripped me; two sisters humiliated at once. 'Have you ever spoken to Rabbia about it?' I asked.

'That would destroy her marriage,' she said.

Before dawn, I was again knocking hard and loud on Uncle Mimoun's door. He was already up, looking smart, and was surprised to see me. I expected a pot of tea, but didn't get one. He seemed preoccupied.

'I am going to Nador,' he said. 'Mimount has been bleeding for weeks. A doctor needs to investigate the problem.' He paused for a few minutes and I could see he was thinking. 'Your father would never forgive me if I withheld my help. A friend of mine, Mr Amakran, loaded with cash, will lend you a quarter of a million francs. I will be the guarantor. You can come with us and start now.' *This is too good to be true!* I thought. 'A taxi will pick us up around ten o'clock.'

In a few leaps, I was home. Anxious, Amina wanted to understand why I was going back to a filthy town, Nador, in a crazy rush. 'I will be back home before dark,' I promised. I saw her tears, but sprinted to catch Uncle Mimoun before the taxi arrived, as I knew he wouldn't wait for me.

In a royal blue Mercedes, I sat at the front beside the driver, who drove carelessly at an excessive speed, steering with one hand and holding a cigarette in the other. Uncle Mimoun sat at the back and gave his wife all the space she needed. She stretched her legs and put her head in his lap. He stroked her head and put a scarf on her face. *He is so close to his wife, with all his tenderness . . . did Uncle Mimoun really need a second wife?* I wondered.

Dropped at the doctor's surgery, we found the waiting room packed. 'We'll be here for the whole day,' I said, watching men and women sitting on the chairs and lying on the floor. An old woman was doubled over, screaming with pain, her hand on her chest.

'You will be first this afternoon,' the receptionist told us.

On top of her bleeding, Mimount complained of carsickness. Travelling from the doctor's surgery to a hotel was all she could bear. There we left her to sleep until early afternoon.

Uncle Mimoun and I went straight to Mr Amakran's warehouse, which was immense and busy. Mr Amakran struck me as a heavy man, fat and lazy; he never moved, but his brother, older but looking younger than he, took the orders and did the work. I watched a man confined at the very back of the shop to whom no one was allowed to talk or distract; he was the bookkeeper. He looked miserable, his head constantly hanging down over the papers, but from time to time, he lifted it. I wondered if this man was going to punch the glass encircling him, as sometimes his cheeks looked red and ready to burst. Mr Amakran kept his eyes on him. *To scratch a living, he has to be caged like Kamil's hamster, deprived of sun, sky and air*, I thought.

Mr Amakran ordered tea from the café on the corner, and the waiter arrived with two pots of tea and a tray full of glasses. Sitting around a low, narrow table, Uncle Mimoun and I, with Mr Amakran and his brother, drank tea, but I couldn't taste it, as I was nervous, wondering when the loan was going to be discussed. When the pot was almost empty, the rest of the tea, strong and cold, was poured in a glass and taken to the bookkeeper, like a dog given the crumbs.

'My compliments; you have a good son,' said Mr Amakran to Uncle Mimoun.

'Thank you. He is the son I never had. If he comes to you, would you recognise him and remember him?' Uncle Mimoun asked.

'Absolutely!' replied Mr Amakran.

'Please make a quarter of a million Moroccan francs available to him and put it on my account,' requested Uncle Mimoun.

'Yes,' said Mr Amakran, but looked puzzled. 'That amount of money for a young boy?' he murmured quietly.

'Jusef is going to meet the daily ship from Malaga,' said Uncle Mimoun.

Mr Amakran understood the game immediately: black market currency trading. Turning to me, he gave me a deep, long look, as though seeing me for the first time. He then left his chair and went to his bookkeeper's office, disappeared for a few minutes and came back carrying a shabby suitcase. Mr Amakran, while never lifting his hand off his suitcase, took me to a large table and opened it.

I couldn't stifle the gasp that escaped from my mouth as I spied the largest variation of currencies I had ever seen in my life: Spanish, German, French and others I didn't even recognise. Mr Amakran looked on, amused at my astonishment. 'Do you like it?' he chuckled.

'If only it were mine!' I answered.

'Never mind!' said Mr Amakran, who was well versed in foreign currency.

Looking at me, he hit a thick stack of French francs with his middle finger. 'Avoid this currency,' he said. Lifting the index finger of his left hand, he pointed to a pile of German notes. 'This bird,' he said, 'never stops soaring,' and he ran back and forth, flapping his arms like birds' wings.

Mr Amakran thought I should know the currency traders as well as the tricks of the trade. 'Did you ever hear of Mr Marosh?' he asked me.

'Yes,' I replied, 'when I was a child. He was cruel, a killer.'

'Then I don't need to bore you,' he replied. 'However, black market currency trading is full of Maroshes. If Newton discovered gravity, Marosh perfected cruelty. There is only one law in currency trading: make big money – and fast!'

From the outset, I had thought Mr Amakran was a holy

man, but now I thought he had no soul. A gigantic grandfather clock chimed one and ended the talk and trading. The bookkeeper emerged from his cage while Uncle Mimoun and I rushed to the hotel with only enough time left for a quick lunch.

'I am starving,' said Mimount when she saw us, 'but I had awful nausea this morning. Maybe I should just fast,' she added.

'Let's go,' said Uncle Mimoun, who was lying on the bed and seemed to have already had a short snooze.

On our way out, Mimount laid her hand on my shoulder. She needed support. Inside the restaurant, she was the only woman, and Uncle Mimoun tried to hide her. Conscious of the lack of other women, he sat Mimount facing the wall. She had never seen city beggars. When she turned to see where she was, as if she had just awakened from a deep coma, two male beggars standing outside the door of the restaurant caught her eye.

'I can't swallow any more,' she said.

Uncle Mimoun looked at her and smiled. 'You've seen nothing yet,' he said.

'Has it to be like that?' she asked.

'Nador has always been like that,' I told her, 'but Fez is worse. It's time to move,' I reminded Uncle Mimoun.

He stood up, turned his shoulder and threw a scarf over his wife's head and around her neck. He moved first, and she dawdled behind him like a leashed dog. Mimount's consultation was not expected to last more than an hour. Doctors were very frugal with their time. Uncle Mimoun and I echoed the meeting time to each other: four o'clock at the taxi station.

I stepped into the bakery next to the doctor's surgery. *Two loaves would please Amina and save me the bother of baking for today*, I thought. Moving toward the market, I succumbed to the bargain offered by the grapes vendor, who was harassed and chased by the police wherever he went, as he could have been unlicensed or a tax dodger.

An eternity passed waiting for Uncle Mimoun to show up. Not conscious of how many grapes I had popped into my mouth, I finished the bag. Six o'clock struck, business died and spooks crept out to hunt. In the dark street, standing alone, I waited. And waited.

Uncle Mimoun and his wife appeared, but I couldn't fathom why both were beside themselves with fury. 'Those two are mad!' the taxi driver told me.

'They've just come out of the doctor's surgery,' I explained.

'They should never have gone to see that quack doctor,' he said. In his late twenties, he was excited to be commissioned for a long journey.

'What a beautiful Mercedes you drive,' I complimented him. Painted royal navy, freshly polished, the taxi had a diplomatic flair. As the driver was conscious of the value and the importance of his car, he made his way carefully, but as we left the paved road, we found the dirt road blocked by stone after stone, impassable. The driver and I tried to move them when suddenly, a pack of boys and girls stormed us from every direction. They dented the car, and we engaged in a stone fight, in which Uncle Mimoun joined. It was a disgraceful battle, but the boys and girls enjoyed it. Somehow, I enjoyed it as well.

At home at dinnertime, Amina pulled gossip from the past. 'Mother used to call me a mindless chicken! Am I really?' she asked me.

'Yes,' I teased her, not unravelling her motive.

'Then find a husband for me!' she replied.

Seriously, I started looking for a husband for her. I went to Mr Kalid, who had no daughters, only sons. I suggested Amina as a wife for one of them. While waiting for his reply, I was horrified to discover that Amina had not been honest with me. She had already been fornicating with our cousin, Moha, temporarily on holiday from Germany. Before she knew it, she was pregnant, and tying her up with her lover proved to be difficult. Thick clothes could not hide a speedily growing baby indefinitely and local gossip hurt. Amina asked me to find an abortionist, but I refused.

* * *

ON THE TWENTY-FIRST OF July, before the sun rose, I was standing at the front door of Mr Amakran's large store. Arriving on his own, without his brother, Mr Amakran didn't look at me, speak to me or greet me. He looked locked into a private world of his own and gave me the impression he didn't want to see me. *Is the offer still on the table?* I wondered, worried.

'Good morning to you, Mr Amakran,' I said, moving closer to him, intending to shake his hand and jolt his memory.

'Morning,' replied Mr Amakran, with a slow, heavy voice.

Neither my physical presence nor my voice jostled Mr Amakran's memory, despite Uncle Mimoun's express request that I be recognised. 'Uncle Mimoun sends you his greeting,' I said, after a few seconds of loss. In fact, I lied. I hadn't seen Uncle Mimoun since the day Mimount had visited the doctor. As if a new sun had arisen or a dark curtain raised, Mr Amakran smiled and every muscle in his face and chin rippled.

'Is your Uncle Mimoun in the town?' he asked.

'No,' I said.

'Pity,' he replied with a sigh. Mr Amakran could not forget his faithful comrade, Uncle Mimoun. As teenagers, just to be fed, they had fought together in the Spanish Civil War and often reminisced about hunting for Spanish girls.

I couldn't believe the heavy bundles of keys Mr Amakran carried on his belt, making him look like a prison warden. Mr Amakran picked the right key and unlocked his massive store. Once inside, I heard a gentle voice. 'Tea and doughnuts, Uncle Amakran?' It was a boy from the café nearby who came every morning to serve him like a king, but with no official crown.

Before the tea and doughnuts were delivered, Mr Amakran's brother arrived, weaving through the aisles, inspecting the stock and jumping on the telephone whenever it rang. With a full plate of doughnuts and a glass of tea each, Mr Amakran, his brother and I sat around the same table as we had with Uncle Mimoun. The tea quenched my thirst and the honey-sweetened doughnuts revived my brain. I would have loved to have more. From the breakfast table, Mr Amakran and I moved to a far smaller table, under which Mr Amakran kept his cash. Notes of different currency were tied in bundles, and with just a small piece of paper indicating the exact amount.

'I have counted each bundle six times, and my brother has

counted eleven times. No one has ever said that I shorted him,'
he said to me. Mr Amakran's extreme precision impressed me.
In one single gesture, Mr Amakran handed me a quarter of a
million Moroccan francs. I signed no paper. Mr Amakran knew
I had to go quickly, so I split the bundles into two breast
pockets, left and right, which made me ripe prey for a pick-
pocket.

I left Mr Amakran and joined a column of men, women
and children, young and old, all heading to the town of Melilla,
some in their private cars and others either by taxi or coach.
It looked like an exodus, but Nador never emptied. A non-stop
flood of people kept pouring in as well as out. To a tourist,
the town looked like chaos; a war with no guns and peace with
no tranquility.

In a coach full of people, there was just enough oxygen to
survive, and most passengers were women, but, unlike those
of Fez, they were unveiled, robust and strong. Very soon, I
realised that everybody was carrying a basket. A teenage girl
sitting beside me asked, 'Where is your basket?'

'I don't need one,' I answered.

Puzzled, the girl smiled. A basket was used as a disguise,
but also the means for an officer, Moroccan or Spanish, to close
his eyes and pocket a few hundred pesetas.

Different from most, with no basket in hand, I became
worried I might be searched. My mouth felt dry and my eyes
itchy. At the border, the queue was long, slow and degrading,
and the officers chose whom to pick and search. Carrying no
basket, I was quickly ushered along. People didn't matter; what
they carried did.

Once beyond the Moroccan frontier and past the Spanish border guards, I remembered how a few years ago, my sister Sanaa had used me to visit Awisha, the Jewish witch, to fix her marital problem. *It wasn't kind of my sister to send me here*, I now realised. *Melilla was, and is, a risky and dangerous place.*

The city centre faced the sea, though a tall row of palm trees stood between it and the gleaming Mediterranean beyond. The main boulevard running through the centre of the town split it in two, where shops of all kinds stood facing each other across the wide, busy street. The fortunes of the street ran from north to south in relation to how close premises were to the top end where, closest to the sea, chic cafés and exclusive banks thrived. At the bottom end, things were different, as beyond the end of the street lay a vast sprawling slum where Awisha lived and practised. Nothing had changed since the last time I was here.

Travellers leaving Africa, like those arriving from Europe, all passed through the city centre, from where the ship connecting the continents could be seen. There was no better place for a currency trader to sit than in the luxurious terraced cafés that lined the broad boulevard.

I hadn't fully appreciated the challenge; it was more than I had bargained for, and I was overwhelmed. I stepped into one of the chic and luxurious cafés and immediately felt sick. It stank of stale beer and too much alcohol. Half a dozen men, talking loudly, were loitering around the bar. They were all focused on one waitress, and she looked very happy to flirt with all of them, and all at once.

I stepped outside and sat on the terrace facing the sea and

palm trees where the air made me feel much better. The terrace was almost full, and everyone was clapping, calling the waiter, who was running to cope with very demanding clients. The waiter pounced on me. '*Qua-quearas, señor?*' he asked.

'Espresso,' I replied. The coffee was too strong and bitter, despite the amount of sugar I poured into it. I couldn't drink it. Nevertheless, I kept sipping, watching and wondering.

At last I was in the right place with the right money, yet didn't know what to do next. At the very end of the terrace, a stocky, burly, middle-aged man was sitting, drinking a beer and smoking a cigar. In front of him, on his white table, were piled many tall stacks of bank notes of different kinds to advertise his business. Not far away, facing him, stood a gigantic bank. Travellers could either step into the bank or exchange currency with him. He was far busier than the bank across the road. Travellers were a shrewd kettle of fish; they wanted the most for their money. The best way to achieve that was to boycott the fat cats, the banks.

The trader was extremely relaxed, either counting his money or just watching people pass by. Whenever patrolling policemen passed by his table, he called them by name. They answered with a nod.

Half an hour later, a man joined him, and a swap followed. The stocky man left; a younger man took his seat, but the money remained on the table. The changeover puzzled me.

Just across the boulevard, two thin-looking men promenaded in front of *Banco de España* and whispered, '*Sarf! Sarf!* (Exchange! Exchange!)' The street was full of colliding passengers, but there were no obvious buyers or sellers. The clock's hands indicated three forty-five; I felt glued to the chair, and my head was simmering. Amina was expecting me, and I first had to take the bus to the border, then catch the coach to Nador, and from there to Moulay-Rachid. From there, it was two hours' walk for a strong man or solid donkey.

It was time for me to go home, and I had achieved nothing except to spend some of Mr Amakran's money and drag my Uncle Mimoun into debt. As I stood up to catch the bus, I decided to saunter up the boulevard in Awisha's direction – one boulevard, but different people, like black and white. It swelled with fatty women in black mourning clothes and many young people parading aimlessly on the street. As I stood peering through the window of one chic shop, I heard a whisper. 'Girls waiting . . .' A few steps farther along, I heard, 'Exchange! German marks, dollars, French francs!' *On this boulevard, you can buy and sell anything*, I thought to myself, *if you know how.*

Relieved to hear the word 'exchange', I made my first gaffe. I stopped and asked, 'What's the rate for Deutschmarks today?'

'Are you buying or selling?' asked the trader, a man in his thirties, whose eyes were dancing as he talked.

'I am buying,' I said.

'How much do you want?'

'One hundred marks,' I replied.

The man's eyes changed immediately. They looked possessed. He invited me to come with him and discuss the rate. I realised I had stepped into dangerous territory and backed off slowly at first, then turned to run. 'Much better rate! Much better rate!' the man shouted behind me. Hurriedly, I vanished into the thick crowd.

Arriving home late, I couldn't disguise the effect of the day on me, and Amina couldn't misread my face: dry, tired and wrinkled before my time. She wanted me to tell her how the day had passed, but all I wanted was a chunk of bread and to fall asleep.

'You are hiding something,' she told me. But she herself was hiding something more serious.

Three days passed, and I seemed to have lost my courage, to have fallen into the old, boring form of life, taking care of the dogs and donkey. But Uncle Mimoun, my loan guarantor, was watching. Mr Amakran would snatch his land if the loan weren't paid in time and in full, and this would be a problem for Uncle Mimoun, not only of land, but also of honour.

'Has Jusef given up after just one rough day? He must have already spent some of Mr Amakran's money. Wouldn't it be preferable to minimise our losses and hand back Mr Amakran's money?' he asked Mimount. It didn't feel good to hear that from her when she told me later.

On Saturday evening, while sitting outside, chewing local barley porridge under the moonlight, I told Amina, 'I am leaving tomorrow at four in the morning . . .'

'Are you crazy?' she said, before I even finished the full sentence.

'I am going to Melilla to meet the *agarabo-na-Melilt* (the ship of Melilla.)'

Amina had never seen a ship. For her, it might have been as small as a frog or as high as a mountain. She had never been near the sea; just the words 'ship' and 'sea' filled her mind with wonder and gave her a thrill. She was unaware of the real peril. I would be carrying a quarter million Moroccan francs, travelling practically all day and night, changing coaches and crossing two merciless borders: Moroccan and Spanish. This had to be kept secret from all my other sisters and their husbands.

I was at the Melilla port two hours before the ship reached African soil. Still miles from land, the huge ship's deck was packed with people. Though still far away, some peered intensively to identify their friends. On the shore hundreds of people, young and old, some well-dressed and others like tramps, buzzed around, going nowhere. They had all come either to receive their relatives or to give a royal reception to the ship. For many, it was just a nice place to be and watch. The juggernaut manoeuvred into port.

Unfamiliar with the port and a novice in the currency trade, I moved closer to the gangplank and observed the passengers disembarking. Many appeared happy, but some, with puckered lips and shrivelled faces, appeared to wish the ship would make a U-turn instead of anchoring. They threw their scornful glances on everyone and in every direction. A few had come to be reunited with their families, or to get married, but others to resolve family disputes or divorce their unfaithful wives . . . it was with these people I had to do business: the rich.

A passenger carrying heavy suitcases, but unable to move and unwilling to trust the porter, burst into a tantrum of rage in front of me. A man quietened him by a few softly spoken words, 'Do you know where you are now? . . . in Africa . . . wait, the worst is still to come,' he added with a smirk. The outraged man kept pulling his cases and grumbling to himself.

He was expecting to be met with trumpets and saxophones, but there was nothing of the kind.

'Exchange!' I whispered in his ear. He elbowed me in the ribs. I whispered again, 'Exchange!' He ignored me. His anger carried him away. I had aimed for a target and missed.

No black market currency trader could afford to miss the arrival of the *agarabo-na-Melilt*, yet I did. The only man I recognised was the multi-millionaire standing by, alone, and travellers vied to shake his hand and go. I marvelled at this nonverbal protocol. I couldn't compete with the multi-millionaire or with those whose voices, like thunder, tore the sky. '*Sarf! Sarf!*' they shouted.

As I had failed either to buy or to sell, I was beginning to understand how tough the game was. From the shore, I moved to the taxi and bus station, which wasn't too far away, but it was like a bottleneck. Travellers heading to Morocco or other parts of Africa all started here, but few had the right currency for a taxi or a bus, let alone the right change. I shouted, 'Exchange! Exchange!' Even here, I failed as I wasn't alone. I moved and stood at the front of the bank door.

'Better than a bank! Better than a bank!' I shouted, trying to make my mark. A white man with grey hair and carrying two heavy bags stopped in front of me and, without much bargaining, sold me five hundred Deutschmarks. This was my first break, a coup. *The spot where I should stand is in front of the bank*, I told myself. The bank manager called the police to move me, but they didn't beat me as I had feared. Fifteen minutes later, I returned to the same spot. Standing there, I bought two hundred Dutch Guilders, but at a higher price than what official banks offered, and even higher than what my competitors proposed. The other traders were furious, and I created dangerous enemies.

Two particular veteran traders were angry to see me. They were outraged by the prices I offered, and the threats started. 'You are breaking the rules,' one of them snarled, as he walked into me and pushed me hard.

'What rules?' I asked.

He spun around and shouted over his shoulder, 'You'll soon find out!' His friend was standing, watching and waiting, under a palm tree nearby. Despite the sickening feeling, I ignored the threat and continued trading until the last of the travellers disappeared with me in their midst.

I serpentined to Café Morina and sat on the terrace, facing the prestigious Banco de España. This was the only place I felt safe, a hectic spot with fat and lazy police patrolling and pedestrians strolling all day long. The rich trader was already there, glued to his chair, gazing at his mountain range of currencies. His jaws were split by a cigar; espresso and a bottle of beer sat on his table.

Returning to the same place in front of the bank, I sold a hundred Dutch guilders to a Moroccan woman travelling alone for the first time. She told me she was determined, but nervous, to cross the sea, as she didn't have all the papers required. For different reasons, I was equally nervous, constantly looking over my shoulder, fearing I might be hit with a potato stuffed with needles and razorblades. Potato crime was common among rival traders, and innocent people were often disfigured.

After the *agarabo-na-Melilt* left late in the afternoon, the port became deserted. It felt as if humans had left and spooks had taken over. The smell of the Mediterranean Sea, with all that was dumped into it, along with the smell of fish, nauseated me.

By the end of August, I had learned a few tricks, but had lived like a yo-yo going back and forth. I proudly repaid Mr Amakran what I had borrowed, and was trading with my own capital.

* * *

THE SIXTEENTH OF SEPTEMBER has stuck forever in my memory like a monument. Trade was very slow and sluggish; the ship brought less happy travellers: extremely frugal, hard-bargaining and not law-abiding. Strolling the street, I witnessed with horror a rough, dangerous skirmish. While a taxi driver, out of his car, was talking to his friends, seven men jumped in and claimed his taxi. In the blink of an eye, they had filled the taxi's boot with heavy bags and suitcases, so it wouldn't close. Whatever luggage they couldn't fit in the boot, they threw on the roof. While the taxi driver shouted at them to get out, they shouted back at him to get in and drive. Refusing, he was pushed and sandwiched against his car. When the police arrived, though armed, the men were intentionally slow to empty the taxi. I was among the witnesses, but I wasn't able to give much of a description, as firstly, I didn't speak Spanish and secondly, it had happened too fast.

I went back to the café after watching the attempted taxi hijacking. The terrace was full except where the millionaire sat alone with one vacant seat beside him. He had never spoken to me or had even nodded his head, though sometimes there were just the two of us sitting on the outdoor terrace. 'May I share the table with you?' I asked him.

'Certainly,' he replied.

I grabbed the spare chair and sat beside him. Undisturbed, he opened his valise and spread out hundreds and hundreds of notes in foreign currencies. I moved my cup to the edge of the table to make room. He lit his cigar and ordered a double espresso. Before finishing his espresso, the rich man, whose name was Mr Timsamani, ordered a beer and anchovies. *This man is very rich, but not a Muslim. He is eating forbidden food and drinking alcohol*, I told myself. Unlike other traders, he didn't chase after the travellers. Upon the arrival of the ship, he stood fifty metres away like a majestic statue with distinctive clothing and a cigar or pipe, and people swarmed to him to pick up their currency, as the deals had already been done in Malaga.

'Where did you come from, sir?' I asked him.

'Local, local,' he answered. '*Akaali, Akaali*. My parents, grandparents and great-grandparents were all born within five miles from here. I am not racist,' he added. 'We are all children of that grumpy old man, Adam, but different . . .'

'Why do you think Adam was grumpy?' I asked him.

'Wasn't it he who pushed his wife to the point she lost her mind?' he said.

I wondered what he was going to come out with next, as it seemed he had already had a few pints of beer somewhere else. While he was still talking, his colleague, Mr Mohand, joined him, pulled a chic packet of cigarettes out of his left jacket pocket and passed it to me to help myself.

'Thank you,' I said. 'I don't smoke. In fact, it gives me headache and nausea.'

'You have escaped the street culture,' said Mr Mohand. 'As a little boy of ten, I used to ask smoking pedestrians to give me a cigarette. When they refused, I followed them until they threw the butt on the ground. I would pick it up and waste nothing of it. As a group of boys, we used to collect the butts, meet every afternoon and feast on them.' Mr Timsamani took no interest in what his colleague was telling me.

Both of them left. I stayed in the café and tried to make sense of what I had heard. Before the bank opened, I was strolling the boulevard in front of it. A couple arrived, looking for a doctor.

'Do you know if there is a doctor nearby?' they asked me.

'There are two on this street,' I said. As the man seemed to be confused, I took him to the door of the surgery. 'I can sell you pesetas, if you need them,' I told him.

He didn't look like it, but he carried a lot of cash. I sold him twenty thousand pesetas. The sale made my day, and I went home early.

The following morning, the seventeenth of September, I was first into the café. Mr Timsamani sat beside me and picked up the conversation that he had missed the day before.

'Where do you come from?' he asked.

'From tribe Kebdana,' I replied.

'It's a long way to commute,' he commented with a grimace.

'Yes, it is,' I answered.

A sound, unpleasant and ominous, filled the air. Br.r.r.r.r.r.

It was the hooting of the *agarabo-na-Melilt*, sailing through a very thick fog. We both prepared to leave, although we still had forty-five minutes to spare. 'Do you expect many travellers today?' I asked.

'My colleague in Malaga has completed a transaction of thirty-seven million six hundred Moroccan. He bought German marks, guilders and francs. Eight people are expected to arrive this morning and pick up their money.'

My ears couldn't contain what I had heard. 'Do they trust you?' I asked him, with surprise on my face.

'Yes,' he said.

'Have they already handed their money to your colleague in Malaga?'

'Yes, they have,' he said with a smile. 'No one loses one single cent,' he added. 'It is a trade regulated by honesty and trust. Capital punishment applies . . .'

Now I understand, I thought.

Before the ship arrived, in fact, before it had even left Malaga, the lucrative business had already been done. Only crumbs were left for traders like me. Mr Timsamani had a far-reaching hand. *The sea is not his limit*, I thought. The ship anchored, and Mr Timsamani stood far away from the crowd, but he knew his own, and they knew their man. It was a code I had now deciphered.

*   *   *

FOR THE NEXT EIGHT days, I stayed at home; I missed some important trading days. I had to arrange to give Amina as a wife to her cousin, Moha. Amina's belly had sprouted fast and big, and loose, thick clothing failed to hide her pregnancy from peering eyes. Her problem had become mine.

I went to Moha's father, my uncle, and told him, 'Amina is expecting and Moha is the father.' He either wasn't interested or didn't believe me. I told the same story to Uncle Mimoun, who looked shocked and surprised.

I went to Moha's father again and told him, 'A marriage must be arranged soon.' I repeated the same story to Uncle Mimoun.

I threatened my uncle. 'Unless we resolve this problem, I have some powerful friends in Melilla who will come and take care of Moha for me.'

First, he shrugged me off, but as I was a currency trader, he reluctantly agreed. He probably thought I was in contact with some important people, most of them criminals. Facing the possibility that Moha might be ambushed as he disembarked in Melilla by some dodgy thugs, he agreed to a marriage *in absentia*, as Moha was expected soon.

The wedding was cooked in a rush. Uncle Mimoun arrived with six elders, and Moha's father with the same number, around five o'clock. A form was completed verbally.

'Jusef, do you give Amina, your sister, as a wife to Moha?' asked the chief elder.

'Yes, I do,' I answered. With that question and answer, the legalities were completed. *It's a degrading ceremony*, I felt. Amina and Moha became husband and wife, but neither Amina, nor I, nor Moha's father knew where he was. All I knew about him was that he worked in Germany and sent money to his father. With four wives, his father needed his son's support.

Three days later, at five-thirty, two flatbed lorries arrived full of women and children, and on the corner of one lorry was a shackled ram. On its own, it made just as much noise as all women and children put together. Amina was upset when she saw the lorries approaching the house without a flag. They had handed the flag to a young girl and the wind had taken it away, beyond reach, we were told.

'A wedding with no flag,' Amina moaned on her own wedding day.

I felt angry with Amina, but I couldn't spoil her day. She was so upset by the missing flag, and yet she herself was marrying with a ragged flag.

I invited our sisters with their husbands and their children, but they were all indignant about not having been consulted about this betrothal before. It was, however, a rare occasion for sisters to meet, insult each other and see changes in each other and in the house, garden and prickly pear that fenced the house.

It was a busy wedding night. The ram was slaughtered by an expert, who enjoyed skinning it and asked me if he could keep the skin for a rug. The ram was big and fat enough to feed the elders, the guests, my sisters, their husbands and children. Bold, artistic women enjoyed themselves singing, while others played homemade drums. Amina liked all the fuss, but she sat in a corner the entire evening and was covered with a gauze tent so she could only watch the festivities. Children, like locusts, were lying asleep all over the house; they played to exhaustion and dropped anywhere.

By dawn, the guests, heavy and dishevelled, didn't know what to do with themselves. At ten-thirty, two lorries arrived.

They picked up the groom's guests and Amina, as the bride, went with them.

By four o'clock, the house was hollow and empty, with just me and the two dogs rattling inside. *Amina has resolved one problem, but she has started a lifelong marital problem*, I predicted. The whole space: the house, courtyard, rear and front garden, and the field became mine, but I didn't know what to do with it, or how to fill it. The house my father built had been the family's holy grail. We had shared the holy shell, but had never drunk the same wine.

Early the next morning, leaving the bruise of the wedding behind, I was in Melilla before nine. I went to my favourite café, sat on the terrace and waited for the *agarabo-na-Melilt* to arrive. Coffee was exceptionally comforting, but the noise of the wedding night was still reverberating in my ears. I forced myself not to think beyond where I was at that moment.

The ship arrived, and hundreds of people rushed to receive it, as if welcoming a war hero or a glorious football team. Trade was brisk, and the traders aggressive. Subject to sneers and threats, I reverted to Café Morina, my hub. It was, however, never easy to find a free seat on the terrace. Waiters, unfriendly and grumpy, squashed people together at the too-small tables.

*   *   *

AS I BECAME A familiar face at the café, I always tipped the headwaiter. I loved sitting outside, watching the pedestrians waving and crashing into each other, but too much coffee and very little solid food often made me sick and weak.

Life in summer at midday in Melilla was consistently under the thumb of the sun, heat, sea, humidity, the massive consumption of fatty fish and a heavy diet enhanced with chickpeas and yellow peas. Pedestrian numbers fell after one o'clock. People headed home and sank into a long, deep siesta. The main street became quiet, and a sense of insecurity could be felt in one or another of its corners depending on who was there at the time. It could be an arms dealer, drug seller or a pimp.

I wasn't immune to Melillan culture or the double sun reflected at close range from the sea. Midday was a particularly hard time for me. My metabolism dropped, my energy dwindled, my eyes got heavy and slow.

I frequently took refuge in Monastery *Parroquia Castrense de Melilla*. Not far from Café Morina, it stood half way along the boulevard. At my first visit, I was overwhelmed. The cathedral was gigantic, awesomely quiet and semi-dark, surrounded with decorated glass windows and full of golden statues. A bed of lit candles added to the sunlight filtering through the windows. An immense statue of the crucified Christ was dangling in the centre of the space above the altar. The Virgin Mary's statue was, even for a non-believer, emotionally evocative, with a settled sadness visible on her face.

No one ever stopped me, asked me to pay or forced me to worship. As the days turned into weeks, I felt happy and comfortable inside this majestic edifice. Going back to Café Morina afterwards, I felt renewed in energy, mind and spirit, and ready to bargain.

Mr Marjosi, the headwaiter, always faced me, nodded and said, 'Did you have a good rest?'

'Not too bad.'

Mr Marjosi was a local man in his late forties, though he looked older; the sun had etched a map on his face. He was too tall to be average, Mediterranean, and looked very wiry. He always combed his shiny hair back to touch his collar. Polite and friendly, he was known to everyone. Spanish poured out of his mouth with ease. His energy, look and age commanded respect on the terrace, but he was not Mr Timsamani's favourite waiter. They hardly spoke.

I never took to Mr Marjosi myself; he was too inquisitive. 'Are your parents dead?' he asked me once.

What a curious question, I thought.

At midday on the second of October, 1963, I went to the cathedral, the same pew as always. It was empty except for two short, fat Spanish women, dressed all in black, standing quietly and genuflecting before the statue of St Mary. This spot had become my solace, but almost became my grave.

Sitting back on the pew, with my eyes fixed on the crucified Christ and my hand busy shovelling Spanish white bread into my mouth, I began to doze. Before finishing my bread, my eyes closed, detaching me from everything around.

Three men awakened me when they entered the church. *They are cleaners*, I thought, *certainly not worshippers*. I gave them no heed. They passed me by in a hurry, making very little noise. All of a sudden, out of nowhere, a filthy black cloth was thrown over my head. There was no chance of moving, talking or yelling; my neck was held in a stranglehold and I struggled to draw breath. Both of my hands were grabbed and forced behind my back. Yanked to my feet, I felt a sudden pressure on my neck; a serrated knife was pushed hard against my throat. I felt the notches digging into my skin. Inside the darkness of the cloth, I kicked my legs with all my might against the attackers, hoping someone would see the scuffle.

'Stand up!' one shouted fiercely. I felt my pockets getting turned inside out. In a second, all the trade of the week was lost. No currency was spared.

A second voice shouted ferociously, 'Don't move until we tell you! Don't dare leave!'

'If you do, we'll slit your throat!' another voice finished.

In an eternity and the silence of a looming death, I heard them scurry through the side door. As it opened, a stream of sunlight snaked into the building. Two-thirds of the floor, pews and statues suddenly came to life in the sunshine. Through the gauzy fabric, I saw the last man in the cathedral streak out. It was the headwaiter, Mr Marjosi!

Without a backward glance, the next thing I knew, I found myself in the middle of the noisy boulevard, not far from Café Morina. *I've been robbed and nearly slaughtered*, I murmured to myself, as the pain stung my neck where the notches had left their mark. Watching the people bustling down the busy street, I realised no one knew or cared much for my fate. *No talisman would have saved me*, I realised. *I'm in a dangerous profession*, and remembered Uncle Mimoun's warning.

I plunged my hands into my pockets, and there was nothing left to grab but a few old crumbs. I didn't know how they had gotten there. Half an hour ago the same pockets had been obese, packed full of foreign currencies. *How am I going to get home now?* I wondered, a rising panic filling my chest.

Headed toward the bus station, I hesitated to jump in. *I don't even have a fare for the bus!* I thought despairingly. Sitting on a quiet bench in the corner of a small park, I felt like a tramp. I felt around my clothes, checked my usual hiding place between my socks and shoes. There, to my relief, was the hidden treasure I had been standing on; there, gleaming in the sunlight, was the little stash Mr Marjosi had not found. Five hundred pesetas were lying hidden between my socks and shoes, as though the inevitable had been expected. The notes often irritated my feet and, like a stone in a shoe, were a niggling source of discomfort throughout the day.

Looking as utterly miserable as I felt, I headed home and arrived earlier than usual in the full light of day, but there was no one there to hear my story; my parents dead, my sisters married. The house was empty. The two dogs that no one wanted spared no energy in showing their happiness; they jumped, danced and courted each other, their tails turning into the blur of a spinning wheel. However, they could not be immune to the sad mood I carried with me into the house. Their enthusiasm quickly turned into apprehensive expectation.

It's good that I've paid Mr Amakran back in full. Uncle Mimoun would have been dragged in if I hadn't. I was proud of myself, trading on my own capital. It's all gone now. What a whopping error to carry all my capital on me. Now it's all in the hands of Mr Marjosi, I mused bitterly. *Can I start from scratch? The same thing might happen again! School resumes in two and a half weeks. I could miss the first week, but then Uncle Mimoun would ask what is holding me back; I don't want him to know what happened. If he knew the robbery had taken place in the most famous cathedral in Melilla, he would only say it was the wrath of God for my being there.*

A stash of money was needed for school, and I had lost most of what I had made. I felt I'd been raped. There was no difference between my ass and my neck. A spirit of vengeance took over. I planned to kill Mr Marjosi.

The night dragged on and on and I didn't blink an eye. I felt tormented, hot and sweaty. *Should I ask Rabbia to lend me some money?* I wondered.

My mother had left four beautiful, heavy silver bracelets, and each sister had tried to steal at least one. They had fought over them like ferrets in a bag and to make a temporary truce, it had been decided the bracelets should stay at home, become a part of the house like the doors, hooks and stones until, of course, one of them managed to steal them away.

I knew how bitter the fight over the bracelets was. But, to raise money to trade again, I could think of no solution but to pawn those precious bracelets, despite knowing a battle would be waiting for me.

On the ninth of October, I got up well before dawn and after two hours of walking, caught the first coach coming from Oujda. It was nearly full; everyone was almost hypnotised by the beauty of nature and the power of the rising sun. The coach was fitted with a radio through which morning music added to the joy of the travellers. Hiding four bracelets in my school bag, I was careful and nervous. The road was dotted with police checkpoints. *What if they ask me where I got the four bracelets?* I worried. I would be accused of either illegal trading or stealing. Luckily, I sneaked through without being frisked.

Searching for jewellers in Nador, I found two, but they were not open yet. Waiting, I sat in a café, under a palm tree, keeping watch on the doors.

One jewellery shop owner came and slowly, delicately, opened his shop door, which had three locks and a massive padlock visibly hanging from the doorknob, a tangible sign of how hard it would be to break into his shop. I was his first client, and the jeweller looked happy, a smile spreading over his face.

'I have four bracelets,' I said, 'but I really don't want to sell them. Could you price them for me, please?'

'Yes, show them to me.'

I pulled out the bracelets, one by one, and put them on the counter. The jeweller was impressed and looked at me suspiciously as if I were a thief. 'Those are antique,' said the jeweller. 'No one makes them anymore. They are heavy and beautifully engraved. I would guess that each one is worth fifty thousand Moroccan francs. This is a conservative estimate. Why not sell them?' he asked.

I hesitated, not knowing how to continue the conversation; a short silence ensued. 'If you give me one hundred thousand francs, I will leave them with you until I redeem them, but I will pay you interest,' I offered.

With some skepticism, the jeweller agreed to the deal, and I went out with one hundred thousand Moroccan francs in my pocket. I felt reconstructed from the dust. On the coach to Melilla, I felt the hills looked higher, the sea wider and bluer, and my mind focused on how to kill Mr Marjosi.

Arriving in Melilla at midday, I had missed the morning trade. On my way to Café Morina, my saliva thickened and my throat dried; I needed water quickly. Before reaching the café, I stopped; hesitation took over.

From across the road, sitting on his chair, Mr Timsamani spotted me and called out, but his voice was lost in the wide road filled with cars and pedestrians. He kept waving. I crossed the road and looked for a free chair. The terrace was full of lazy old men come to discuss America and Russia, hell and heaven.

'Hi! Hi!' shouted Mr Timsamani to me, and offered me a seat at his table.

'You haven't traded for days,' he said.

'I haven't,' I said.

'A herd of travellers arrived two days ago and were desperate for Moroccan currency. The traders did very well,' he said. While he was still talking, Mr Marjosi arrived with a tray full of bottles of water and hot espresso steaming up into his face.

'What can I get for you?' he asked me, his criminal eyes spinning fast.

'Coffee,' I said.

It was almost one o'clock, and Mr Timsamani's Mercedes arrived to collect him. Full of trepidation, I glued myself to the terrace.

Later in the afternoon, like an earthquake, the ship's horn shook the air. Traders, as well as spectators, all dashed to meet the ship. It was jam-packed. As passengers poured down the gangplank, small traders like me were waiting at its foot whispering, 'Exchange. Currency exchange.' Mr Timsamani, far away from the travellers and the traders, did business just by nodding his head. I watched him and admired his achievement.

Though travellers were desperate to convert their money and go home, pulling teeth would have been far easier than doing business with them. Shrewd bargaining reaped a profit, but the success of the day didn't extinguish the deep anger I felt for having to pawn my mother's bracelets. I couldn't be this miserable and leave Mr Marjosi happy.

*   *   *

THE JEWELLER'S FACE FELL when just two weeks later I stepped into his shop and told him, 'I am here to redeem my mother's bracelets.' He counted the stack that I handed him several times and said nothing.

'What's the interest?' I asked him.

'I won't charge you,' he replied. 'You're the boy Mr Amakran spoke to me about.'

The jeweller's words touched me, but nothing could assuage my anger toward Mr Marjosi. I redeemed my mother's bracelets and went straight home.

I felt happy and so did the two dogs. *My mother would be pleased to see her bracelets back in the cubbyhole. How sad she would be if she had seen her bracelets pawned and worn by another woman.*

I had just a week or, at the very most, ten days before returning to school. I endeavoured to sort out the fate of the two loyal and beautiful dogs, plus the quiet donkey, as there would be no one in the house once I left.

'Do you need a donkey?' I asked Uncle Mimoun on a visit.

'Of course I don't,' he shrugged.

'Why not sell the donkey?' Mimount asked.

'It's an old donkey. It dates from Father's days,' I said. 'It has lost practically all its teeth. It's very slow chewing barley and straw. However, I will do some publicity through Baghdad. He might be able to sell it at the bingo club.'

'Clever,' said Mimount. Uncle Mimoun didn't budge. 'What about the dogs?' Mimount asked.

'Maybe Uncle Mimoun would like to have one or both,' I suggested.

'Let's stop talking about dogs,' he said shortly.

*   *   *

AMINA WAS IN LIMBO, married, but unmarried, and sent a messenger to ask me to visit her. Reluctantly, I went. Waiting for a husband who might not even come home was painful to her; meanwhile her husband's father played like a rooster in the middle of four wives plus daughters-in-law.

After a two-day visit, I resumed my trade. I went to Melilla and sat on the Café Morina terrace. I felt a light chill in the air, indicating that summer was on its way out. I saw that the waiters' uniforms had changed to heavier clothes in a darker colour.

As the morning trade wore on, I ventured deeper into the sprawling slums. I took the main avenue past the Catholic cathedral until I reached the end, where deprived life began with the small shops. I took a narrow, right-hand street where very tiny cubicles cascaded one into another, and further down men, bored to death, were selling second-hand clothes laid on the ground. At a grocery shop, I stopped to buy a couple of bananas.

Passing the rag-cloth market, I descended the gentle hill until I reached the bottom, a large, dusty, open intersection. Here, I remembered the stack of melons and my pilgrimage to Awisha the witch. The flag of poverty and depravity flew high and the people bustling or sitting all looked like marionettes up to no good. At the entrance to a narrow street, a tiny boy with dark hair and a long neck barked like a parrot, 'Girls! Girls! Brunette or blonde!'

Behind him, forty metres away, a middle-aged man stood still and eyed the boy. A few metres farther down, a second boy offered the same product, but he didn't look as smart as the first and his heart wasn't in the job. 'Gun,' I murmured to myself, a little too loudly, on my way past.

Walking away, I felt a tugging on my jacket and whirled sharply like a dervish. 'What are you up to?' I shouted, fist at the ready, Mr Marjosi in my mind.

'I will provide you with a gun,' said the boy gently and confidently. 'They are very cheap and come in all sizes to fit the pocket and the price.'

'Show me one,' I said defiantly.

'No, I can't, but I will put you in contact with a trader,' he said.

'Who and where is he?'

'He's a retired army officer,' replied the boy. Reading the doubt on my face, he added, 'He's a very serious man.'

This boy is not as stupid as he looks, I thought, *but he might lure me to a second Marjosi.* The thought of buying a gun, let alone pulling the trigger, worried me, but to be 'raped' by a bully weighed on my pride.

*　　*　　*

THE NEXT DAY WHEN I had decided, I went back to find the little boy, and to my surprise, there he was, identically the same, looking deeply bored. He moved slowly from the corner where he had been standing idle and rushed toward me. 'Did you find what you wanted?' he asked.

'No.'

'Listen to me. Listen,' he whispered. 'Coming down the street, you might have noticed a watch repair shop on your left. It's not always open. It's a front. Give me five minutes, and the trader will be there and the shop will open.' The boy spoke convincingly, so I made a sharp U-turn. A small shop with two narrow glass windows packed with cheap Japanese watches stood beside a Spanish butcher's. Dangling sausages were visible, and I smelled ham from metres away.

Peering through the window, I spied a short, fat woman, olive-skinned and dark-haired, busy polishing some watches with a white cloth. No man was visible inside. *Is this the shop?* I wondered. Despite my doubts, I entered. Immediately, a man stood before me. His wife joined him and both smiled as if they had known me since birth. The boy had certainly given them some description of me. The man, tall, heavily built, with extremely blue, unsettling eyes, hung over the counter and overshadowed his wife.

Fidgeting, I didn't know how to start. Sharply calibrating

my movements, the woman asked me, 'Is there anything that you want to see?' She smiled and closed rank with her husband, who was settled back into his armchair.

'A pistol,' I whispered, my heart beating. The man carefully and gently pulled open a drawer full of pistols, all different sizes and origins. None looked dusty. They all looked shiny and surprisingly cheaply priced. With an impulse, my hand dove to the smallest pistol. *It's easy to hide*, I thought, *but maybe not easy to use*. The man took over and the demonstration was quick and exciting. I paid five hundred pesetas for a pistol the size of my palm.

'The bullets?' I asked.

'We don't sell them,' responded the wife with a crooked smile and pursed lips.

Quizzically, I looked up at the ceiling and then again at the woman. 'Why not?' I asked politely.

'Many reasons,' said the woman, eyes fixed on her husband.

'The law,' the man said.

'A pistol with no bullets is harmless,' said the woman.

I felt cheated. 'Where can I buy bullets?' I asked incredulously.

'One street over,' motioned the wife. 'The shop has two glass windows, radios on one side and leather belts on the other.'

Angrily, I scrambled through the crowd, skirting some meaty and fat Spanish women, to the luxuriously stocked shop that the woman had described, with leather belts on one side and Philips radios on the other. Peering through the window, I spied two middle-aged men playing chess.

The shop was stuffed with merchandise both antique and modern, shirts and ties, women's pants, leather wallets, but mainly radios of all sizes. The men were glued to their chairs playing chess, unaware if I, or anyone else, was inside. Their complete silence was filled with light melancholic music emanating from invisible speakers.

One of them seemed to be deep in thought and was a slow player, so the other had a chance to lift up his head. 'May I help you?' he called.

His partner interrupted his pondering and both advanced to the counter. They stood side by side, looking calm and patient, but eyed each other constantly, and they certainly wondered what I was up to. I pulled the pistol out of my left jacket pocket and asked, 'Do you sell bullets to fit this gun?'

'Yes,' replied one.

Though they had bullets to suit many types of pistol, they couldn't find the one that I needed. They kept searching and wrecking the drawers. While they were rummaging, they cracked jokes and I wondered whether they were in love with each other; they were never more than half a metre apart. Nothing could split them until a Siamese cat with a pink furry collar around its neck jumped on the counter. It was picked up and cuddled with affection by first one man, then the other.

A bullet, with the price and date marked upon it, was found, but looked just slightly bigger than the dropping of a full-sized mouse. The snag was the price, far higher than the price of the pistol itself. I wanted three bullets. The price of the second bullet was higher than the price of the first, and the price of the third, higher than the price of the second. I had never come across such nonsense and became visibly annoyed. 'Why is the second bullet more expensive than the first?' I asked, my hands palms up.

'The more bullets you carry, the more power you have, and we sell power,' said one of them, smiling. I wasn't able to purchase more than one bullet and was glad to get out of the shop and away from the two crooked men.

*   *   *

NOW ARMED, I FELT strong enough to kill Mr Marjosi. Twice I planned to ambush him, but twice aborted. On my last trading day, the twenty-fifth of October, I arrived early at Café Morina and waited for the ship that never came, and no one knew why. It had either sunk or been cancelled. Mr Timsamani might have known about it. He showed up at eleven, only to leave immediately.

Without the ship, trade was paper-thin. Mr Marjosi was on duty, looking bored and sneering sarcastically. 'It's a wicked day for wicked people,' he said loudly, referring to currency traders. *He wouldn't have said that had Mr Timsamani been around*, I thought.

That day, Mr Marjosi looked tired. Throwing his head back with a gaping yawn, he traipsed lazily off to the bathroom. Stealthily following him, I pushed the door open and found him standing, pissing into the urinal, struggling to hold his trousers up.

As loudly as I could, I shouted, '*Arriba la mano!*', an expression feared and lethal with gangs. At the speed of light, Mr Marjosi turned and found me clutching a pistol with both hands, my face intent and set, one leg lunged forward toward him. With lightning reflex, Mr Marjosi came alive. His trousers below his knees, he jumped very high, dodged to the left and kicked, aiming at my face, and with two fingers pointed, flew at my eyes. Unfortunately for him, the floor was very wet with water and urine. He missed his mark, slipped, fell back and knocked himself unconscious. With the pistol still in my hand, I spat on his butt. I decided not to empty my gun into his head.

In a panic, I rummaged through his pockets, but sadly, it hadn't been a good business day. I knew Mr Marjosi would get up at some stage and launch a search to kill me, so I ran out and avoided public transport.

I arrived home late that evening, safe, but deeply shaken. Still with my pistol loaded with one single bullet, I felt comforted by two dogs, each at my side, and ready to maul any undesirable intruder. When my blood pressure came down, I counted the notes and coins from Mr Marjosi's pockets. A loss! I had reaped less than a tenth of what I had paid for the pistol, let alone the bullet. Angry with myself, I hurled the pistol against the wall, and it went off! I heard a yelp and realised the ricocheted bullet had hit the white dog, Dina. I sank into despair. It was the power of vengeance, the feeling of pride, that had killed my dog.

Horrified by the accident, I endeavoured to find a home for the remaining dog. Mrs Zinab had taken the donkey, and I thought she might want the dog. I went to see her, and she was shocked at the sight of me. Probably she thought I had come to take the donkey back, but although I smiled to re-assure her, she didn't seem relaxed.

'Would you be interested in our black dog?' I asked, hoping to hear 'yes'.

'Alas,' she said, 'I can't feed a dog.'

'Can't you feed him with husks?' I asked.

'If I had husks to feed the dog, I would have enough flour to feed the boys,' she replied.

Now what? I wondered.

If Dargan were left to wander among farmers, he would be stoned to death, so I took him to the wide valley dividing the two high mountains Makran and Tassamat, and abandoned him to fight for his own survival. I hoped Dargan would baptise himself into nature, join the foxes, and become a strong wild dog.

Back in my empty home, in the past full and noisy, my conscience began to thump. *Was abandoning Dargan in the valley the best thing I could do?* I wondered, feeling the burden of guilt. At night, sleep deserted me. I wondered where Dargan might be. Was he sleeping on this chilly night, or fighting other animals, stronger than himself and less hungry? What the night aroused, the day swept away. As dawn shook the night, I heard a faint barking nearby. As it was windy, blowing south, I thought it was the bark of Uncle Mimoun's dog, Sobbi, carried and distorted by the intermittent gusts. I hoped the wind would stop and the barking would die, but it continued, disturbingly.

The barking voice began to be clearer and nearer. Still undecided about what to make of the confused sound, I moved slowly to locate a scratching noise. I opened the main door and there was Dargan, using all the power his paws could wield to get in. His presence broke my heart, but I was leaving soon and had to find a home for him.

At the shrine of Sidi Mimoun, far, far away, was a small oasis, where water could be found and birds could be heard singing. Dargan had never been there before and I thought it would be a good place for him to live.

One early morning, still intending to get rid of him, to set him free, I trekked with him to the oasis. While he was sniffing the ground, I turned around and took a twisted road home, thinking he would never be able to find his way. The night was long and lonely without Dargan, but before the sun rose, empowered with an intrinsic compass that I had failed to trick and confuse, he was back.

The time to return to school neared, but I had failed to find a home for Dargan and he refused to be independent. I locked my room, the house, and trailed by Dargan, left to catch the coach to Nador, to leave behind the boiling, dusty summer and the bleeding memories of Mr Marjosi. Standing on the side of the road, waiting for the coach, Dargan became frightened of the cars and their noise. When the coach arrived, I jumped in and Dargan made no attempt to follow. The companionship ended there, at Moulay-Rachid checkpost, but not the sadness.

22

When my coach arrived at Bab Ftouh, the gate to hell, I found Faissal waiting desperately for his brother, who was on his way to Meknes and had promised to bring him pocket money. Spotting me stepping off the coach, Faissal rushed towards me and gave up on his brother. We hired a French Simca, a small car with an underpowered engine at the back, which struggled to climb even the small, twisted hill from Bab Ftouh to the New Town.

Faissal had arrived at the very start of the term. I wanted to know about the new pavilion, what dormitory we were in, and the new professors, but Faissal had far more intriguing news to tell. 'Do you know what?' he said. 'We have six girls in our class. They're the only girls in the entire school!'

'Wow!' I exclaimed. 'Are they beautiful?'

'They joined our class because their school could not afford to pay professors for just six girls,' said Faissal.

'They must be clever,' I replied, my mind still occupied with what the rector might ask me about my late arrival. 'Are they modern?'

'Four are veiled and provincial, one is semi-modern and the other is ultra-modern.' Still excited, Faissal added,

'Tomorrow morning at eleven o'clock we will have a meeting with the rector – our first instruction in sexual behaviour. Aren't you lucky not to miss lessons in how to . . . Ha! Ha! Ha!'

Arriving at the school, Faissal entered his dormitory and I went to the office. 'Rumours have circulated that you might not come back, and that you had already joined the military school,' the officer said.

'Where did you get that from, sir?' I asked.

'Your class mates,' he answered.

The dinner siren sounded, and I scurried to the refectory. As a baccalaureate student, I joined the private table, separate from junior students. Faissal and I were on different planes; his mind was full of girls and sexual fantasies, and my mind was still drowsy. I was happy to leave the table and find my bed.

The following morning, the rector called my class to have sex education in his office, a large room furnished with a red rug, a world map on the wall and a wooden desk with a telephone system on it. We stood in a semi-circle, facing the rector.

Full of energy, the rector stood, faced us and peered at me. 'You're late,' he told me from behind his green-tinted glasses. Then he addressed the whole group. 'It is the first time in the history of this prestigious school that we have had both sexes in the same class, with the same professors, and facing the same important exams – the baccalaureate,' he said. 'The six girls in your class could be a deadly distraction. Some of them, I am told, are motor-mouthed. The professor of Arabic rhetoric has already filed a complaint against two of them. That, however, is my problem. A big mouth is a medical condition, and I will deal with it. Some of the girls are modern, some semi-modern and the rest just like your stone-age granny; I beg you to treat them all the same. As for your careers and your exams, those girls could be a dangerous distraction, so God help you all.'

Faissal, standing beside me, was gob-smacked by the lesson. He had seen some pictures in men's magazines and had expected an exposé, picture-based. We left the rector's office and the girls were ushered in for their lesson in sex education. They were secretive about what they had learned except the semi-modern girl, who wasn't embarrassed to tell everything. 'In the rector's own words, "be wary of the beasts",' she told us.

*   *   *

THERE WERE RUMOURS CIRCULATING that anarchists and anti-regime activists would force the school into a strike. On the twenty-first of December, mid-morning, while we were in class, a large group of agitators gathered outside the school were gaining momentum. We didn't know why they were there; they would have looked just like a group of unhappy tourists if it were not for their massive numbers. The gate-keeper, seduced by his tiny transistor radio, noticed nothing. The anarchists craftily concealed sticks, knives and slingshots in their pockets and tucked into their trousers.

Like an Indian chief, the ringleader whipped through the gang, whispering and readying his troops. They swarmed like wasps, entirely flooding the school grounds, and were immediately followed by a second and bigger mob. Reminiscent of Indians attacking a fort in the Wild West, they kicked everything in their way, knocked the gatekeeper out of his chair and stamped on his hands. Filling the school grounds, they shouted, 'Out! Out! School's closed!'

The noise of shouting filled the air. Listening to the professor's lecture, but drawn by the noise, I shoved my chair back and peered through the window. Hundreds of men were pulling students and motioning them out of their classes. Horrified, I watched as one boy was dragged out by his long hair, a passing group of thugs kicking and beating him with their heavy boots and wooden sticks. A few brutal minutes later, the boy was silent and still. While groups of thugs were roving through the buildings, others ran off to find fresh quarries and pound them into submission. As though hit by an earthquake, students, like sheep, rushed out of their classes and flooded through the open school grounds, while professors scurried to take refuge in the rector's luxurious office. The thugs met no resistance and gloriously continued their scourge unabated.

In a flash my class, refusing to leave, became the thugs' focus; two windows were shattered by slingshots, and the air was suddenly thickened with threatening, angry voices. 'Scabs! Scabs!' shouted the mob.

'Here they are!' responded a swarming crowd with sticks, knives and chains.

Shocked and terrified, the professor was the first to jump through the window, leaving us to face the peril. A few of my classmates and I imitated the professor and escaped through the second back window, but a student called Larbi was caught by the back of his shirt and held by three pursuers, who mercilessly competed to stomp on his head.

'Pass me a knife!' shouted one of the crowd.

'Kill him! Kill him!' shouted another.

A few of my classmates ran and took refuge in neighbouring houses where, luckily, they were hidden and smuggled out by the workers' wives. Some boys and I ran in confusion past the dormitories and the laundry, then took refuge in the school kitchen, a huge complex. The mob stampeded behind us and destroyed everything they came across as they stormed the kitchen. They pulled down the water tanks and flooded the grounds. Those who were unarmed picked up kitchen knives, forks and whatever else they could grab.

Hassan and I slipped into a narrow closet with a white door, the same colour as the wall. Inexplicably, the mob kept passing us by. I crouched down, but Hassan, unable to control his nerves, kept mumbling and watching through a small window at the top of the closet door.

'Get down! Get down!' I whispered. 'They will spot us!' Hassan entirely lost control, fainted and dropped to the floor of the closet.

During the mêlée, one of my classmates, Mehdi, was caught and a knife plunged into his eyes, but another classmate, Shamlali, was able to put his hand on a knife when he was caught, turn on his attacker and split his face in two.

Najib pretended to be one of the mob, grabbed a long stick, and started swinging and shouting, 'Show me the scabs! Show me the scabs!' Within half an hour, the kitchen was in a shambles with the injured lying around the room, and the mob, like a sea wave, disappeared as quickly as it had come.

Taking advantage of the dying storm, Hassan and I

ventured out of the closet, and I ran straight to the rector's office. The rector was standing in the courtyard with his boss, the Regional Director, watching without moving a finger. I hurried to the boss and shouted, 'Sir! Sir! They would have killed us if they'd found us!'

'With no doubt! With no doubt!' he replied.

'Don't we have the right to be protected?' I demanded angrily.

Butting in, a classmate's father who was a high court judge, advanced aggressively and shouted to the rector, 'Sir! If you are not able to protect these boys, then it is our duty to protect them!' He thrust his hand into his pocket, pulled out a pistol and waved it in the air.

'Put that away!' shouted the rector, a metre away. He rushed toward the judge, grabbed him by the shoulders and led him away.

Knowing this was just the beginning, my roommates and I packed up and left the dormitory immediately, each going his own way. Some went into hiding and some went home for good, badly traumatised.

With nowhere to go in the town, I headed to Ali, a young grocer I had met through Abdu, and who rented a small room on a bridge over the river. By the time I reached Ali's room, it was dusk. The door was closed and there was no sign of him. Nervous, I knocked harder and louder.

'Wrecking the door won't open it!' shouted a passing tramp with a thickly bearded face, while picking food from his bowl.

Standing on the dilapidated bridge, I jumped at any noise from up above or underneath. Ali arrived an hour later and the sight of me gave him a fright. 'You look awful!' he exclaimed. 'What's the matter?'

'Could I stay with you for three or four days?' I asked.

'Sure. You've been expelled, haven't you?' he asked.

'Worse than that,' I answered.

Ali's room was small and dark, and the floorboards left gaping holes. Peering through the huge cracks, I saw the rushing, murky water and the stench pierced the room. Distasteful as it was, it was heaven.

Ali's hospitality was unstinting. He went out and came back with eggs, tomatoes and peppers . . . but he couldn't find bread nearby. While he was cooking, I went to fetch a loaf of bread while fearfully looking over my shoulder.

Frying eggs was Ali's forte. 'No one can emulate me. I never cook eggs the same way twice,' he said. He fried tomatoes in olive oil and vinegar. Watching him, I wondered if the room was going to be set alight. Despite the splashing sparks, Ali was the master of the fire. When the tomatoes were over two-thirds fried, he poured scrambled eggs over them. I had never seen this done before. The end result looked like a cake of tomatoes and eggs.

Ali fell asleep like a child, but I couldn't sleep. I kept the light on and looked at my study programme; Ali was undisturbed. *I wish I could sleep deeply and peacefully like him*, I thought.

At five o'clock in the morning, Ali's birds vibrated the room. He had four birds, two in each cage. They all looked well-fed and healthy, but the noise they produced could awaken the dead and dement angels. For Ali, their voices were nature's pure and unpolluted music, but I realised this was not the place for me.

After listening to the birds' songs, Ali went to a corner and spent half an hour meditating like a Buddhist, detached from the world. 'Morning prayer for me,' he said, 'is the key to the day.' Despite being a believer, my practice was sporadic, hindered by lack of water and clean clothes for prayer.

Ali wanted to be a wholesale grocer, but his clairvoyant, who lived close by, had told him to wait, as his stars were not in his favour. We had a quick breakfast, which was tasty although it was just bread and tea, as Ali had to go to the market.

'When you are ready,' he said, 'on your way out, bring me the key.'

'Where is the key?' I asked.

'On the floor under your shoes,' he replied. 'Can't you see it?'

Only a tip of the key was showing from under the shoes. Looking at it, as in a rearview mirror, my memory spiralled years into the past and Samir and Moussa came to mind. I could almost see Moussa spilling his tea over Samir's trousers and a squabble beginning.

Ali prepared himself to go. Half an hour later, I left to hunt for a room to rent where I could hide before falling into the hand of the protestors. I rushed to Bab Talaa to find a *samsar* (a broker), an old man who billed himself as a paragon of virtue. He sat in a pigeon-hole shop a metre and a half above the street, only four metres high and two metres wide. Sitting cross-legged, he never had a chance to stand up and could only get in or out by grabbing the rope hanging from the ceiling and catapulting himself. He jumped like a hen on and off its roost.

The *samsar* wore a blood-red hat twice the size of his head. He was very fat and waddled when he walked, in a conscious effort not to lose his *babouche* shoes.

'What is in your heart?' he asked with a lazy voice.

'I need a room to rent,' I replied.

Silence fell, as no quick answer was forthcoming. He stretched his hand slowly to light a half-cigarette he had saved and looked deep in thought. Nothing was urgent for the *samsar*. His eyes browsed the wall where a few keys were hanging and a few murmurs came out of his mouth.

'Is your mother going to be with you?' he asked.

'No, sir,' I responded, stunned by the question.

'We have a few big houses with rooms to rent, but you are a bachelor!' he remarked, shaking his head and sucking his lips. 'The tenants, all married, refuse to have a bachelor in their midst.'

I had heard that before. From there, I moved to a second *samsar*. Based in a Jewish ghetto, he was an orthodox Jew, clothed entirely in black, including his hat, and his beard looked enormous, long and white, covering his whole face and touching the floor when he sat. 'Sir,' I asked, 'do you have a room for rent?'

'No,' he replied. 'Go and look in the *medina*,' he advised, meaning he thought I was poor and of no importance.

At quarter to one, lunchtime, people, like birds, flocked to their homes. Streets became deserted; some were dangerous, and not even armed police could safely patrol the hidden, crooked corners. Back in Ali's room, I found Abdu reclining against the wall, and Ali struggling to cook a meal of camel mince mixed with potatoes, coriander and cumin. Excitedly, Abdu spoke of the university, where he was a first-year student. He looked different, was wearing new clothes, and looked much better fed.

'Any joy with the *samsar*?' he asked.

'Not a thing,' I replied.

'Vipers, aren't they?' he said with a cynical and aborted smile. 'Why not look into *funduq*s?' he asked.

'Anything but that!' I replied, disgusted at his suggestion.

The cooked meal settled the mood. Ali couldn't keep his eyes open after lunch. His birds made a lot of noise, but that only added to his deep sleep. He had bought a new transistor radio, tiny and tinny, which he clasped against his chest. When he left for his shop, I continued hunting for a hideout in the sprawling slums.

I didn't return to Ali's room until late that night, but with good news: I had found a single-car garage to rent. I rapped on the door; no one answered, yet the light was on. *Ali wouldn't go to sleep and leave the light on*, I reasoned. *He's a penny pincher.* With a second rap on the door that left my knuckles burning, the door opened a crack.

Abdu's face looked like a patchwork quilt. 'Was it a fight in the street?' I shouted.

'No!' answered Abdu. 'Around eight o'clock, five big thugs knocked on the door and flooded in the moment Ali opened it. They saw me lying on the floor and mistook me for you, kept calling me Jusef. They pulled me out and began pummelling and kicking me, and one of them with a big stick. They shouted, "Son of whore! Poof! Scab!"'

'I managed to reach the kitchen knife and slashed out, not caring where my blow landed. I split one of their buttocks in two. He yelped like a beaten dog. The blood poured on the floor, and he couldn't move. With the help of the others, he scurried away, leaving no trace except the blood, but I've got bruises and cuts all over, and my face is swollen. It's you they tried to get!' screamed Abdu to me, as he studied his face in a small mirror the size of his palm.

Hot-headed Abdu wanted revenge. Convinced they would come back soon, despite the slashed buttock, he wove a plot and wanted me to play a part in it.

'We should switch off the light and leave the door half open,' he said. 'We'll let the first one in and immediately bar the door. We'll jump on him and snap his neck. By the time they force in, if they ever do, their chief will be a cadaver to drag away.'

I rejected the plot, and angrily Abdu pointed to his face and shouted, 'Look what they've done to me and think what they might do to you!'

'The plot is full of flaws. They won't come in twos, but in a group. If the door is open, they'll just throw a petrol bomb inside and fry us! We must all leave this room now,' I insisted.

'And go where?' exploded Abdu.

'To the garage I rented this afternoon,' I said. I hadn't had a chance to tell them about it.

Convinced and in a chaotic rush, Ali hurriedly grabbed a

blanket, rolled it up, stuck it under his arm and held the key in his hand, ready to lock the door and follow me.

Neither Abdu nor I had any bedding. 'Do you have any blankets?' I asked Ali.

'What you see is what I have!' he replied. He had one or two blankets, dusty and old, thrown in the corner. Abdu and I each grabbed a blanket, rushed out, and Ali locked the door.

We vacated the room, but left the light on. We wove our way through the stenchy bowel of the town, each of us with a rolled-up blanket under his arm, heading for the garage that was miles away. Empty and deserted streets, dimly lit, echoed the sound of our footsteps. Secluded corners and empty doorways were home to tramps. Grouped together, it was hard to know their number. They were not all happy to be disturbed. One, tall and hairy, stood and shouted, 'Tramps of the town, give me peace! Don't disturb the tired, the elderly and us hard-working people!'

As we emerged from the city slums, the sky opened and stars dangled from heaven. The night was over and a crisp, early morning began. There were no pedestrians on the road, but heavy lorries with smelly diesel engines heading either south or north were out in force.

Gendarmes were on the lookout for overweight lorries, careless and drunken drivers. We were their first catch of the day. An American jeep stopped abruptly in front of us and two armed policemen jumped out, blinding us with a spotlight. Abdu's face showed marks of a fight, impossible to hide or deny.

'Look at the injuries you've sustained stealing that blanket!' said the captain to Abdu.

'*Nous ne sommes pas voleurs!* (We're not thieves!)' I jumped to defend Abdu.

'Drop those blankets!' said one of them. They kicked the blankets with their steel-toed boots, but nothing was inside, neither hashish nor gold.

As if on cue, Abdu shouted, 'Thugs attacked me!'

'In your house?' asked the captain.

'In my room!' replied Ali.

'Why did they choose you?' the captain asked.

'Because Jusef stayed with me,' said Ali, in tears.

'Where are you going now?' they asked.

'To a garage that I rent,' I answered.

Confused and suspicious, the captain demanded, 'Jump in the jeep!'

'To go where?' I asked.

'You'll see,' he said. I refused. 'Do you want to jump in cuffed or uncuffed?'

The gendarmes drove us not to the interrogation centre, but to a forest fifteen miles out of town, and there we were dumped to find our way back.

Swollen with anger and mounting frustration, Abdu turned into a digging horse. He kicked the ground until half his shoe broke off. Ali, who had never ventured out of the town, felt disoriented with no clue of where he was. 'How can we ever find the way home?' he kept asking me.

'It could have been worse!' I shouted.

'Worse? Worse?' yelled Abdu.

'Yes! Had they dumped us at the central police station, we wouldn't see the sun for days, weeks, maybe months.'

'Are we criminals?' asked Abdu.

'It's easier for them to charge us as criminals than for us to prove our innocence.'

'Ridiculous! Ridiculous!' shouted Abdu, his face upturned to the sky.

'Absurd!' cried Ali.

'Do you have a receipt for those blankets?' I asked Ali.

'No,' he said.

'What would stop them from charging you as a thief?' I challenged, 'And that's not all! Abdu's been in a fight. What happened to the man he fought? Did Abdu kill him and dispose of him? Unless the other fighter is found, Abdu could be suspected of murder. We are more lucky than unlucky. Let's move,' I pleaded.

The path out of the forest, where north, south, east and west were indistinguishable, was physically rocky. Abdu couldn't keep up; the sole of one shoe was dangling. Twice he nearly fell on his face. Lorries' headlights, like fireflies, drew us to the main road like a beacon. Reaching the road, we saw how far we were from the town. Many cars, heading to the town, passed us, but no driver dared to stop and pick us up. At best, we looked like tramps; at worst, like thugs.

As we were approaching a café, my bruised toes started to hurt. The café was packed. The *garçon*, rattling back and forth, was a small boy of ten. He was polite and quick. His boss prepared tea and coffee behind the counter, his eyes constantly upon him. The boy ran eagerly to please everyone, but that didn't save him from being called a donkey when a clumsy client spilled his tea over the table. The boy wasn't new to this; he looked immune to the abuse. Before noon, his ears had collected several titles.

Before leaving the café, I felt unwell. 'I have a stomach ache and nausea. The garage isn't too far, and we should move quickly,' I told the others.

'My shop . . . my shop!' shouted Ali. 'I must go.'

'Your room is no longer safe,' I said. 'The mob, organised into teams and unchallenged, will get you and whoever is found in the room with you.'

'You brought that on me!' he accused me.

He jumped up, picked up his small sack, grabbed his blanket and made one step to leave. Abdu shot out his hand and pulled him back to his chair. Ali was surprised by how aggressive Abdu could be. By the time I had paid the bill and joined them again, my pain was worse. The garage was only half an hour's walk, and I could barely make it.

The area was unfamiliar to Abdu and Ali. The garage was built as part of a terraced house, and designed to harbour a small Simca. I opened the door and collapsed instantly. I wrapped myself into a blanket.

'Is this your new room?' asked Ali, looking around. 'It's just walls!'

'Yes,' I said. Reading Ali's mind, I continued, 'Your room has no water or toilet either. The window that you have comes from the crack in your floor and a dirty river runs underneath. Would you like to share this room with me?'

'No,' replied Ali. 'My room is central, close to my shop.'

After a few hours of sleep, I got up and felt much better. Hearing voices talking loudly and sometimes over each other, the landlady realised there was more than one person in the garage, and this wasn't what she had agreed to. She came out of her house and stood in the doorway of the garage. She looked physically unfinished, with a beefy and large trunk, legs only a few inches long and a tummy pushing hard against her clothes. She peered at Abdu and sneered at me.

'Face of an angel and heart of a devil, you brought not one but two with you!' she shouted at me.

'*Lalla*, my friends will soon leave.'

'Do they need a blanket each to visit you?' she asked.

'No, *Lalla*.' I ran out of truth. Had I told her I was hiding from thugs, her husband would have refused to rent me the garage. If I told her that Abdu and Ali intended to spend the night with me in the garage, she would be outraged. Abdu had endured enough of her sarcasm and clever talking. Impulsively, he stood up and pulled his trousers down. Ali and I vibrated with shock.

'I know what you carry under your trousers! You don't need to show me,' she said, still blocking the garage door and any light coming through.

'Do you want to increase the rate?' I asked.

'Yes,' she said, 'if more than one lives here.' Undisturbed, she turned her back on us and began conversing across the street with a black woman with shiny teeth who was three times her size.

'I am leaving,' said Ali, shocked by the audacity of Abdu and the unshakable confidence of this odd-looking, sawn-off woman.

'I am leaving too,' chimed in Abdu.

I had some books and clothes to pick up from Ali's room. On our way there, Ali told me, 'I wish you'd never come to me!'

I wish I had never needed you, I thought to myself. *Had we been allowed to study, this wouldn't have happened.*

'I want to get to my room, cook something, hold my transistor against my chest and be first in the market tomorrow. This has been my daily life since the age of eleven, when I left my mother and abusive stepfather,' said Ali.

His hope was dashed. When we reached his room, the door was open wide. Ali knew he had locked the door, as double-checking was his daily obsession. Sliding into the room, his ears swelled and got red as tomatoes. No words were uttered by either Abdu or me. Inside the room, Ali gasped and collapsed, his head against the wall, just like an orthodox Jewish pilgrim at the wailing wall. The room's walls had been hammered full of gaping holes, the birds were lying dead at the bottom of their cages and mountains of dust and debris were everywhere as if a cyclone had hit. Like a hen, I scratched the rubble to see what I could find.

Suddenly, I spotted an envelope with my name on it stuck on the wall; no one could miss it. I yanked it down. It was one and a half pages long, and it read:

Jusef, you and your baccalaureate classmates refused to join us in the strike and disobeyed the committee's will and order; you swept aside, for your personal benefit, the interest of struggling people and attended your classes. We know how stubborn you are and how clever you think you are. We know you scabs will hide and emerge to sit the national baccalau-reate exams, but before that, we will catch you, skin you and scalp you.

Signed: The Committee — God is Great —

Fearfully, I read the note and wadded it into my pocket so Ali and Abdu wouldn't see it. Abdu, deeply stunned, lamented over Ali's room. Ali seemed to have been struck by a lightning bolt.

Looking at him and the state he was in, I said to him, 'Ali! Come with me! If the garage can hold a French Simca, it can hold two people.'

'That's it!' said Abdu, lightened by my suggestion. Ali showed no enthusiasm; he looked stunned.

'We must move, and quickly!' I shouted.

'Do I have time to go and see my clairvoyant, Zui?' asked Ali.

'Do you need to see Zui even when you have no roof?' I asked him.

'Yes, that's exactly why I need him,' he answered.

I realised the only way to move quickly was to accompany Ali to see Zui. He spent less than fifteen minutes there. Coming out, he looked a different person, calm and relaxed.

'How much will the landlady charge me?' Ali asked.

'No idea, but we will strike a bargain,' I replied.

'She will go berserk if she finds me living there without paying rent,' murmured Ali.

'Such a woman's wrath should be avoided,' I said. We all left just like the night before.

Hearing me unlocking the bolt, the landlady and her husband rushed out one after the other. Under the scrutiny of her spotlight-like and razor-sharp intuition, she welcomed Ali with a smile that left nothing of her face but her shiny front teeth and the receding gums above.

Quickly and without the usual seesaw bargaining, she charged Ali forty-five per cent less than she had charged me. She took the money and Ali picked up the key. Both smiled at their own success. I thought the total rent should be divided equally. For Ali, however, what the lady charged each of us must remain set in stone.

23

The garage was truly a new environment for me. It was a tiny part of a small mud house sandwiched in the midst of a terraced block, right on the narrow mud street. Children, free-range, filled the street, and constantly looked for something to do, to eat or to steal. Before I rented the garage, it had been a wasted space, but now it was a lived-in area and so attracted the children. They knocked on the door, threw stones in whenever the door was open, peeped in, shouted and ran, or blocked the garage door by simply standing and watching. Yet, they all feared the landlady; she was a fierce watchdog.

Settled in the garage, Ali and I became the landlady's wards. Her property was a shrine pedestrians could watch but never touch. Had she been allowed to carry a gun, she would have.

A peculiar boy of unknown age and parentage kept knocking on the garage door and running away, but one Friday morning was his unlucky day. When he passed and gave in to his maniacal knocking habit the landlady was baking. She went out, hands wet, and followed him to a tree that he had climbed to hide and enjoy her tantrum. She pulled him down to the ground and squeezed him against the tree. In a frenzy, he flooded her with kicks and punches. She couldn't grab either a foot or an arm. In her final attempt, she grabbed his head and, being the same height as he, gnashed his ear with her powerful jaw and sharp teeth. With all his power, he jerked away, leaving half of his ear in her mouth. The boy yelped and yelled. When I rushed to the scene, all was over, but her chin was blotted with blood.

'I got a bit of him!' she told me.

I felt sorry for the boy. *He should be in school*, I thought. *Had his parents been sterilised, he wouldn't have lost half of his ear and be left with the other half mashed.*

For weeks, I rarely ventured out except to go to the Catholic centre to have my French lesson with my new teacher Suzanne on Friday afternoons, to the Turkish bath two miles away, or to get bread from the unlicensed shops nearby.

Puzzled, the landlady told me, 'How weird you are, Jusef! Students go to school and you nest on your books just like a hen!'

'I have to teach myself,' I said, finding the woman both curious and peculiar.

'Don't let what you have learned from the big masters leak out of your head,' she advised me.

'I don't have very much in my head,' I answered.

'Make sure, then, you don't fatten your ignorance,' she said, looking serious. 'If you give me your palm, I will tell you a lot. I am a gifted palm reader.'

She is one of them, I thought to myself. *She reminds me of the witch in Oujda years ago when she told me I had run away from home. She also reminds me of Awisha in Melilla.*

In an act of impulse and audacity, expecting nothing dramatic, I stretched my palm out for her to read. She looked puzzled and confused. I laughed at her face dancing in waves.

'How is your mother?' she asked, her eyes on the ground.

'My mother is dead.'

'That's a lie!' she said. 'She isn't, but it's not your fault. They have kept you in a pit of darkness.'

'Can you tell me where she lives?' I challenged her.

'No, I can't. The onus is on you. Your mother is alive and she works like a doctor. She is extremely beautiful, but unfortunately, a born romantic.'

I wondered when she was going to stop and lift her eyes off my palm. She became serious and her appearance changed. 'Your father was a genuine aristocrat,' she continued. 'He died young, I think, and tragically . . .' She closed her eyes as if going to sleep and said, 'Your mother knows where you are and is eternally sad. She prays for you and sends you her silent greeting every morning.'

'I don't believe a word of what you say,' I said, anxious to go back to my book and keen to get rid of her.

She didn't look offended, politely left the garage and slid into her house next door. *What a woman! I should never enter into conversation with her*, I thought. *God only knows what she will say next; I could be killed on my way to sit my exams, be executed, spend my life in prison . . . I don't give a damn about what she said.* I reassured myself, intending to concentrate my mind on my work.

I found it difficult to navigate through all the baccalaureate subjects without the help of professors. *One can hide from the thugs, but not from the examiners*, I thought. *Oral exams are particularly hard as they are so fluid. The examiners can take any direction, unlike the written exams.*

Late one afternoon, I took a risk and ran down the long, narrow, twisted descent to the *medina* to visit Kadija, a girl who had sat in front of me in class. Having worked in Melilla, I was wary of potato throwers, so I watched over my shoulder. My heart thumped when I lifted the knocker on her door.

She was first to the door. Behind her stood a boy, his big eyes full of curiosity. Kadija didn't smile or say 'come in', let alone offer tea according to tradition. 'I can't navigate through maths. I need some help,' I said.

'What about me! I haven't even started yet. Honestly, I can't even think about it. Those thugs have crushed my hopes,' she said, tears cascading down her cheeks.

'Faissal is keen to sit his exams. He would be happy to pay for private lessons. Do you want to join us?' I asked.

'Absolutely!' she responded.

'Let the other girls know. They all live in the *medina*.'

'I know where they live,' she said. 'They are deeply upset, and so are their parents. They are frightened to venture out.'

I tried to find Faissal, but he was elusive. Coming out of my French lesson with Suzanne and going through a busy street where boys and girls spent the entire afternoon exhibiting themselves to each other, I spotted Faissal and Najib together. Faissal was doing all the talking and Najib all the listening, nodding his head to keep Faissal talking.

They left the wide street and turned into a narrow lane. Fearing I would lose them, I hurried behind and anchored my hand on Faissal's shoulder. Both were happily surprised to see me, and with so much to talk about in a street that echoed every word and every footstep, I invited them to my room for tea.

Faissal never refused an invitation and Najib never contradicted him. 'I live away from the town centre. Where do you live?' I asked Faissal.

'Hiding with Najib, whose father owns a small terraced house in the *medina*.'

When we arrived, Ali was not in the room, and Faissal wondered who else lived there. 'Ali, an old friend of Abdu,' I explained.

'In which class is he?' asked Faissal.

'He's not a student,' I said. 'He's a grocer.'

'That's quite strange,' said Najib, speaking for the first time.

'Ali's room was vandalised,' I said, 'but I was the intended target.'

'The thugs are cracking down on all baccalaureate students. My nephew Hamidi, a baccalaureate student from class B, was assaulted. Coming back to his room, bending down to look for his room key amidst his shopping, he was hammered by a heavy stick across his back. Two hooligans pushed him against the door, thinking the door was open so he could be beaten in private. But Hamidi is Hamidi! His hand is never far away from his mortal knife. In a quick dance, he pulled it out and slashed the cheek of one attacker. I'm lucky. Nothing has happened to me,' said Faissal.

'You spoke to Kadija about clandestine lessons!' burst in Najib, his eyes flashing at me.

'Yes, I spoke to Kadija,' I said.

344

'She lives on the street only a few doors away from us,' said Najib. 'From time to time, she knocks on our door to ask what's going on and if there is an end to the strike.'

'Would you like to pay for private lessons?' I asked them.

'Which professors should we ask? And which subjects should we tackle?' asked Faissal.

'The Egyptian professor, Nassiri,' I said. 'We had him last year. He's good at maths and serious, with a real sense of urgency, never a minute wasted.'

'He is a mean marker,' said Najib.

'For baccalaureate, that doesn't count,' I said. 'The marker will be the luck of the draw.'

'What about chemistry?' asked Faissal.

'The Christian Lebanese Professor Naimy is excellent at teaching chemistry. He is patient and never gets angry, even when the lab is on fire,' I said. 'But we have no lab,' I added.

Listening to the discussion through the paper-thin wall, the landlady came to see what was going on. She glared at Faissal and Najib, and didn't seem to like either of them. 'You have a lot of friends!' she barked at me. 'Where did you pick them up?' she asked, nose scrunched.

'What a funny woman!' Faissal said when she had left.

While we were still anxiously debating our lessons, Ali, accompanied by Abdu, came in from work. He immediately dropped his bag and a few apples spilled out of it. They looked overripe and badly bruised. Whatever Ali couldn't sell, he brought back and charged me for a part of it. The garage was small to seat five people. Ali and Abdu went for shopping, to a nearby café, expecting Faissal and Najib to leave soon.

'He shares the garage with me,' I said, facing Faissal. 'You were wondering. He's an exile like I am. We can't cook here. We live on cold food, and we will soon be sick,' I said.

Ali and Abdu returned sooner than expected, as it was drizzling. They both squeezed in and joined the discussion. 'Who is going to see Professor Nassiri?' I asked.

'Certainly not me,' responded Najib, his eyes widened in fright.

'I'll do it,' I said. 'I will offer to pay him exactly the amount he gets from the government.'

'This is the key to success!' shouted Abdu.

By the time Abdu, Faissal and Najib left, it was dark, and the landlady had been eavesdropping the whole time. 'Their noise vibrated my house and the garage so much that any more of it and the walls would have needed to be replastered,' she told me afterward.

*　　*　　*

WITH THE STRIKE GOING on indefinitely, and thugs policing the town, the professors enjoyed a full year's holiday. Obliged to show up at the school, they gathered in the grounds and formed a circle that reminded me of Baghdad's bingo club. Professor Nassiri frequently took his family on Friday afternoons to a posh French café on the main boulevard. I put on a clean shirt, trousers, and shoes that had broken soles, and went to find him. Watching him from a distance, I thought he looked like a real pharaoh, surrounded by his large wife and two equally large daughters. He appeared happy and relaxed, smoking a cigarette and sipping his espresso from a tiny cup, while his wife and daughters hoovered Coca-Cola through straws.

'Good afternoon,' I said, facing him and his wife.

Recognition showed on his face, but he didn't call me by name. 'Take a seat,' he told me. 'Is the strike over?' he asked.

'No,' I replied. 'My classmates and I would like you to help us cover a part of the baccalaureate programme. We will meet the cost.'

'Pity, I thought you had come to ask for the hand of one of my daughters! They are beautiful, aren't they? Look at them,' he said.

They looked beefy, well-fed and well-dressed, while I looked like an emaciated waif. His wife burst into laughter, and his daughters also seemed amused. 'I am prepared to help, but be well aware you can only cover a part of the intended programme. Too much time has already been lost,' he added. 'The school gate is open, but would you dare put your foot in it? I can't convert my house into a school; I can't teach in a café either, though it would be best.'

'We will be taught in Kadija's house in Medina.'

'Is Kadija one of your group?' he asked.

'Yes.'

'Here is my telephone number. Tell me when the tea is ready. Four o'clock in the afternoon would be best.'

Full of hope, I scurried to see Kadija in the old town. When I knocked, Kadija's father, looking puzzled and out of breath, opened the door. 'I've come to speak to Kadija,' I said.

'She's not here. I am her father. What's this about?' he asked, suspiciously.

'I am one of her classmates. I saw her a few days ago, and we talked of private tutoring.'

'What's your name?'

'Jusef.'

Kadija's father changed his tone and spoke politely, calling Kadija, as if he hadn't just lied about where she was. Barefooted, she ran to the front door. Her father stood watching and listening to each word that was said.

'I saw Professor Nassiri; he agreed to help, and I have his telephone number,' I said.

Kadija's mouth opened with surprise and so did her father's. 'Come in,' she said. While I was waiting, she hurried to bring Faissal and Najib, rousting them from their boredom and depression.

We quickly scrambled to the post office. 'Who is going to talk to the professor first?' asked Kadija.

'You,' said Najib.

'No, he'll remember the mess I made of my exercise book.'

'Jusef will speak to him,' said Faissal.

At the post office, there was a huge queue waiting to make phone calls. It took an age to get to the attendant at the window, and even longer to be directed to the right booth where the call was connected. We all tried to squeeze into the phone booth, but bulged out the sides. It was the first time I had ever held a telephone.

'Hold your hand steady, Jusef!' whispered Kadija.

'I would if I could,' I whispered back. The professor's wife picked up the phone and spoke with an Egyptian dialect. The confusion grew, and she hung up on me.

'It's not going to work,' said Najib.

'Let's try again,' said Kadija, disgusted with Najib's pessimism.

'What did Madame Nassiri say?' asked Faissal, fully frustrated.

'I don't know. She spoke too fast in Egyptian, and seemed angry,' I explained. 'Do you want to give it a shot, Najib?'

'No. They don't speak Arabic, but claim to be Arabs,' Najib said.

'Stupid!' said Faissal. 'They're not Arabs; they're Egyptians, not Berbers.'

I returned to the attendant at the window and asked to be reconnected. Professor Nassiri himself picked up this time. He didn't seem happy to be called, but I reminded him of his promise. A wave of hesitation vibrated through his voice. *Was he just acting like a comedian in front of his family and daughters?* I wondered. He had good reason to go back on his promise to help us; thugs wouldn't spare his head should they discover he had taught baccalaureate students in hiding.

My hope was plummeting when he suddenly asked, 'What is Kadija's address?'

She whispered the address into my ear, he took note and fixed the day and the time at five o'clock the next day.

Coming out of the booth, Kadija threw her arms around me, turning Najib green with envy. Faissal, burdened with a huge ego, looked dejected and left out.

True to his word, Professor Nassiri, smiling and out of breath, arrived at Kadija's house the next day. She had anticipated his passion for mint tea and almond cakes, so there were plenty, but just for him. With his massive constitution, and everybody else small and tiny, he became Barnabas surrounded by fearful, diminutive students. He didn't know the name of each student, and two of Kadija's close friends, Rahma and Bajia, joined us. I hadn't seen them since the day we had been chased from the classroom.

Bajia was very short and fat, but pleasant. Rahma was completely covered; only one third of her face was exposed; she occasionally sucked in her veil when she breathed. She was extremely bitter, and her words sharper than a sword.

Faissal and Najib brought another student, Shami. He was a short, thin, ambitious boy with a jealous nature, who was from a poverty-stricken family, neither white nor black.

Professor Nassiri was impressed with the number of people attending, but refused to do class teaching. He outlined the required programme and made us feel small and shivery, but without completely crushing our hope.

'I am here when you are stuck and will be enjoying my tea,' he said. 'Divide yourselves into groups any way you like.'

Unfortunately, our personal chemistries didn't combine well. Faissal and Najib were cemented together. Rahma and Bajia were forced to work with each other so Kadija, Shami and I formed the third group. No tension showed within the groups in the first week. But, severe tension began to build between Rahma and Bajia. Soon they were behaving just like two minks in a sack and Professor Nassiri failed to muzzle them. Frustrated, he split them up. Bajia joined Faissal and Najib; Rahma joined Kadija, Shami and me.

Enthused by the success of Professor Nassiri, Faissal and

I decided to hire Professor Naimy. He didn't show himself much, but his wife owned a yarn shop in New Town.

His wife was surprised when Faissal and I entered her shop. 'Do you boys want to knit?' she asked us.

'May we speak to Professor Naimy?' I asked her.

'He's abroad and won't be back until the end of the year,' she said, turning away.

That can't be true, I thought. It was term time and though the school had been closed by the rioters, it did not give the professors licence to cruise through Europe. *This woman is taking us for fools!* I thought.

'We should leave a note for him,' suggested Faissal.

'We would need a note of one hundred pages to get his support,' I replied. 'Face to face is the best. He can't lead the life of a rat. He'll surface sometime.'

Shami, wandering aimlessly, happened upon Professor Naimy acting as a tourist guide, showing the darkest corners of the old town to a mixed group of French-speaking visitors. Two days later, Faissal and I went back to his wife's shop. It was a Saturday, near lunchtime. The sun was beating down and nature was as happy as a bride.

Two middle-aged French women, busy talking over each other, were in the shop bargain hunting. Faissal couldn't understand a word of what was said; he hated different languages, especially French. Thanks to Michelle, now in France, and Suzanne, I was able to grasp most of the conversation. The French women left, looking happy; the Professor's wife recognised us and shot me a disdainful and suspicious look.

Faissal's appearance and gesticulations were not reassuring

for her. He was broad-shouldered with an exceedingly prominent and thin chin. His manner and questions were not what a modern woman living in New Town would expect.

'May we speak with Professor Naimy, please?' I asked.

She slipped into the back room and disappeared for a few moments. The shop was quiet and empty, except for us.

'*Vite!*' I heard her say.

'The Professor is coming. She's called him,' I whispered to Faissal.

Anxiously, she emerged from the back room, her face bright red and mouth completely zipped. We stood stick-like, waiting for Professor Naimy.

Out of the blue, a police van halted abruptly in front of the shop, and armed police flooded in. The surrounding area was cordoned off, as if the President of the United States were in danger.

'*Ces deux garçons* refuse to give me peace. This is the second time . . .' she shouted at the police.

My heart jumped into my throat. '*Quoi? Quoi?*' I exclaimed.

'Shut that hole!' shouted a police officer.

'Your identity card!' another demanded.

I handed him my school card, but Faissal had none on him. The policeman was not very happy. Faissal began to murmur to himself. 'Tube! Shut up!' a police officer shouted at him.

Our arms twisted and cuffed behind our backs, we were pushed into a van then shoved onto hard seats. We heard the doors slam.

'We've done nothing!' I shouted.

'We were called,' said a policeman in the front.

As the van stopped, four policemen yanked us out, pulled us by the scruff of our necks and led us to the waiting hall, a long, narrow dungeon-like basement corridor with an endless row of low-ceilinged rooms. Time froze in eternity, the long corridor cold, dark and filled with unrecognisable faces.

'Are we ever going to see the light again?' whispered Faissal fearfully.

'Undoubtedly,' I answered with animated bravado. 'We're not criminals, or worse, politicians!'

From time to time Faissal seemed to fall into a snooze. A cry of a man made him jump, and he asked, 'Are we still here? Next time that'll be us!'

Before being led to the interrogation room, a policewoman made a psychological analysis of us. She seemed convinced we had been wrongfully arrested, but that didn't spare me a formal and rigorous interrogation.

Inside the interrogation room I faced a man, his face nearly fully covered with heavy tinted glasses. He might have been anyone, even a customer in the café that morning.

'You are from Kebdana,' he said. 'We have never had any trouble with anyone from that tribe. I wouldn't expect to have trouble with you, either.' *Is he honest, or just conning me?* I wondered anxiously. 'You should be at school,' he said.

'The school is a no-go area! A death trap! I was nearly killed!' I told him.

He must have known about the strike and the thugs, but pretended not to. 'Can you tell me more?' he asked.

'I can't tell you more than you already know,' I answered. The man bobbed his head as if it were a heavy weight.

'What brought you to Madame Naimy's shop?' he asked. 'And twice!' he added.

'Her husband was our professor, and we thought he could tutor us,' I answered.

'Who is "us"?' asked the interrogator. 'Give me everyone's full name. Where do you meet and what is the purpose of your gathering?'

'Simply to cover the baccalaureate programme with Professor Nassiri.'

'Did you invite him or did he volunteer?'

'We invited him,' I answered.

'Who is "we"?'

'It was me, sir.'

'Do you pay him?' he asked.

'Yes, we do,' I answered.

'Hmmmm,' he grumbled, nodding. 'You are intelligent people. I am assuming you talk about many things: art, music, sport, religion, politics and what-have-you. What's your favourite topic?'

'We don't talk of any subjects, sir. We do academic work, and that's it.'

'So you just wanted Professor Naimy to teach you?' he confirmed.

'Yes, sir.'

'Madame Naimy is intelligent, not a little girl. You must have given her a fright. If not, why should she call the police?'

'I am surprised, sir, that she did.'

'How were you able to contact Professor Nassiri and not Professor Naimy?' he asked.

'Professor Nassiri gave me his telephone number.'

'Did he? Do you know the boy who is with you well?'

'Yes, I've known him for many years.'

'If your group gets any bigger, we need to know,' he said. 'I'm counting on you to inform me.'

'No, sir.'

'What do you intend to do next year?'

'I'm going to Europe,' I said.

He pressed the buzzer under his desk, and I was whisked out. I grabbed Faissal's hand and followed the corridor to the exit sign. Faissal bathed himself in the late afternoon light, but raising a smile proved impossible. He embarked on bitter criticism. 'Had the school provided us with protection, we would not be left to the mercy of the thugs. You see the police in the street, but still feel unsafe. To study, you have to pay and hide.' He kept murmuring until he lost his balance and was nearly hit by the mirror of a huge lorry at the hand of a careless driver.

'Keep away from the road!' I shouted, but Faissal's ears were deafened by his own tirade, just as his eyes were blinded by what he had gone through that day. Pulled back to the pavement, he took a deep breath and his mind came alive.

'Are we going to tell the others what we've encountered and where we've been?' he asked.

'Don't be silly!' I replied. 'We'll lose Professor Nassiri if we do. He's an academic and ultra-sensitive. He would be terrified to be accused of forming a clandestine political cell.'

'Chickens don't form political parties!' said Faissal with a roaring laugh.

'See you soon. See you soon,' we echoed each other. Faissal went east to join Najib, and I went west, hoping Ali would be back from his shop.

Ali was not in the room when I arrived. He had come earlier and had started peeling potatoes and onions. A dirty knife was left on the floor, and the red bucket was full of water. *Ali is very tidy*, I thought. *Once he is in, he never goes out again.* Time passed, but no Ali.

Worried, I knocked on the landlady's door. 'Have you seen Ali?' I asked.

'I had a long chat with him late this afternoon,' she said.

Back in the room, I finished the cooking Ali had started and waited for him. He arrived, looking perplexed.

'What's the matter?' I asked.

'The landlady came while I was cutting onions, and she poured my family history and genealogy on me,' he said.

'Did she get it right?' I asked.

'Not all, but a lot. My father's first wife was a divorcee, she said, and that was true. I have a brother in France, working as a farmer, she said, and I have. She said my young sister got married too young and, in fact, she is not yet married, but she has always wished and talked of nothing but getting married since she was seven. We've often teased her.'

'She's just a mad witch!' I told him. 'She advised me to go and look for my mother, that she is still alive! My mother is dead and dust.'

A sharp knock on the door was heard, followed by a voice. 'Jusef! Is Ali back?' shouted the landlady.

'Yes,' I replied. I was anxious to go back to my books. Ali

threw his tinny, tiny transistor radio around his neck and swayed with the music like a drunk.

The disc jockey reminded his listeners to reduce the volume of the music, as students might be nearby, struggling with their exams. He gave the date, place and the exam subjects, orals and written. A quiet anxiety seeped through my skin.

Kadija heard the announcement and wanted me to know. She knew I lived far away, but not exactly where. She rushed to Najib's home nearby and insisted Faissal inform me right away. As she left, Faissal told me later, Najib scowled and mumbled, 'She has a crush on him, doesn't she?'

24

On the twenty-fourth of May, I awakened struggling to breathe. Inhaling was hard and painful; it felt as if my lungs were tethered to the floor and had lost the power to expand. At first, I thought I was lying in a bad position. I stood up and walked around the garage, but it made absolutely no difference. A day passed, and the pain tightened its anchor.

'You look like an old man,' said Ali, watching me bent over, trying to dampen the agony.

In unbearable pain, I went to the hospital a few miles away; arriving early in the morning, the queue seemed more than a mile long, with men, women and children of all ages shouting and fighting. A policeman was shoving patients into line with his baton. A tall tent was set up for women. In pain, they were careless about how they undressed or who might be watching them.

Obsessed with sheltering the women's tent from men's eyes, the policeman, baton at the ready, shouted at the men, 'Don't look at the tent!'

He came and shoved me out of the queue and said, 'Don't gaze at the tent! Turn your head! You are dying and still you are twisting that giraffe's neck to watch women!'

I felt furious. 'You are here to keep order, not to police men's eyes!' I told him and went back to the queue. He moved away.

To treat the thick crowd of patients, there was just one French woman doctor and one male Moroccan nurse. I didn't like the look of the doctor, and didn't expect too much from her either. She was thin as a plucked chicken with skin to match, wore pyjama-like clothes and flip-flops on her feet that made her unable to move. She looked sluggish and lazy. In this endless queue, I had no chance of seeing the doctor, but was lucky to see the nurse, who took my temperature. The gate of the hospital closed like an iron curtain, and many were turned away.

Leaving the hospital, I was glad to find Abdu sitting outside waiting for me, but he looked deeply depressed. He immediately noticed my restricted breathing.

'Was it your lungs that brought you here?' he asked me.

'Correct,' I answered.

'You might have tuberculosis,' said Abdu.

'I'm worried. Time is crucial, and I have very little money left,' I said. 'I'll need all I have to spend on doctors and drugs, so I might write to Rabbia to lend me some money. I hate that, but if it's the only way to stay alive, I'll have to do it.'

'One day, you will not recognise me or talk to me. You might even try to avoid me,' Abdu then told me.

'Are you going to fail your exams?' I asked, thinking of what had happened to my cousin, Ahmed.

'No. I've been told that I have a venereal disease. Madness might crown my life.'

'Some madness is desirable. It allows you to laugh at yourself and enjoy people different from you,' I said, not believing him. Abdu didn't laugh at my joke, became visibly upset and his fingers twitched. Trying to cheer him, I had failed.

'What type of drugs has the nurse given you?' asked Abdu.

'None,' I answered.

'What are you reading?' Abdu enquired.

'Physics, maths, biology. When I am bored, Simone de Beauvoir. Unfortunately, my French is not good enough yet,' I said.

I left Abdu and went to the private clinic of Dr Salah in Batha, the most affluent part of town. The waiting room was cluttered with men and women, veiled and unveiled. The air was stuffy with mouths and noses exhaling carbon dioxide, and the atmosphere was spooky. A middle-aged woman screamed with pain, her hand resting on the bottom of her tummy, her back bowed forward, but her screams didn't bother the doctor. A little girl, about eleven, was roaming the room. Her left arm was swollen and grey, with a deep gaping cut.

'What's wrong with your arm?' I asked her.

'My brother attacked me with a knife,' she sobbed.

'My son is a monster,' added her mother, overhearing. 'Because of him, his father left me.'

'You should starve him,' bellowed the woman sitting beside me.

'How could I?' asked his mother. 'He rules the house with a kitchen knife in his hand.'

'Is he really your son?' another curious woman asked.

'Yes, he came from the pit of my womb,' she said.

'You bore a brute!' an old woman who looked a thousand years old quietly said. 'Hang him from the ceiling by his ears!' she counselled with a wicked laugh.

The mother looked hurt. A middle-aged woman leaned over and whispered into her ear, 'Forgive her,' she said. 'She is my mother.'

'The older they get, the more wicked they grow!' cried the old woman.

Dr Salah opened the door, called the girl, and her mother followed. His thunderous pronouncement was heard. 'This girl needs a tetanus shot!'

A woman stood up, bobbed through the room and glued her ears to the doctor's door. 'You're a busy-body!' a small, thin woman shouted at her.

'Mind your own business or I'll sit on you!' the woman retorted. The mother came out, her eyes weepy and her hands firmly holding a prescription.

With a gruff voice, the nurse called me, 'Jusef!'

Sitting in his leather and mahogany chair facing the door, Dr Salah observed his patients from the moment their feet slipped over the threshold. I had heard that by the time they reached his desk and sat in the low, intimidating chair across from him, he had already made a primary diagnosis and opinion. I sat down full of hope, but his telediagnosis had failed.

'You should be in school, young lad,' he said. 'You have been skiving, are now in trouble, and need a medical certificate to cover up!'

'I am not skiving, but barred from school,' I answered.

I coughed, and the doctor realised this was not a skiving

case. Though he had a small x-ray cabinet, he disliked using it in case it affected him. I stood in the tight-fitting box and he began reading. The diagnosis was quick, sharp and bad.

'You have diseased lungs,' he said. 'I suppose you don't want to go to the hospital, as no one does, but if you wish to go, I will write a letter for you. Whether they would take you in a month or a year, I can only guess.'

'Private treatment?' I asked.

'Yes, but it is costly, lengthy and ineffective.' He slung the prescription across the desk and said. 'Come back in two weeks. You are significantly underweight and malnourished. Eat more, especially grapes.'

Armed with the presciption I rushed to the pharmacy nearby, five minutes before it closed. 'Is that all for you?' the pharmacist asked me, reading the prescription with a magnifying glass.

'Yes,' I answered.

The pharmacist nodded, pulled the drugs out and threw them chaotically on the counter. Looking at the growing stack, I became terrified. Paying the rent and buying food was all I could cope with. I paid for the drugs and was left with nothing to live on.

Back in the garage, I found a letter from Kadija lying on my blanket. She had come with Faissal and Najib. The exam method had changed, and they had come to inform me. Cut off from the world, I hadn't heard of the change. Ali's radio played rattling music most of the time, so I rarely heard the news.

I felt sad to have missed Kadija's visit, although both garage and the street were an embarrassment. I slowly picked up the letter. 'If I pass my exams, I will fight to get a scholarship to study law at Paris University. Would you like to come with me?' she wrote.

The letter shook me. I was ill and on the brink of destitution. I toyed with the letter. Reality. *It would be easier to ride a rhino in this garage than untangle the web woven around Kadija by her parents*, I thought. *She is beautiful, sweet and intelligent.* I dwelled on the dream until I fell asleep.

A violent pounding vibrated the entire garage. The landlady heard the thundering knock and hurried to catch the hooligan. I scurried, a kitchen knife in my hand, thinking I was being attacked by a thug. It was Abdu. Focusing on his face, I couldn't fathom what the last few days had done to him.

He looked aged, his forehead ridged in grooves, and his unshaven beard faded with heavy, thick dust. 'Are you all right?' I asked with surprise.

'Why?' he replied. Inside the garage, he refused to sit down. Out of the blue, he burst into tears.

This is not the Abdu I know.

'I want to be a martyr,' he told me.

'A Martyr? Martyr!' I shouted.

'Yes! Yes, boy!' he responded.

The word 'martyr' disturbed me. I made some distorted, uncomfortable faces and subjected him to some burning looks that pierced deeply into his skull. 'Is there any cause worth more than your life?' I asked him.

'The life I would like isn't the one I am living. Why not at least die the way I wish?'

'Martyrs come to a terrible death,' I said, clenching my teeth.

'Pain is not intrinsic to martyrdom, but to death itself, whether you are a king or queen, prince or princess, young or old, rich or poor. The only way man can overcome the pain of death is by death itself. I prefer my body to be pierced by bullets rather than capitulate to a swarm of flies, a pool of worms, bacteria and germs,' explained Abdu.

'Why don't you unload your heart in a book?' I asked.

'In a book, stupid boy! Intelligent in class and living in a filthy garage!' he told me. 'God wanted to explain his bothers with man in one book, he couldn't, and he ended by writing many books! He neither resolved his problem with man nor finished his books! My heart is full and heavier than any book could ever express.'

*　　*　　*

TWO AND A HALF weeks passed, and despite suffering badly, I didn't return to be re-examined. The doctor's fees were high and the cost of medicine prohibitive. I had finished all my drugs, and yet my breathing was still restricted. I looked like a vampire escaped from the graveyard. Desperately short of money, I began composing a letter to Rabbia that took me hours to finish.

Dear Rabbia,

I know that you have always wished to build a house in Sabbab. I am happy and willing to sell you my share for any money that you could send to me. If my share is added

to yours, you will be the major landowner and the rest is
between you and the other sisters to swap.

According to the medical tests, my lungs are diseased,
and I need more treatment. I have started, but as I am out
of money, am unable to continue. Because thugs have closed
the school, I am no longer boarded there, but hiding from
them in a garage. If my proposal is agreeable, use Uncle
Mimoun and Mrs Malani as witnesses.

Jusef

Rabbia received my letter, but as she was illiterate, she
needed the local *hafiz* to read it to her. That brought about a
sad occasion for her, face-to-face with the *hafiz*. For her, *hafizs*
were certified idiots. They tried to dwarf heaven, wrote and
sold talismans for the wealthy and poor, healthy and ill. They
scribbled talismans for headaches, migraines and diarrhoea,
but also to cure impotence, irrespective of age, barrenness and
other conditions. The local *hafiz* made no secret of his suspicion
that she was a shrewd witch and thought it was a pity the days
of burning them had passed.

I imagined Rabbia going back home, sitting on a solid
stone, turning her head against the grilling sun and her mind
going wild. Building a house in Sabbab, such a beautiful field
in the middle of a vast valley between two mountains and
bordering a dried river only a few kilometres from the public
fountain, had been the ultimate dream for all my sisters. I
thought her husband would be livid if he were to miss an
opportunity to own Sabbab.

Rabbia's husband loved to bring trashy bingo gossip, made

up by physically crippled old men, to the dinner table. Single women bore the brunt of it. 'That night was special,' she later told me. 'At the start of dinner, I gently pulled the letter out of my sash. I looked at it, wished I could read it and my husband hear it. Instead, he asked what the talisman was for. I had already decided not to mention Sabbab, the beloved piece of land. "Dr Salah has diagnosed Jusef with a lung disease," I told him, "and he has written to me seeking help."

'"Help! What type?" My husband asked me. "Financial," I told him. "Why doesn't he sell Sabbab," he asked. "That's exactly what he has offered," I told him.

'I asked him to go with me to Fez. "I would never put my foot in Fez, Sodom and Gomorrah!" he said. I didn't dare travel south to Fez on my own. I feared getting lost and making myself the butt of jokes. I bombarded my husband for days, but he dropped his ears like a donkey.'

*   *   *

WHILE I WAS WAITING for Rabbia to reply, my pain didn't get any better. I struggled to draw a breath. 'I'm going to see Dr Salah tomorrow,' I said to Ali, who was counting his earnings.

'And pay with what? You haven't received any money yet,' he said.

'Credit,' I answered.

'Your illness is going to your head,' he said with a subdued laugh.

I walked from my room to the doctor's clinic the following morning and felt as though I had crossed the entire desert. As usual, Dr Salah's clinic was full.

I went to the receptionist and whispered in her ear, 'May I pay the doctor by credit?'

'I've never heard of such a thing!' she said. 'Go and ask your parents for money.'

'I'm from the north, from Rif,' I answered.

'So what?' she replied. She sashayed away and entered the doctor's room without knocking, in spite of the red light flashing above his door.

'Someone wants to see you on credit,' I heard her say to the doctor while he was taking a patient's blood pressure.

'Bring him in next!' he shouted loudly.

When I entered, he looked me up and down. 'Do you feel any better since I saw you last?' he asked me.

'No.'

'You need a hospital; my clinic is small and inadequate. We doctors prescribe painkillers, people go home, feel better and claim miracles. Apart from antibiotics, thanks to a Scot, ninety-five per cent of our pharmaceutical drugs are not even worth the bin they are thrown in.'

With a new antibiotic prescription in hand, I left to spend my last penny. The chemist refused to give me drugs on credit. I could only buy one-third of what the doctor had prescribed.

*   *   *

ALI REALISED I HAD run out of money and stopped sharing food with me. I dreamed about food; I smelled food on Ali's clothes and knew he was eating out. I thought this was his revenge against me for making him lose his room.

For six days, I lived on water. Already weak, I got

physically weaker, but was mentally intact. I thought of several solutions. If I lied and pretended to have converted to Catholicism, I would have the right to ask for food from the Catholic Church. I toyed with the idea more than once. I went to the Church, but my ego and principles wouldn't let me go in. I also thought of going home to plead with Mrs Malani to lend me some money.

I never believed Rabbia would ignore my letter. I figured the offer was too good to miss. I also figured Mrs Malani might be away, and I was right.

Rabbia told me later, 'When I saw Mrs Malani's house under billowing smoke, I knew she was back. My husband scooted off to the bingo club, so I went to see her. As usual, Mrs Malani had some stories to tell, but I spoke first. "Jusef wrote to me," I told her, "and he's never done that before."

'She asked if it was good news. "No, he's ill and has run out of money," I told her.

'She asked me how ill you were. I told her your doctor had diagnosed you with a lung problem, and it must be serious because you offered to relinquish Sabbab for some money. I told her I had asked my husband to go to Fez with me, but he had refused.

'Mrs Malani told me she would go with me right then, and if my husband didn't let me go, she would go on her own the following day. I was surprised. Not yet unpacked from her long trip, she began packing and I left to do the same.

'My husband was shocked when he found my clothes, bag and shoes already packed. He knew Mrs Malani had a hand in it. Being a member of the bingo club, he had learned, like others, how to trick his wife. To frighten me, he said, "Going to Fez even for a man is dangerous, and you are a woman, aren't you? You don't have either a *jellabah* or a veil. Let me buy you a veil before you go."

'To stem the gossip, Mrs Malani and I left before any bingo player or kif smoker woke up; the trip was hidden and secret. The journey was, however, rocky and peppered with stops and checkpoints. We were neither short of patience, nor money, nor wisdom. Sleazy old men buzzed around us like flies that could find no place to land and feed.

'It was late afternoon when we were dropped in Fez. "To a good hotel, please," Mrs Malani asked the driver of a small French taxi. And do you know what? The driver tried to exhibit his charm, then he turned into a spy. We met him with a barricade of silence, and from the language we spoke, he understood we were provincial, from Rif, and that we could be treacherous.

'We checked into the hotel and neither of us spoke French or looked citified. We were an enigma to all. Via the hotel receptionist, we ordered a taxi late in the evening. A small, shabby taxi arrived, but the driver hadn't a clue how to get to you, in spite of the long address you had written.

'"I will get directions at the taxi station," he told us, but when we got there, no one knew more than he did, so he ploughed on, bit by bit, by stopping and asking, until we reached the right street.

'"Can you see a garage?" asked Mrs Malani.

'"Not from here," the taxi driver responded.

'"Can you drive to the end, please?" she asked him.

'As he drove slowly, peering right and left, a dim light came from a single-door garage, which was part of a teeny house.

'"This might be it!" I said to Mrs Malani.

'She was not sure, but she turned her face far from me, leaned toward the driver and shouted, "Wait for us just for five minutes or so. We must go back to the hotel." We jumped out of either side of the taxi, our bags and sacks in our hands.'

* * *

IT WAS NEARLY MIDNIGHT when Ali and I heard a car engine roaring just a metre away from the garage door, then a gentle tapping and the muffled voices of two women. Neither of us dared to open the door. Thugs were ever-present in my mind. They had increased in confidence and grown in number; the streets could be a death trap. The knocking on the door stopped for a few seconds, and that was enough to give me a real fright.

Rabbia confessed she was not sure that she had reached the right door, but that was as far as the address could go. She and Mrs Malani had bought a ticket to go back the following day at two-thirty in the afternoon and her husband was already enraged. A second night away would certainly be asking for trouble.

Rabbia gave a frustrated, hard knock and Mrs Malani shouted, 'It's your sister, Rabbia!'

'It's me!' confirmed Rabbia. Full of doubt, I jumped over Ali's blanket and opened the door. In the pitch-black darkness, Rabbia and I hugged each other. Then I turned to Mrs Malani, who gave me a warm hug.

Once inside, Rabbia took in the entirety of the room in a

blink while Mrs Malani spoke to Ali, sitting cross-legged on his blanket, gaping, with his small radio lying almost dead on his lap. Mrs Malani would have been shocked if she had known how mean Ali had been to me. She was appalled at my living conditions.

'From boarding school to this!' she told me, shaking her head, looking at me, emaciated, rasping and pale.

Hearing the taxi roaring in the street and two females talking through the thin wall, the landlady, in a nightdress, jumped out of her bed, pushed the garage door, burst into the little space left and shouted at me, 'Women are not allowed in this room!'

'This is my sister!' I shouted back.

'She's still a woman!' she yelled even louder. Mrs Malani and Rabbia tasted their first dose of the city. Ignoring the thundering landlady, Rabbia handed me a heavy bag, while Mrs Malani poked a pouch filled with coins into my jacket. With the speed of light, they whispered farewells to me and rushed to the taxi.

The moment the bag was brought into the room, Ali and I knew its contents. The fried chicken smell burst through the bag to fill the tiny room. The feast started when the door shut behind the landlady. We tore into the chicken like vultures. With steely teeth, we mashed the meat and bones with a vengeance.

More food was in the bag than we expected. Small buns of barley bread, homemade, were wrapped in a small piece of white cloth. Boiled eggs rolled out when I moved the bag. A tiny amount of salt and black pepper was tied up in a small red cloth.

Eating our fill, we got thirsty. Though the room had no water, we had never bothered filling our jug at night. 'Why don't we go out and get water?' I asked.

'We could have tea,' Ali added, forgetting that we no longer shared food. We went out happily, but stupidly left the door ajar and the light on, to act as a fog light in the dark street. A passing tramp smelled the food, peered through the door, saw nobody in, and decided to make it his personal Eden. He went in, switched off the light and rolled himself up in Ali's blanket, head and feet covered.

The tramp's switching the light off confused us. The street was dark and all its tiny houses interwoven into each other looked alike with no trees, no gates, no fences, just streets and tiny doors. On our way back, Ali asked, 'Do you know where we're going?'

'We left the light on,' I said. 'The landlady, that rotten witch, must have switched it off.' The garage was not far away from the intersection with another street just one metre wide, I remembered. 'Let's look for the narrow street,' I said.

'Here it is!' said Ali, with eyes open like an owl's.

The street was like a tunnel. From the narrow street, I counted doors and one was ajar. We both recognised the room, which was still emanating a smell of fried chicken. As I turned on the light, the tramp jumped and shouted, 'Switch off the light!'

Ali released an inhuman yell and we both backed into the street. *This is the thugs' tricks and a trap*, I thought to myself, looking around to see what would come next, but no one emerged from the room. It was dark and quiet, and I couldn't see Ali, who'd run away. I knocked on the landlady's door for help, but there was no sign of her.

I quietly opened the garage door, switched the light on and yanked the blanket off the tramp. Confronted with a bearded face and long hair, I jumped back, hitting the wall behind. The tramp didn't move, was deep in sleep and I didn't know if he was dead or alive. *Ali will come soon*, I hoped, but he didn't. *Shall I awaken this man? Shall I threaten him with a kitchen knife? But he might kill me in self-defence. He has nothing to live for. I don't want Rabbia and Mrs Malani's visit to turn into a burial.*

Time passed with still no Ali. The landlady hadn't bothered answering the door though my knocks had carried distress. I ran back to her door and kept knocking until she and her husband came out in a rage.

'A tramp! A tramp in our room! Wrapped in Ali's blanket!' I shouted.

They looked confused. 'You're walking in your sleep!' the husband thundered at me.

'The tramp sneaked in while we were fetching water,' I said emotionally.

'That's what you get when you rent your precious property to kids from the street!' the husband told his wife.

'I've been awakened twice: by Jusef's sister and now by a tramp in Ali's blanket!' said the landlady.

In the silence of the night and the darkness of the street, we heard footsteps coming nearer and nearer, but we couldn't see who it was. It was Ali coming back. He saw the light, the landlady's door open, me talking to them and shouted, 'Is he still in my blanket?'

The landlady and her husband faced and stepped back from each other, then stopped talking. She broke alliance with her husband and pushed him back into the house, so the tramp wouldn't choose him as a target because of his height and girth. He went back in, quietly, like a reprimanded child.

'Follow me,' she told me. She burst into the garage with me behind, and mercilessly jumped up and down on the tramp like on a trampoline. She flattened him like a mouse under an elephant's foot.

He dodged and shouted, 'Woman! Have you never been taught to respect a man?'

'Certainly not you!' she retorted.

He stood up, glowered at her and edged toward the door. With her two hands up, just reaching his shoulders, she shoved him into the street, cold and dark, where he had come from. 'He's a seasonal tramp,' she told me. 'Young, but with no youth left.'

I expected a row, but she quickly disappeared into her house and didn't show up until afternoon the following day. The tramp hadn't touched our food.

Scared to fall asleep, Ali kept talking to me. 'What a long journey your sister has made with chicken and bread in her bag!' he said.

'She knew how mean and stingy the inhabitants of this town are,' I replied with him in my mind.

In the morning, I joined Rabbia and Mrs Malani. The hotel restaurant was big and attractive, and its French patron, with no hair or neck but as large as an ox, was in command of everything. Waiters, all Moroccan males, bowed in every direction he went.

Breakfast was light, but tasty. The waiter brought croissants and *café au lait*. Rabbia couldn't believe how hollow and empty French croissants were. 'Do French people really live on that?' she asked me.

'No,' I said, but I didn't really know what their diet was.

'How did you allow yourself to get this run down?' Mrs Malani asked me.

'Rioters and thugs have imposed a strike and closed the school. With no classes, the bursar closed the dormitories and the kitchen to save money.'

'Which he pocketed for himself, I suppose,' she said.

'The school did nothing to protect us; neither did the town authorities,' I said. 'They almost killed me twice, and they would now if they could catch me.'

'This is crazy!' exclaimed Mrs Malani. 'A school is not a shrine! It can't be run with spells! It needs an iron rector. The non-strikers' rights should be protected.' She shook her fists angrily.

'How can a few thugs hunt people, beat them, and still run free?' asked Rabbia.

'It's a fact of life!' I answered.

'If a single pistol would protect you, I would have brought you one,' said Rabbia. She didn't know I had bought a pistol just last summer, but now the game was different. Her hand dove into her sack and picked out a small bag, hand-made with white cloth, cash inside, small notes. 'This is the Sabbab money,' she said.

I felt both happy and sad, for the money I had received and the Sabbab I had lost.

Mrs Malani immersed her left hand into her battered, hand-made leather sack, and picked out a medium-sized bottle of crystal clear glass filled with a dark green liquid, dotted with some floating bits. 'This is for your chest,' she told me. 'It's honey and herbs.'

It was time for them to go, and I ordered a taxi. We all lurched out to the waiting taxi. It was not the usual tiny, tired French Simca, but a royal blue German Mercedes. Most likely, the taxi driver had been expecting an Arab diplomat, a sheik, a rich man, but certainly not two provincial women. He wasn't convinced we were the right passengers. He left us, the engine on, the doors open, and scurried to the receptionist.

'Passenger room nineteen?' he shouted at the receptionist, a retired French woman.

'They are already in your car,' yelled a uniformed girl, moving in and out.

I believe the driver couldn't reconcile his luxury car with two peasant women and me beside them.

'This car is far more spacious than the room we slept in,' whispered Mrs Malani.

'But the bath is missing!' grinned Rabbia.

At the station, the coach to Nador was late, and I asked the ticket vendor, 'Is the coach on its way?'

'It might be,' he said. 'It might also be in a garage waiting to be repaired.'

His words fell on Rabbia's ears like stones. She knocked on the door of the office manager not far away and asked angrily, 'When will the coach be here?'

'God knows, I don't,' he replied. 'We offer one departure

a day, but we never guarantee the time. Don't lose hope until midnight.' He slammed the door and disappeared behind one with steel bars.

Just across the road, there was a café with loud music, scattered chairs and the unmistakable smell of mint tea. I grabbed Rabbia's hand, called Mrs Malani and crossed the dangerous road where one car was worth far more than ten pedestrians.

'Take the chair, Mrs Malani,' I said. Rabbia grabbed her own.

'I have never seen such anomie, such unstructured, disorganised time-wasters as I have today. Do they really know what time it is?' Rabbia asked me.

'This is a city,' said Mrs Malani. 'Honey for flies. Those with no will or strength will get stuck.'

It was two-thirty, and the coach still hadn't arrived. Rabbia and Mrs Malani drank plenty, switching from tea to coffee and back again, whiling away the time.

'Look! Look!' I shouted. 'The coach has arrived!'

All its doors were open, and people were going in and out as if it were on exhibit. As the coach honked its horn, Mrs Malani and Rabbia jumped across the road. Real travellers boarded, and those who had just gotten on for a rest were unceremoniously dethroned. Weaving through the crowd, I looked for seat numbers fourteen and fifteen, but they were already occupied. Two women, comfortably settled in, refused to move.

'We have tickets and we can sit wherever we like,' one of them barked at me.

'Fuck off!' exclaimed the older one.

The matter couldn't be settled until the driver and his assistant intervened, both wearing dark black and red uniforms. Neither Rabbia nor Mrs Malani had expected to be denied their seats by two respectable-looking females, let alone be told to fuck off.

After some nasty verbal skirmishes, the coach took off to Nador with the speed of an aircraft heading into the sky.

*　　*　　*

WHILE I WAS WITH my sister and Mrs Malani, the landlady spent the entire afternoon waiting for me. Mrs Malani and Rabbia had left her with perplexing impressions. Her look disturbed me, and she was the last person I wished to see, let alone talk to.

'I know more about you now,' she confronted me.

I didn't answer. All I wished to see was her back.

'Your sister doesn't look like you, does she?' she said.

'It never occurred to me,' I answered.

'It's just as well,' she said. 'She has blue eyes, and yours are brown. Your hair is black and hers is ginger. That is peculiar in this land, where people and even the soil look alike. What does she do, anyway?'

'She's a witch like you,' I said, hoping to get rid of her.

'She came from the north to the south without a man at her side?' she exclaimed.

'She's married,' I told her.

Swollen, taking all the air in the room with her, she turned to leave, her hand already on the doorknob when she suddenly changed her mind and twirled on her heel toward me.

'Is your sister coming back?' she asked.

'No,' I answered.

With a glowering look at me, she straightened her back and shouted, 'Rat! Rat! A rat lives here!'

I stood up, jumped and shouted, 'There's more than one rat here!'

'Do you mean me?' she asked.

'Yes!' I answered. She went away and I expected her to return, but she didn't. Now that I had money in my pocket from Mrs Malani and Sabbab, I had the confidence to challenge her and change accommodation if I needed to.

Only two weeks were left before the start of the first exam: physical and aerobic fitness. I was well aware of my medical condition. I couldn't complete a one-hundred-metre run with incapacitated lungs. The physical test decided whether a student was worth the nation's grant. The Ministry of Education wouldn't waste the country's wealth on a student whose body wouldn't hold up.

With the pouch of coins from Mrs Malani, I bought five kilos of grapes, three kilos of oranges, and two dozen eggs. I set myself on a course of outdoor therapy to breathe fresh air into my lungs, and walked every morning for two hours. I gradually increased my speed and distance until I could run a hundred metres without stopping.

One very hot early morning in mid-June, I went back to Dr Salah's clinic. The reception quarters and the waiting room were flooded with patients; those who couldn't find a seat or space poured out of the door to sit or stand outside, a test of fitness in itself. The receptionist had a hard job coping. Three or four people were crowded around her, talking to her frantically. They forgot she had only one mouth. 'Just wait! Just wait!' was all she could say.

'I am here to pay,' I told her, when I finally reached her desk.

She looked confused, but soon remembered me. She disappeared into a small side room and came back out trailing behind a French woman with salt-and-pepper hair, who was smart, small, thin, confident and terrifyingly serious.

'I am the doctor's wife,' she said, touting her French. 'Do you have the right change?' she asked me.

'Yes,' I replied. She took the payment and slipped off in the blink of an eye.

*   *   *

ON THE EVE OF my physical fitness test, I packed all my books, pens, pencils and erasers in a suitcase; blankets and towels were left to be packed in the morning. The test would start in the morning at eight o'clock on the French football pitch, near the New Town.

Coming back from his shop, Ali was hit by the emptiness. The corner where my books had been chaotically scattered looked bare. 'Are you leaving?' he asked, startled.

'Yes,' I replied, 'immediately after the test. From tomorrow, this room will be yours and yours alone.'

Ali kept silent, biting his lips. 'I am trapped here,' he said. 'I came to Fez as a young boy and now I am in my late twenties. I am no richer now than when I arrived in the first week.'

'You are in the wrong trade,' I told him. 'Switch to hashish.'

I left in the morning while Ali was sleeping; my quarters were cleared and tidy, and the room looked bigger. By seven-thirty I was miles away, cold and standing waiting at the gate of the football pitch. Two girls from a different school were already there. Four hundred metres away, their parents were squatting, watching over them. A police van passed, and I wished it would stop, if only for two seconds, as a show of strength and a warning to the thugs. Faissal arrived with two heavy, muscular brothers at his side, then Kadija and her girl-friends were the last, her old, fragile father with them. Seeing Kadija for the first time after weeks in hiding, I left Faissal and walked with her toward the gate.

The janitor opened the gate and segregation by sex started – boys to one side, girls to the other. A group of arrogant French teachers took over. No one was called by his name, just by a number. Within half an hour, even usage of numbers faded, and nicknames were used. '*Le petit! Le petit!* Move! *Vite!* Run! Run!' ordered one French woman in a gym uniform with a whistle in her mouth.

Another teacher shouted, '*Le grand!* Jump! Jump!' As there were many '*petit*' and '*grand*,' the titles grew more specific, personal and unflattering.

'*Le noir! Le noir, avec le pantalon noir!* Move!'

By one o'clock, all the physical exams were over. We were all sweaty, thirsty, hungry and completely unaware of the outside world. Leaving the pitch, each student grabbed his clothes and peered left and right, on the lookout for thugs. Everyone dispersed within sixty seconds, as if falcons had struck a flock of hens and their chicks. Faissal, escorted by his brothers, was one of the lucky ones. I didn't see Kadija; she had escaped invisibly like everyone else, with her father.

Off the pitch, I grabbed a dilapidated taxi to the coach station, boarded the coach and headed east for two hundred fifty miles, to impose myself as an unwanted guest on my sister Sakina and her husband.

Sakina had endured an arranged marriage. She was illiterate, and her husband was twice her age. The attraction for him had been her beauty; with her olive complexion and rosy cheeks, she had stood out from the local girls. She loved talking, it didn't matter if it made sense, and dancing whenever she was invited to a wedding. He loved food, especially meat, but never shared a meal with her at table. He had to be fed first and would only have the best of everything. There was only ever gravy left for Sakina and the children. He had a dangerous temper; not one single day passed without his anger bursting.

I knew Sakina was far from happy, but it was in her home that I took refuge. I tried to be invisible and discreet, not part of the family. I awakened every morning before sunrise, before anyone else was up, and never stood in the way of anyone who wanted access to the toilet. One and a half miles away stood a majestic mosque, open nearly all day and night. Like a hermit, I took refuge in one of its corners. It was a quiet and peaceful spot, facing a stained glass window. I sat cross-legged, read, revised for my exams and sometimes slept. It was only at night, when the mosque was closed and no worshippers were expected, that I headed to Sakina's house. I would walk back as slowly as possible, hoping to avoid her husband.

Sakina always kept the third-class dinner leftovers, after she and the children had eaten, for me.

Revising one afternoon at the mosque, I had forgotten some vital books and went back to collect them while Sakina's husband was teaching. Inside the house, I couldn't hear or see Sakina.

'Sakina!' I shouted twice. *She's not allowed out, so where is she?* I wondered. Going farther into the back of the house and into the cemented yard, I heard a loud cry from the toilet. 'Are you there, Sakina?' I yelled.

I waited for her to come out, but she didn't. Again I heard crying, so I went nearer to the toilet door and asked, 'Are you locked in?'

'Yes,' she replied with a quivering voice.

'Have you lost the key?' I asked.

'No. My husband locked me in and went away, as usual.'

'Where does he put the key?'

'I don't know.'

I searched everywhere, floor and windows, table, but found no key. When I discovered an old nail, I used it to try to unlock the door of the single toilet. Sakina didn't want me to force the door or break the lock. I stayed outside and kept her talking, hoping her husband would return soon. It was five o'clock and there was no sign of him. She had been locked in a toilet, one square metre, with no seat or window and no air except what could pass through the cracks since two o'clock. Her children would be back from school shortly, and her main worry was hiding the drama from them. Tinkering with the lock, I finally managed to open the door. Inside, Sakina was squatting on one side then the other, straddling the toilet hole and its contents.

I felt sorry for my sister, but had no solution to offer, as she was economically trapped. Hoping to shame him, I wrote an angry note in the evening and handed it to him myself in the morning. I grabbed my bag and boarded the coach headed home, miles to the north.

25

B ack home, I was all alone in an empty house, with no life,
no sisters, no dogs, donkey or even a wild cat. Silence was
all that God had left in the previously noisy house, but with
the silence came peace; I didn't fear thugs or need the police.

The house was like a mausoleum. My mother had been
terrifyingly superstitious. She had often spoken of death and
the dead and connected herself more with the dead than with
the living. Though my father had died years ago, she had still
kept his turban on a hook. His shoes were still behind the door.
Leaving everything as it was created a silent montage of the
past. I felt the distance between me and the dead, paper-thin.

I had run away from the thugs and my sister's house to be
invisible for a few days before going back to sit the rest of my
exams. My wish, however, was unachievable. As it was built
on a hill, anyone moving in and out of the house was visible
from a higher hill behind, from neighbouring hills, or just
from the valley beneath.

Uncle Mimoun spent two-thirds of his time cruising from
hill to hill, his rifle ready to kill any edible rodents. Failing
rabbits or pigeons, there were always beautiful robins in the
sky to shoot down, for thrills if not for food.

I later learned that Mimount had been the first to spot me. 'A strange man was coming out of your brother's house and quickly disappeared,' she had told her husband. Uncle Mimoun had feared an intruder, important family documents on his mind. Mimount hadn't wanted him to go and confront the intruder. She knew how quick-tempered he could be, so the two of them had decided to investigate.

Nervous and worried about what might happen, she had led the way. Uncle Mimoun had not been complacent, and his finger, though trembling, had been on the trigger.

Fifty metres away from the house, as the local creed stipulated, Mimount called, 'Mohammed! Mohammed! Mohammed!' Mimoun stood side by side with his wife, his rifle directed at the main door.

Though I heard the voice, I didn't go out. *The caller might be a beggar*, I thought, as many were roaming around. As the calling continued to be a bother, I couldn't ignore it. *An intruder might get in if I don't go out*, I thought to myself.

Slowly, I edged the door open. Steadily, Mimoun cocked the trigger. When I popped my head out, Mimount recognised me and abruptly shoved the rifle barrel up into the air as the rifle discharged with a bang. She shouted with horror, 'Jusef! Jusef! Who would have thought it was you! Your uncle nearly killed you!'

With a sigh of relief, Uncle Mimoun laid his rifle far away against the wall. He had had every reason to worry. If an intruder had gotten into the house and made off with the family documents, Uncle Mimoun could have lost his house and every plot of land he owned.

Being a *hafiz*, my father had been the family registrar. All documents relating to divorce, marriage and land purchases had been kept in my mother's trunk. Despite the suspected intruder turning out to be me, Uncle Mimoun still didn't want to leave until he saw that the trunk was still heavy with documents, even though he was illiterate.

Relaxed and smiling, Mimount followed me. 'I remember when girls popped in and out of this big house. Which room are you using?' she asked me, probably hoping not to go to the main bedroom, which was where the trunk had lain under the dust and where Uncle Mimoun was headed. The bedroom door was unlocked, and Uncle Mimoun was the first in.

The trunk had been a fixture for as long as I remembered and was full to bursting. My mother, my sisters and I had all been taught not to tamper with it. No daughter had ever put her hand inside; I had some years earlier when I was young and naïve, looking for magic, and had discovered the book of spells, all meticulously handwritten, but none of them had been any good; I had never turned water into honey and a talisman hung on the branch of a tree had never brought my beloved, or any other girl, to me.

Mimount appeared as though she had been sucked through space, weeping and sweeping her tears away at the same time. Moving her hand as if it had fallen asleep, she pointed behind the door. My father's shoes were lying there neatly, as if he might come back and put them on. Watching Mimount, I kept my ready tears to myself.

Uncle Mimoun caressed the trunk, opened the latch, lifted the lid and smiled when he saw no documents were missing.

Land documents were all rolled up and carefully pushed inside bamboo reeds, similar to the one from which I had made a flute. Uncle Mimoun grabbed as much as his right hand could hold, and he grimaced when he saw a long, white worm inside one bamboo reed. One document carrying his name was unreadable. It looked like a fishnet; the worm had eaten its way in and out.

Each handwritten document was stylised, and the language used was a mishmash; some words were Arabic, some dialect, and some Tarifit words written with the Arabic alphabet. The wind was the main tool, apart from the river, that marked the border between fields. 'Mr Hamza's field ends at the point of rustling wind and the peak of the hill,' read one document. 'Mr Bohali's field ends at the hugging wind,' read another. As the wind never stopped and kept changing strength, so did the farmers' arguments. Fighting and death had been woven into the hearts and life of this deceptively peaceful community for years.

Watching her husband's enthralled face, Mimount asked innocently, 'What is in this trunk?'

'Our history, our land, our religion, everything we are!' replied Uncle Mimoun loudly. Squatting down, he kissed the trunk. For me, it was a history that I disliked and the cause of my endless misery.

'Tonight you will have your dinner with us,' offered Mimount just before leaving and standing in the shadow of Uncle Mimoun.

'Thank you. I will,' I replied.

Mimount never lacked generosity. A big plate of cous cous,

adorned with chickpeas and a stewed chicken on the top of it, was put in the middle of the crowded family. With his rough hands, Uncle Mimoun ripped the chicken apart with joy and vengeance.

Still eating around the plate, Uncle Mimoun shouted, 'The land documents must be moved here before you go back to Fez!'

Going back home in the pitch-dark night, I couldn't shake off the tales of ghosts and demons and became fearful of them as if they were real. I trembled as I reached the dry riverbed. I had hoped Uncle Mimoun would give me company going home, as his rifle inspired confidence, but he hadn't offered.

Going across the valley, I heard footsteps, but couldn't tell where they were going or coming from. *This could be a ghost, a vampire, a demon, a genie, or just my blood pulsating in my head,* I thought to myself. Still moving slowly in complete darkness, concentrating on the scattered white stones marking the path, the sound of someone or something walking came nearer and nearer, but there was still nothing to be seen. *Should I go back to Uncle Mimoun's house?* I wondered. Fearful, I heard the shuffling footfalls get very much closer. *It's real,* I thought. I clenched two heavy stones, one in each hand, ready to throw them if the shadow got too close.

Ready for the worst, I continued until I reached the cross-path, where I walked in a semi-circle; so did Rabbia (for it was she), and unknowingly we avoided each other.

Passing the paths' intersection, listening to the footsteps dying away, I breathed relief, but still kept my ears on full alert until I reached the fence of my house, built of solid stone in front of thick, high prickly pear. Climbing the short hill and reaching the main double door, I noticed a flickering candlelight coming from the main room. Jumping back in fright, I gasped to myself, 'What's this?'

I had heard of people who had found lit candles in their rooms or on top of a hill, often under trees. Frightened, they had moved house or emigrated to run away from the mysterious lit candles. The common advice was not to react to the light, not to use it, and certainly not to extinguish it, because a group of genies or demons was using it.

Afraid to go into the house, I stayed outside the whole night. The sun rose slowly and bathed the house in light. I entered the house and went to the main room where the mysterious light was. The door had no lock, but was closed. As I opened it, sunlight spilled in. There was no sign that anything had changed, but the beeswax candle was extinguished, choked by hundreds of spit bits of wax.

When Rabbia came that afternoon, I learned the mysterious candle had been her trick to deter intruders. Worried about the house and the trunk, she came now and again and lit a candle. She turned her fury to Uncle Mimoun when I told her of his desire to hold the land documents in his house; they had never seen eye to eye. He had accused her of being a witch and a disgrace, and she thought he was a bully and out of touch.

'Are you happy to hand him the documents?' she asked me with a look of dismay.

'No,' I replied.

'I'm certainly not!' she retorted. 'I've always kept an eye

on the house and trunk. I come late most nights and light a candle. Do you have any idea what else is in the trunk apart from the land documents?' she asked me.

'No, I lost interest the day I went to school, but I do remember a notebook of spells,' I explained.

'Don't lose them,' she said. 'People will pay a fortune for them.'

Before the end of the week, she came twice. She brought her husband and their donkey to empty the trunk, but I wouldn't allow it.

Out of his bed after a bout of summer flu, Uncle Mimoun did the same. He came on his mule, his rifle on his shoulder, and asked to load the land documents into his saddlebags. I refused. I had run from the thugs, from Sakina's husband, and was now caught in a tussle with both Rabbia and Uncle Mimoun.

Intrigued by the interest of Rabbia and Uncle Mimoun in the family heritage in my mother's trunk, I started a disturbing journey of discovery. Tucked deep in the trunk lay three medium-sized books, all with hard covers. Their beauty caught my eye – maroon, brocade covers with pink paper, well printed, and each page with sketches. They were all written in the Arabic alphabet, but not in the Arabic language. Challenged and defeated, I couldn't decipher them. Their meaning was locked into their pages as a mystery, just as it was a mystery how they happened to be here in this land and in the hand of someone who hadn't written them and couldn't read them, let alone understand them.

I was stressed by the looming exams, the overwhelming

task of revision, and frightened of what the thugs might be plotting, yet I was compelled to thumb through the contents of the trunk. I found a notebook filled with papers of different sizes and colours. *This is my father's writing!* I realised.

Artistically written notes, but in mixed languages, Berber and Arabic words meshed together, were so difficult to make out that I struggled to decode the meaning. One page however, struck me like a hammer on the head:

Jusef's father was a true nationalist. He loved freedom just as much as he loved nature. 'Colonialism,' he told us, 'is rape in the daylight.' He was not a romantic or a visionary. When the time came, he sailed courageously with his men to provide arms for nationalists. In the middle of the Mediterranean Sea, his ship was encircled. The blockade lasted for days, and when he ran out of fuel, the battle started. Sadly, he was killed along with Mr Omar, Mr Jaloun, and Mr Sohbi. Mr Ishram was wounded, but miraculously picked out of the sea by a passing merchant vessel . . .

Blinded with love for her lost husband, very young herself and left with an infant son, the young widow was unable to function. Her widowed mother, traumatised by the experience of her only daughter, moved in with her for months, but had seven boys of her own living miles away, to keep her eyes on. The young widow, heartbroken, tearfully entrusted her infant son to Sabah, my wife.

Perplexed and numb, I moved to the goat room, a large room with only three walls. There, I pulled down my old flute.

It had been stuck between bamboo rafters in the middle of the ceiling, hidden from Uncle Mimoun's tyranny. I played the flute to block out my thoughts, but it only brought back the past. My shepherding days had been hard and lonely. The sound of the flute vibrating through my ears brought back every scorpion that I had killed and every snake I had chased, my movements from hill to hill, mountain to mountain, valley to valley, the chasing of foxes, the feeding of goats and sheep who never once expressed thanks.

Unable to focus despite my looming exams, I went back to the notebook. Disappointed, I found no more on how the infant, like a bag of groceries, had changed hands. Trying to digest what I had read, I had so many unanswered questions . . . and no one to ask.

*   *   *

THERE WAS A WEDDING just a few days before I left for Fez. Mrs Robbi was outside watching the bridal procession slowly ascending the hill to reach the house adjacent to hers on the top. She was all alone, sitting on a large grey stone, her legs outstretched and spread ungracefully.

'Hello, Mrs Robbi,' I greeted her with a nod and a wide grin.

It took her a few minutes to recognise me. Pleased that someone had bothered to notice her, she called me to her side. I sat next to her, and we both watched the bride nearing the house where she was received with fireworks. Once it was over and the bride, blanketed with a clumsy cloth, was conducted to the room where she would later be tested for virginity, the time came for Mrs Robbi and me to leave, but she couldn't pull her legs back to stand up.

'I suffer from arthritis,' she told me. 'Being heavy-boned doesn't help.' As I helped her to stand up, she leaned heavily on my shoulder. I propped her up until she reached home. Her face flickered with pain; we stopped here and there to allow her to take a deep breath, but the smile cascaded from her face when she reached home.

'Why don't you slip into my orchard and pick some fruit?' she offered to me.

'I like apricots,' I said.

'Well, there are plenty and they are ripe,' she answered.

Her orchard was immense, though deceiving as its entry was narrow and dark like a dungeon. The apricots were ripe, but more sunny days were needed to ripen off the figs, peaches and grapes. I counted twenty-four beehives in four rows with walkways in between. Bees darting in and out like bullets made the orchard like a battleground. Sadly, I was stung on my cheek by one of the bees.

Watching me from her tiny window, Mrs Robbi realised I wasn't picking fruit, but swatting bees left and right. My reaction amused her, and she came out. 'It's like a bee chasing an elephant!' she said sarcastically.

'It takes up to two weeks for a bee's sting to fade. I don't want to go back with swollen cheeks,' I told her, feeling embarrassed.

'I don't want you to look odd!' she said, smiling at my expense. 'Your father was pretty clumsy with bees. He never placed hives in the right spot, and never renewed them when they got old. His bees died prematurely, and your mother used to get frustrated with him and envious of my honey.'

'Did you know my father very well?' I asked.

'I always thought so,' she replied with a shrug.

'Did you know my mother just as well?'

'I wouldn't say so,' she replied. 'There was a hell of a difference between them. Your mother worked pretty hard to tame her two piglet daughters. They tattooed their faces beyond recognition with long stitches on the forehead, both cheeks, the chin and neck, driving her to tears. It would have taken a blind man to marry either one of them, but that didn't bother your father, which was an additional pain to your mother. How did you do in your exams?' she asked.

'I haven't sat them yet,' I answered.

'Why are you strolling around here, then?' she queried.

'I'm hiding from thugs. I also had to run from my brother-in-law, but as soon as I arrived home, Uncle Mimoun forced me to read the land documents stored in my mother's trunk. Thumbing through the suitcase, I chanced upon my father's notebook. In two and a half pages, he described how Jusef (I'm assuming that's me) ended up in their hands; that my real father was killed at sea and my mother was unable to cope. They took me in as their own. Has my father filled his notebook with fiction?' I asked her.

Visibly at a loss for words, she threw her hands up in the air, turned on her heel and hobbled back toward the house. *That's a strange reaction!* I thought. At that moment, she must have thought better of it and turned around to face me. 'I never knew your father to be a liar!' she stated forcefully. 'The story is, they weren't your natural parents, but I don't know who your parents actually were. I have wondered that for many years.' She backed a few steps and disappeared behind the door.

How can she not know? I wondered. *She was a close friend of my father.*

*   *   *

HAVING BEEN ABSENT FOR a month, I felt like a raven in a land of penguins when I arrived back in Fez. Looking for a safe haven, I hired a room in a small, respectable-looking lodging, owned by a French couple and managed by a local woman. I soon found that female and male prostitutes, black and blond, were hustled about like trains at the station, and kept the manageress busy cashing in. When I asked for the front door key, she refused.

'It's already dark. You're not going out now, are you?'

'Yes, I need to see a friend,' I replied, with Kadija in my mind.

'We never give the front door key to anyone. I can't give it to you.'

'I'll be back early,' I promised.

'I'll wait for you,' she said.

It was dark and the street was empty, no cars or pedestrians were around, and I was alone walking down from the New Town to the *medina*. In the narrow, dimly lit streets, I couldn't see who might be behind or in front of me, so, like a bat, I depended on my ears. Beggars were everywhere.

I reached Kadija's house and wondered what her father might think or say to me. The house number was not easy to read, but I remembered the door, the sign above the lock, and the tiles on each side. I knocked on the door and a tall boy came out. He gave me a suspicious look, and asked, 'What do you want?' The tone of his voice said it all.

'Kadija,' I answered.

'There's no such person here,' he answered with a sneer.

'I am Jusef, her classmate. We had some lessons here not long ago, and our exams will start on Wednesday,' I explained.

The boy didn't budge. Kadija must have heard us talking and rushed, bare-footed, to the front door. I might have gotten a hug had her brother not been around. 'Where have you been?' she asked.

'I went to my sister's, then to our house in Kebdana.'

'I have been working day and night,' she said.

'Have you seen Faissal and Najib?' I asked.

'No. They are hiding. It's such a shame! But, I've seen Rahma and Bajia,' she added. 'Now that I've seen you, I'll work harder!' she whispered with a smile, checking that she hadn't been overheard.

'I came to see you as soon as I arrived,' I said.

'Exams start on Wednesday at eight. Do you think it's safe?' she asked, frightened. 'I've heard they mistook a girl for a baccalaureate student and threw acid on her face. What is left if a girl is defaced?'

'Nowhere is safe. Anyway, don't forget to take your exam ID. They won't let you in otherwise,' I responded, noticing her brother's menacing look. 'I'm afraid I have to go. I promised the manageress of my room to be in on time. Otherwise I will be locked out.'

'I'm glad you're back,' she smiled sweetly.

The manageress was pleased when I arrived before closing time. Seeing that I was tired and sweaty, she said, 'You're a sight!'

'Yes, I was running.'

Inside my room, I felt exhausted and hungry. I avoided looking at myself in the mirror beside my bed. For three days, I lived on bread and milk. The manageress discovered how dedicated I was to my studies and how poor my diet was. 'You need more than bread and milk,' she told me.

Wednesday couldn't arrive too soon. I hired a taxi and mapped a circuitous route. Puzzled, the taxi driver wondered why I was wasting my money.

Each examinee had to come and go at his own peril. Escorted by her father, Kadija arrived in a taxi with Rahma and Bajia. They were immediately ushered into the hall and then to their seats. I was already seated at the very front, near the window, face-to-face with the proctor. Faissal and Najib were far away and apart, for once. Kadija was seated in the middle and waved to me as she sat down. Rahma and Bajia were somewhere, but invisible to me.

Four hours of maths exams debrained me, and I was the first to hand in my paper and leave the room.

Kadija came out almost in tears, shouting, 'Hard! Hard!'

'It would have been harder if Professor Nassiri hadn't given us those private tutorials!' I answered.

'Horrible as horrible can be!' remarked Faissal as he lumbered out of the hall.

At lunchtime, Kadija's father was already outside waiting

for her. Some parents came to pick up their children; Faissal, Najib and I stayed in and shared our lunch. I had brought bread and a couple of mandarins; Faissal and Najib had brought bread and dates.

The second morning was different. Crafty, rough-looking and pretending to be tradesmen, thugs arrived at the exam complex at five-fifty in the morning, ten minutes before the real cleaners were to start, ingenious timing. Carrying buckets and brushes, they passed the gate, spoke to the janitor and penetrated the building, undetected and undeterred. They knew it was a short time before the janitor would raise the alarm. At lightning-speed, they sloshed petrol here and there, threw a match into the middle, engulfing part of the building in fire, and scurried away. The janitor realised that he had been duped, and when the real cleaners arrived, they could only watch the blaze. The building had been turned into a war zone. In the smoke, the police, fire brigade and undercover police watched and listened, but there was no one to cuff and no fish in the net.

On the third morning, the weather was out of character: cloudy, misty and surprisingly chilly; weather no one expected or enjoyed. Overnight, the school ground became a military camp. Vehicles of all sizes and soldiers of all ages and ranks were waiting for action, but all was calm; the moles were underground. The entrance hall was a football ground flooded with undercover police, eyes and ears strained. Leaving the dirty lodge early, I arrived at the building at seven-thirty with a black bag on my back and a suitcase.

At each side of the gate stood two tall undercover policemen, nervous and facing each other; not even a tiny fly could sneak in. 'Your name and your ID,' one of them asked me. *This is going to be the morning from hell*, I thought.

'Your exam number,' asked the other one. The documents were in my pocket. Behind the policemen stood the janitor and his assistant son, whose task was to identify any suspect and to tip the police with a wink of his eye.

'What have you got there?' the janitor asked me at the gate. 'You're not going to sleep here, are you?'

In seconds, two police jumped on me. Two burly men, their eyes popping, focused on the bag. 'Open this bag!' the commander shouted to me. I was slow to do so.

'Are donkeys' ears implanted on you?!' one shouted at me.

Face scrunched, I unzipped the bag. No petrol was found, just dirty old worn-out books. 'Jusef is here to sit his exams!' said the janitor, trying to soften their harsh treatment of me.

'Let him go!' the commander replied, a pistol hanging on his belt, pushing his jacket out.

Passing the gate, I asked the janitor's son if I could leave my luggage with him until six that evening.

'If my father allows it,' he answered. Shouldering his way through the police line, he shouted, 'Are we allowed to keep Jusef's luggage?'

'Yes,' replied his father.

Carrying my lunch wrapped in newspaper, I went straight to the biology lab. Access to it was shut and a few students were waiting nervously by the door. In their midst was Driss, an extremely tall, thin student with a moustache. Because of his height, he could talk to people in either the front or the back of a queue. He and I had never hit it off.

During his exam, Driss sat beside Kadija, and embarked on a very laborious technique of cheating. His arm was covered with writing, and each time he got stuck, he stretched his arm, allowing his shirtsleeve to pull back. The professor spotted his bizarre movement, and at first thought he was just nervous, but soon realised writing appeared each time Driss' arm moved. The professor called his colleague next door, and both of them observed his aerobic art of cheating. At a quarter past twelve, Driss was expelled.

Exams over, the six o'clock siren sounded, and the janitor swept everybody out. Abdu-Rahim didn't heed the janitor and an undercover policeman cuffed him. He was put outside and set free like a mouse from a trap.

I picked up my bag, my suitcase and searched for Kadija. Her face changed and her voice dropped when I told her, 'I mustn't miss the eight o'clock train.'

'Couldn't you stay until tomorrow at least?' she asked.

'By this time tomorrow, I will be in Kebdana. I have no money left,' I responded.

Kadija moved away, faced the wall, covered her face with a book, and broke into tears. I stood beside her, knowing I was not allowed to touch her, and wished all had been designed differently.

'I have applied to read pharmacology,' she said. 'You have applied to do medicine. I will change and do medicine as well.'

'I hope they will give us a grant,' I said. 'As you know, you only get a grant if you don't need one.'

'Can I go home with you?' she whispered to me so no one would hear.

'I wish you could, but my life in Kebdana is tough. Like they did in the Stone Age, you have to grind your own barley to make bread,' I answered, my heart pounding. 'As a currency trader, I narrowly escaped death last summer in Melilla. I have nothing to go home to, and I will have to resume trading again, though I have no capital.'

'I would be good to your mother. I would help,' she pleaded.

Until now, I had been undisturbed by my father's notebook, but was now stirred by Kadija's mention of my mother. Just then, Kadija's father lost his patience. The taxi driver hadn't switched off his engine and had kept the meter running. 'Kadija! Kadija!' her father called. She feigned deafness. Angry, he leaped out of the taxi, and she was unaware of him until he grabbed her with both hands and bellowed, 'Child! The taxi isn't free!'

26

Not meaning to, Kadija left me standing alone with my feelings for her apparent on my face. Fortunately, there was no one to notice. Already lonely and with barely enough money to get home, I had no choice but to move on.

To get a ticket at the train station was a matter of strength. Travellers, wrestling and shoving, swarmed the ticket booth, and the shoving ended only with the train's departure. I pushed and swerved to buy a fourth-class ticket on bare wooden benches. Men, women, children, the fit, the sick and some animals all shared the car. The train was long and slow. I imagined it had been built by French colonialists to transport their armed soldiers and livestock. However, it was the fastest engine I could afford.

Kariat Arkmane was lifeless when I arrived. Shops and cafés were closed, except Café Marhaba, where professional gamblers and hashish consumers spent the long nights fighting, sipping and smoking. Belly dancing crowned the nights.

Racing against the darkness, making a beeline, I found myself on Rabbia's doorstep. She seemed pleased to see me. 'Mrs Malani asked when you were coming and whether I had heard from you,' she told me.

Heavy, dragging footsteps thumped outside the main door; it was her husband. He looked tired, his face spotted with dust. He threw his sandals chaotically behind the door and dropped himself on a small rug woven by my mother. He fell asleep lying on his back. His mouth dropped open and he began to snore.

'Was it a busy day for you and Baghdad?' I asked him later. 'Rabbia told me that you and Baghdad trade produce in the village.'

'We do,' he said, declining to chat further.

After my long journey, the evening was comfortable and it was late when I arrived at my empty house.

At dawn, I was awakened abruptly by a heavy thumping that sounded like a drum. It was Uncle Mimoun banging on the door, frustrated by having to wait. Surprised to see him, I wondered why he was there so early and how he knew I was back home. He was desperate for my help. His daughter, Haloma, was getting married soon and, full of pride and trepidation, he wanted to impress and offer the best possible wedding in the region.

'The wedding is in a few days,' he told me. 'I have invited over a hundred people but, as you know, two-thirds more will turn up with no invitation. I want you to fill my barrels, all ten of them, with water and buy fourteen kilos of grapes.' I couldn't say no to Uncle Mimoun, even though he lived five kilometres away from the water pipe.

'Running out of water on a wedding day is second only to my daughter turning out not to be a virgin and being brought back to me as damaged goods, with compensation due to the groom!' he stewed.

For three days, I did nothing but transport water on an old donkey to fill the barrels for the wedding. When the donkey was not carrying water, I rode him like a yo-yo, back and forth, passing Mrs Malani's house.

As I ploughed along the dusty and rocky path, several metres below her prickly-pear fortified wall, she rushed out of her house and, descending the hill, stopped me on one of my trips. Tense and unsmiling, her large eyes were red-rimmed and puffy. 'How many more trips will you make?' she asked me.

'Until the barrels are filled, provided not too much water is wasted,' I answered.

'Expect that. The bride bathes six times before leaving!' she told me. 'Why didn't Uncle Mimoun hire one of those lazy lumps from the bingo club to fill his barrels?'

'I don't know,' I answered. I didn't understand Mrs Malani's hostile tone. Overburdened, the donkey was restless and I tried to hold it steady.

'How is your mother, Mrs Malani?' I asked, to change the subject.

'Old and frail. Her bones are one of her main problems, but she's in marvellous form, spiritually satisfied. When are your exam results due?' she asked me.

'In three weeks, I hope. It's been a very tough year for me,' I answered.

Mrs Malani noticed the donkey struggling, stomping the ground, carrying its heavy weight and not moving. She touched its head with a gentle stroke and said, 'Sorry, donkey. I kept Jusef talking and you waiting. Has Mr Mimoun more tasks for you?'

'Yes,' I responded. 'He needs grapes for the wedding.'

'Ah, can he not buy them from Baghdad and Rabbia's husband? They know all the farmers and who has what.'

'I've already thought of Baghdad. Now that you mention it, it's a perfect idea,' I told her, but then remembered that Uncle Mimoun hated Baghdad.

She smiled, went away, and I continued my chore. Then I began to think, *Uncle Mimoun wants me to get good quality grapes: seedless, sweet, fully matured in the sun, with no sign of ageing or shrinkage. All that to glorify Haloma's wedding and collect praise for himself.*

I went to Arkmane and strolled, looking for good grapes, in the open market. I found Baghdad standing behind a huge pile of grapes on the ground, with pears and mint beside him.

'Good morning to you!' he shouted at me. 'Taste! Taste! Today grapes are from Boya-Bach, sweet and thin-skinned.'

'Fantastic!' I said, after tasting some. They were spicy and sweet, but I was hungry, having walked for three hours with nothing to eat. 'I need about fourteen kilos of white and black grapes for Uncle Mimoun.'

'Ah-h-h! For Haloma's wedding!' said Baghdad, realising I was serious. 'Do the rest of your shopping and return at eleven. The best is still to arrive. I am expecting a farmer about eleven.'

I whiled away the time at the beach and returned to Baghdad at eleven. I was alarmed to find no new grapes had arrived as promised. Knowing the importance of grapes at a wedding and the intransigence of Uncle Mimoun, Baghdad said, 'Let's go and see Largo.' Leaving Rabbia's husband to struggle with the business, Baghdad and I rushed to Largo's stand one hundred metres down the row.

'Jusef needs about fourteen kilos of grapes of the best quality to impress undeserving wedding guests,' Baghdad said.

'You know me! I sell only good quality, but of course, I'll have to charge more. That's why I always finish after you,' Largo answered with a smile.

Largo was called from every corner, encircled by his clients. Some knew his name, some didn't. 'Two kilos of grapes, please!' shouted a client who didn't know him.

'Largo! Largo! One kilo of plums,' called someone who knew his nickname.

'Mr Ishram! Mr Ishram! One kilo and a half of peppers!' shouted another.

'I heard you! I will be with you!' Largo said when he wasn't able to cope with the barking clients.

True to his word, Largo sold the best grapes in the village Arkmane, but at a price. Sadly, Uncle Mimoun had not given me enough money for the purchase. Not wanting to hurt his pride or let him down, I bought the grapes on credit. Having spent every penny on presents for his daughter's wedding, Uncle Mimoun had starved himself of cash, and burdened himself with all sorts of debt.

Haloma got married, went to a new home, but took away her father's pride and wealth, and sank him into debt. Unfortunately, I found myself lumbered with Uncle Mimoun's bill. Rabbia and Mrs Malani were livid that I had been stupid and sucked into Uncle Mimoun's wedding extravaganza.

*　　*　　*

THE SUMMER DAYS, JUST like the winter nights, wore slowly, and gave rise to anxiety or boredom. Haloma's marriage failed; all my efforts to fill the empty barrels had been in vain. The time came to discover whether I had failed or passed my exams and where life would next be taking me. With the Sabbab's money, I travelled to Fez. My heart pounded the moment I reached the entrance to the school, the barricade and the two massive French doors. It was quiet and hot with no cars or pedestrians passing, no thugs to be feared; it was peace from heaven. The doors were wide open and the janitor was bustling from his office to the bathroom, cooling himself by flushing water on his face and bare feet. As I sneaked in, he grabbed me, but soon recognised me.

'You passed!' he shouted.

I rushed to the board to see for myself. On the corner, a white page with black ink, the same as all the rest but somehow more important, carried the following heading: 'BAC Passes', and not more than a dozen names were listed. I saw my name and kept reading.

'Are you obsessed by that page?' the janitor shouted at me.

'Yes,' I said.

'You defied the odds,' he replied.

Leaving the school behind for good, I took the pedestrian path crossing the cemetery where I had seen and heard people making love and went down into the bowels of the town.

Before reaching the centre, I stopped at the Catholic library and picked up a letter, an acceptance from a Belgian university to study medicine. Blind with joy, I ran to see Kadija.

Her mother answered and peeped around the door. Knowing who I was, she said, 'Kadija is in Casablanca.' On my way to the coach station, I came upon Kadija coming out of the Turkish bath. Both surprised and ecstatically happy to find one another, we moved to a corner where we hid, we talked, we shyly embraced. We both knew that what we wanted couldn't be. She was forbidden from taking me home, and I wasn't in any better position to take her with me.

She went with me to the station where the coach already had its diesel engine revving, ready to go. Leaving her there, watching her through the coach window, I wanted nothing but to bask in her presence, but cried inwardly knowing I never would again.

I had applied and hoped for a grant to allow me to go to university in Belgium. While at home, bored and waiting, an intimidating, official letter arrived, written on green paper. 'No grant awarded,' it said. Devastated, I thought of pleading. I made the long, expensive journey to the grant office in Rabat and hoped to be helped by someone.

The chairman was a Frenchman and refused to see me. 'I am busy,' he told his secretary. 'He should go home and read the letter,' I overheard, as if I didn't know the content!

'I won't move from here until I see the chairman,' I told the secretary.

I sat outside the office, keeping vigil, for the entire week, but I was ignored. The chairman relented and called me in just before six o'clock on the seventh day. His secretary opened the door to the inner office and motioned me to enter. The chairman stood behind a massive desk covered with rich brown leather. He struck me as being too tall compared with the locals, and so well-dressed with a paisley tie that few natives could compete with him. I remained standing.

'Are there any academic reasons for my grant application to be refused?' I asked him.

'Not that I am aware of,' he answered.

'Any other reason?' I queried.

'No,' he answered.

'Is it the luck of the draw, then?'

'No,' he responded.

'And yet my application is refused?' I asked.

'Yes. It's in the letter,' he responded. 'Take my advice. Apply to be a teacher.'

I told him, 'I am a native Moroccan, come from far away to seek a native grant . . . from a Frenchman! Nepotism is thriving, but I am not going to be crushed!' I paused for his reaction. Getting none, I nodded my head and left.

His secretary ushered me out.

Back home, every day I looked for a job, even the most menial (except shepherding), but there were none. I was forced to face the danger of going back to black market currency trading, but anxiety gripped me. *Can I really go back to Melilla, trade as I did, and stay alive?* I wondered. *All trades takes place either in Café Morina or nearby. Mr Marjosi is a dangerous man. I was stupid to challenge him and lucky to get away with my life. I don't have money to start with. Uncle Mimoun is no longer solvent, and Mr Amakran knows it. Would he still trust my ability to make money, now that Uncle Mimoun is no longer my backer?*

I was stuck, and the only stepping stone was currency trading. Melilla was a hub for men and women looking for money and one-night stands. Spanish women, married and unmarried, sailed from the mainland to make some money and taste the difference. Local girls did much the same. A booming illegal trade, from sophisticated perfume to socks, forced smugglers to carry guns that they were only too willing to use on whoever dared challenge them.

Without anyone knowing, I ventured to Melilla, but with no money to trade except a few hundred pesetas. There was no safe place to go except Café Morina, despite the threat of Mr Marjosi.

When I arrived, the street was busy, and the café was full, but there were no traders offering currency exchange. *Something has changed*, I observed. With two hands, I grabbed a heavy chair and sat across from a middle-aged man, chicly dressed, well-groomed, with sunglasses covering two-thirds of his face, making him look like a Mafioso. He was sipping a *demitasse* of espresso. Glancing at him sideways, not wanting to stare, I wondered if he was Mr Timsamani.

I ordered a coffee, and the moment I opened my mouth, Mr Timsamani recognised my voice and looked at me. 'I never thought you would dare set foot in this café again. Mr Marjosi still describes how wicked you were,' he said. 'What has brought you here?' he asked me. 'Not the trade, I hope!'

'Exactly that!' I confirmed.

'Things have changed,' he said. 'The bankers have caught

up with the small traders and are buying Deutschmarks, French francs, sterling and dollars at competitive rates. They have silenced the boys.'

'I had hoped to work with you,' I told him.

'Sorry. Impossible. I have changed trades. I live and sleep in my yacht, under no nation's jurisdiction in international waters,' he explained, nodding.

'Has Mr Marjosi changed as well?' I asked.

'Of course. A Spanish doctor put him on some medication that blew him up just like a Spanish *toro*. Now he's belligerent and dangerous, always looking to gore something or someone. In the absence of people, he gores the walls and doors,' laughed Mr Timsamani.

Mr Marjosi suddenly emerged from inside the café, saw me and rushed back inside, picked up the telephone and made several calls. I felt a chill when I saw him and, listening to him, heard Spanish words pouring out of his mouth like water bursting out of a pipe, but I could make no sense of them. Mr Marjosi emerged again with two trays, one with coffee and the other with beer, and walked with a wobble, his enormous tummy bulging from his trousers.

Ten minutes later, two men in their late twenties arrived. They hurried inside and came out immediately to grab two chairs. Instinctively, I knew they were on to me and planned to corner me when leaving. I kept talking to Mr Timsamani. *I am not going to leave until a taxi passes by*, I thought to myself. That didn't happen, and Mr Timsamani left. The two men, guzzling beer, grabbed Mr Timsamani's chair, and pulled another one to my other side to sandwich me.

'You're not local, are you?' asked one.

'No,' I answered.

'We are local. We could show you the town,' one offered.

'No, thank you. What's your job?' I asked.

'We're doing our job now!' They laughed and winked at each other. 'And what's yours?'

'Last summer, I was a currency trader, and now I sell passports,' I answered.

'Has the man you were speaking with bought a passport from you?' asked one.

'Yes, I am in the process of providing him with three,' I said.

'Amazing! Could you get passports for us?' asked the other.

'Yes, if you pay.'

'How much?'

'Three thousand pesetas.'

'How long will it take?'

'One week, but I need your name, address, and a picture,' I answered.

'It took my cousin five years,' said one, watching his friend bite his lip.

'What's the time?' said the older-looking one, looking at his watch.

'One o'clock.'

'Is the photographer in the park?' asked the older-looking one.

'Yes, he's always there, like a magician poking his head under a black cloak. We could get one now,' said the clever one.

'Do you really think he will procure a passport for us?' I overheard the smaller one ask.

'Yes, yes,' answered the other. 'He's a friend of Mr Timsamani. Mr Timsamani doesn't chat to just anyone.' They rushed away, bickering, to the park. I knew the photographer was there and it would take him forty-five minutes to deliver two photos.

By that time, I was in the second coach, heading to Nador. *I will only go back to Melilla to take a boat to Europe. Life stops, good perishes, but evil always survives. There are people who don't trade themselves, but they won't let you trade. There are others who don't study, but they won't let you study . . . and so it goes,* I concluded.

Not knowing what to expect, I headed straight to Mr Amakran's shop in the late afternoon to seek a loan. I found he had changed. He had shaved his long beard, thrown his hat away and grown grey hair. Facing him, I bowed; probably he thought I was one of the beggars who invaded his shop daily.

Full of himself, he didn't spend more than one and a half minutes with me. Knowing Uncle Mimoun was bankrupt, he asked me for security, which I didn't have, so he declined the loan.

I felt my dream begin to crumble; I left the shop, my head down like a sheep's. I headed to the coach station, destination Arkmane.

On that quiet moonlit night, on a dirt road, with no sounds of any kind, I struggled to get home. It was about eleven at night when I knocked on Rabbia's door. She had visitors: Mrs Malani, Uncle Mimoun and Mimount. For fresh air and to escape the heat of the sitting room, they sat outside in the courtyard. I heard them talking well before reaching the door.

'It's my brother!' said Rabbia when she opened the door.

'This late?' asked Mrs Malani in surprise.

I joined Uncle Mimoun. Talking to him, I heard Mimount crying in the living room.

'Monster! Monster!' she shouted.

'Who is this monster?' I asked Uncle Mimoun.

'My new son-in-law,' he answered.

I crossed over to speak to Mimount. 'What's the matter?' I asked her.

'The groom is a monster! The marriage was arranged with his full agreement. Now he's seen my youngest daughter, and he's accused me of tricking him and giving him the ugliest daughter. The bounty of gifts he received from us was just a cover-up, he claims. He demanded I go to the mosque to swear in the presence of the mullah that I hadn't swapped daughters. Still unhappy, he now wants to exchange his wife for my other daughter!' explained Mimount. 'Haloma is despised and unwanted.'

Feeling sorry for Mimount, I took her to the courtyard to join the others. To change the subject, Mrs Malani asked me, 'How was your day?'

'Mr Amakran has refused to give me a loan,' I answered. 'He needs collateral.'

'You could use my jewellery, my bracelets, Jusef,' offered Mrs Malani.

'I will give you mine as well,' said Mimount.

I had thought of using my mother's bracelets, but they had disappeared from the house. I suspected one of my sisters had stolen them, but didn't know which one.

I went home excited and full of hope, wondering when Mrs Malani and Mimount would entrust me with their jewellery. A few days passed and I didn't hear a word. I occupied myself by chopping an old, dried tree, a substantial source of energy for cooking.

Deeply anxious, I visited Uncle Mimoun. When Mimount heard my voice, she came, wearing her bracelet on her arm. She gently pried it off and handed it to me. I held the bracelet carefully, surprised at how heavy it was, and marvelled at its intricate artistry.

Excited, I rushed to see Mrs Malani. She was having elevenses outside in her orchard. I saw her rushing to meet me when I called. Watching her hurrying toward me, I wondered why she lived alone. She met me with a smile and teased, 'Have you just gotten up?'

'I've come from Uncle Mimoun's house,' I said.

She insisted that I have a cup of tea with her. 'What do you want to do next?' she asked me. 'Is marriage in your mind?'

'I'm happy that I've gotten my baccalaureate. It was a real struggle – the strikers almost killed me. I've been offered a place to do medicine in one of the best universities in Europe, but I have no grant and no money.'

She went in the house and came back with a pouch in her hand. She untied it slowly and gently eased two bracelets out. They were in perfect condition, as shiny as gold ever could be. 'I hope these bracelets will make a difference. You are the bravest boy I've ever known,' she said, with a quiver in her voice. 'May the Lord help you.' With that, she stood up and hurried away.

I left Mrs Malani, Mr Amakran in my mind. *He will not give me a loan if the jewellery is defective or chipped, and even if it is perfect, he will only loan half the value. I'm sure he lends on the basis the borrower will default, then he can sell the jewellery at its full value*, I thought to myself.

The following day, I took the dilapidated, archaic coach from Arkmane village to Nador. I arrived, nervous, my mind full of scenarios, the worst being Mr Amakran would just say no! The shop was open when I arrived. Mr Amakran was inside his office, dozing in an armchair in the corner, a wooden table in front of him.

'Good morning to you, Mr Amakran,' I said with a cheerful confidence I didn't feel.

Mr Amakran looked surprised to see me. I watched his gaze drop from my face to the pouch in my hand and he said, 'Is that hashish on its way to Malaga, crossing the sea?'

If it were, I wouldn't need you. I would be rich, I told myself.

'Take that seat beside me,' he said.

I sat down and moved the chair closer to the table, a few inches away from Mr Amakran's beard. I displayed three beautiful, shiny bracelets on the table like a sacrifice on the altar for him to examine and admire, valuate, or reject.

'Are they for sale?' he asked me.

'No, they belong to Uncle Mimoun's wife and Mrs Malani,' I answered.

'Who is Mrs Malani?' he asked. 'I recall a Captain Malani

killed in a sea battle nearly eighteen years ago. He was a captain in the National Liberation Army, supplying its members with arms.'

'I have no idea,' I said.

'Obviously, they have faith in you and your project. I will hold the bracelets and give you a loan,' he told me.

I couldn't believe my luck. I asked if there were any papers to sign.

'No need,' said Mr Amakran. He stood up, moved out of his armchair, turned around and opened a closet with two doors. The closet was full of jewellery, bracelets, necklaces, rings and watches.

Watching him take the bracelets away, I felt sad, but kept quiet. Back in his armchair, Mr Amakran wanted to know about his old friend, Uncle Mimoun, whom he hadn't seen for a while. 'He's all right, but he refused to let Mr Mahria exchange one of his daughters for another,' I told him.

'A curse from hell!' exclaimed Mr Amakran.

Surprisingly, he invited me and his brother to have lunch with him in a restaurant a few yards away from his shop. The restaurant was packed, and the menu was simple but attractive. Mr Amakran didn't open his mouth or move his eyes away from his dish. His brother didn't seem to be interested in anything; not uttering a word, he just laid his head back against his chair. He was tired, I assumed.

A waiter came, the bill in his hand, and carelessly tossed it in front of Mr Amakran, nearly skimming his nose. 'Take this bill away! Have I asked for it? Have I finished? More tea! And clean the table!' bellowed Mr Amakran. The rude waiter hadn't known Mr Amakran was the owner of the restaurant.

*   *   *

AS I FELT BARRED from Melilla, I rented a café on a monthly basis from an old retired man, Mr Bouaza, in Arkmane. During the day, I served tea and coffee, but at night, beer and wine. Gamblers from the whole region came to the beach to bet, bring their lovers and feel free. Nights were lucrative, but fraught with danger from hashish traders, gamblers and prostitutes, some of them armed.

One night, danger became a near-disaster. A group of Moroccans and one Frenchman spent the night gambling. The Frenchman won consistently. As the Moroccan loser realised how much he had lost, a group plotted to hit the Frenchman and retake the winnings. Hearing the plotting, I whispered to the Frenchman to run. Very proud of himself, he yanked a gun out of his pocket, but soon came to his senses. He jumped out of the café and into his car.

To liven things up, a group of men brought a woman singer and young girls of different ages, colours and sizes. The heat and the sand outside made the beach a comfortable place to lie around. The singer sang the entire night, and everyone called her Fatoma. Each time she got tired and stopped, someone would shout, '*Lalla* Fatoma, *ẕid!* (More!) *Zid!*' She would revive, enjoying the attention and the fuss.

During the day, life in the café was normal. Baghdad came in often, to order a pot of tea, and talk to Mr Bouaza and me. Charismatic and generous, Baghdad pulled in other people. I served them tea, and they told their life stories crowded around little tables.

On the twenty-first of August, after he had sold his goods and the market had thinned to a few men, Baghdad, looking very tired, came into the café. In a torpor, he nearly fell asleep on an uncomfortable wooden chair. Twenty minutes later, Mr Ishram popped in with Mr Ali. Their rough voices woke Baghdad. Mr Ishram ordered two pots of tea, which I served with fresh mint.

'It's my birthday today,' announced Mr Ishram in a shrill voice, holding his head high.

'How old are you?' asked Baghdad, who never missed making a joke, knowing that Mr Ishram had no birth certificate.

'Nineteen!' he replied, chuckling.

Mr Ali said nothing but enjoyed Mr Ishram's fantasy. 'I was born on the sea. It's now been nineteen years since our ship capsized. Captain Malani, the brave captain, died and so did the other six men. I was the only survivor,' said Mr Ishram.

'Do you know Mrs Malani?' I asked, suddenly interested.

'I know of her, but not personally; but Captain Malani lived near the Tassamat and Makran mountains. When he died, he left behind his wife and a boy a few weeks old.' Mr Ishram's description of the gun battle on the Mediterranean Sea sounded to me like a cowboy film. The difference was that seven men actually died, and their bodies were never recovered.

'Do you regret that adventure?' I asked.

'I don't regret joining that noble team, headed by such a heroic captain, but I lament the absence of recognition,' he said.

On my way home, my memory retrieved every word that

Mr Ishram had uttered. *Mrs Malani has been a widow as long as I remember. The captain must have been her husband, but what happened to her son?* I wondered. *Do I dare ask her?*

I had not forgotten the document I had found in my mother's trunk, though my subconscious was reticent to delve further into the story. The document, without mentioning Mrs Malani by name, had described the gun battle on the Mediterranean Sea with the captain and six of his men losing their lives. Though I couldn't shake off my resistance to find out the truth, I couldn't account for it either.

My night-time business prospered. The seekers and gamblers came to meet and take revenge on life and moved from the café to the beach nearby. They feared neither man nor God. They rid themselves of all codes, be they social or religious, overflowed with youth and never resorted to the hopeless witches and wizards. Each time the sun set, they tipped their hats in full respect and believed it might never rise again. Every time the sun rose, they sang and danced.

Mr Ali, a Tarzan lookalike, was addicted to the nightlife of the café and owned a massive yacht. The Mediterranean Sea was, for him, just a creek. He sailed along the Spanish coast and knew every nightclub around Marbella. He and Mr Ishram had grown up in the same village. They had sniffed the same air and the same dust had filled their nostrils, but they had ended up in different worlds – Mr Ishram, a broken man and defeated idealist, but Mr Ali, a joy-seeker and sailor of yachts. Despite their entwined paths and final score, they respected each other.

Mr Ali always bought his groceries from Mr Ishram. As

close friends, nothing could disconnect them. Nothing cheered shopkeepers like Mr Ali's entrance. Butchers bowed to him and called him by name. He bought in large quantities and paid cash. Three-quarters of a lamb was never enough for him; a few lambs' heads, livers and bowels were always added to his basket.

Whenever he popped into my café, he had Mr Ishram by his side. They both loved Moroccan tea. They drank and talked, which enraptured Mr Bouaza, who heard every word and understood none. They never tried to include him, which was perhaps his fault. They thought he was stubborn like a dark donkey; his below-average height and broad shoulders made it an obvious comparison.

When Baghdad was present, the café became heated and the talk rousing. Baghdad threw provocative and sometimes nonsensical arguments into the conversation, and Mr Ali couldn't resist contradicting and challenging him. 'I know the world! You don't!' Ali would boast, to zip Baghdad's mouth.

'You know Malaga, Marbella and Algeciras!' Baghdad retorted. 'What about China? You live on the sea! You just emerge to breathe in some oxygen!' he added, jeeringly. 'Have you given up on Belgium?' Baghdad called to me.

'If I had, I wouldn't be here!' I answered.

'What is stopping you?' Mr Ali butted in.

'Money!' I answered.

'I will give you a discount on my yacht to Malaga,' he offered.

'How much?' I asked.

'Half price!' he answered.

I paid him immediately. Desperate to cross the sea, reach

Belgium and study medicine, I paid to be dropped in Malaga one month later, on the twenty-sixth of December, 1967. I had made enough money to redeem Mrs Malani's and Mimount's bracelets.

*   *   *

TALKING TO A CLIENT and watching through the window, I saw Mr Ali and Mr Ishram side by side, hand in hand, fingers interwoven, heading toward the café. 'Mr Ali and Mr Ishram are coming,' I blurted to Mr Bouaza who was sitting on a low chair. Smartening himself, pulling his jacket around him, he stood up and leaned lightly on the chair.

Stepping inside, Mr Ali immediately ordered two pots of tea. In the middle of tea, Baghdad arrived, complaining of the sea air drying his skin. 'Turtles shouldn't worry about their skin!' joked Mr Ali.

Direct and indiscreet, Mr Ali told me, 'I've cancelled your seat to Malaga. I couldn't go against the wish of your mother.'

I pretended not to hear Mr Ali and moved to serve another client. Mr Ishram, his jaw dropping, looking serious, tense, wanted to speak, but his lips failed him. His look lent credibility to Mr Ali's words.

Loudly, Mr Ali said, 'My boy! Your mother spoke first to Mr Ishram, then to me.'

'She came to see me three times and spoke to Mr Ali twice,' Mr Ishram told me.

'Who are you talking about?' I shrugged, not willing to understand.

'Mrs Malani!' replied Mr Ishram. 'Your mother knows Mr

Ali's activities; some of them are dodgy, I must confess, but don't get me wrong, he is a great fellow. Your father, like him, was a hero of the sea. He died for us all. Hell is not fire, evil is not just black against white. I saw your father wounded, blood pouring out of him, but still fighting. The tide of the sea took him away. I was the only survivor, by the grace of God.'

Mr Ali, not knowing what else to say, stood up to leave. I grabbed his arm, faced him closely, and said, 'Have I paid you?'

'Yes,' he replied.

'I will wait for you on the twenty-sixth of December at nine o'clock at the Melilla harbour,' I replied, my jaw set.

Mr Ali left, and Mr Ishram followed suit. They each went in a different direction.

'Do you know this woman?' Mr Bouaza asked me.

'Very well.'

'Can your father be Captain Malani?'

'This story is new to me, and disturbing,' I answered and sat down. The document in my mother's trunk kept flashing in my head.

Back home, before the darkness settled, Baghdad had told Rabbia and Uncle Mimoun that my father and mother were Captain and Mrs Malani. Full of doubt himself, not everybody believed him. The thin boundaries between reality and fiction in Baghdad's life and mind didn't stop Rabbia from saying, 'Could my mother and Mrs Malani have kept this deceit all these years?'

'Baghdad is a devil mouth!' said Uncle Mimoun. 'From a

dirty village, he brought us this gossip. Because of who he is, God deprived him of offspring. God knows evil comes from evil, and decided enough of it!'

Mimount, not knowing upon whom to pour her love or hatred, whom to be against or for, asked Uncle Mimoun, 'Was there a secret pact between those two women, both highly respectable? Can such a thing of that magnitude happen in our small quarter, from pregnancy to birth, through infancy? Unbelievable!'

Rabbia waited impatiently, deep into the night, for me to come home so she could learn more, but I didn't go home. She didn't know that I frequently spent the night in Nador to avoid the long trip and the loneliness of the empty house.

That night in Nador wasn't peaceful for me, and I didn't expect a happy day either. I entered Mr Amakran's warehouse in the early morning, peered up and down the aisles, but couldn't see him. Yet he was there, facing the shelves and surveying a row of newly arrived boxes. He was wearing jeans tucked into his boots and a short, brown leather jacket made especially for him. He looked completely foreign and totally ridiculous. This was his way of giving a clear, strong signal that he was tough and cowboy-minded.

'I didn't recognise you, Mr Amakran,' I said, colliding face-to-face with him.

"Now you have,' he replied with a fake smile. Away from his clients and brother, in his private corner, business started.

'I am here to redeem the bracelets,' I said.

'Are you?' he replied, eyes twinkling.

'Yes,' I confirmed.

'I never thought you would make that much money, and so quickly,' he said. A long pause followed.

Mr Amakran flew the coop like a chicken and went straight to his private stash, where he kept his treasure trove. He picked up the bracelets and tossed them on the table. 'You've redeemed your bracelets. What is next?' he asked me.

'A long, difficult journey is ahead,' I answered. 'With Mr Ali on his yacht, I hope to reach Belgium soon.'

'I know him. He's a great fellow, immortal and invincible. He is a master of tricks. He tricks the Spanish police and keeps them running like rabid dogs. He provokes them; they block him just as the American hero Kennedy encircled Castro. Inch by inch they reach him, then they find him sleeping, nothing on board except an empty tin of sardines. Other times, he provokes them to test his speed. They race behind him, and if they catch him, the yacht is empty. But, sometimes, his boat is full, and only he knows of what and when. Maybe full of ha..ha..ha...'

I left Mr Amakran and Nador behind and rushed to serve my night-time clients. Carrying three bracelets in a pouch worried me. *What if I lose them or someone snatches them?* My mind kept processing and producing different scenarios. On the coach to Arkmane, I began to count the number of times I had been in this coach. I couldn't remember; there had been so many. I felt safe only when I entered the café and was sure no one was watching me. I hid the bracelets, boiled the water in the urn and later a taxi stopped abruptly at the front door. Happy to see some clients, I turned the volume up on the radio.

Two men and two beefy girls emerged from the taxi. They stepped in and took the largest table by the window. I was expecting them to order wine, but they asked for Coca-Cola. I didn't make very much money on them. When they left, no more clients came.

Normally, I would have gone home, but I couldn't face Mrs Malani, watching her, talking to her, and wondering whether she was my mother. I tried to dismiss what I had heard, but the document, the presence of Mr Ishram and the unsolicited intervention of Mrs Malani herself left me deeply disturbed, disoriented and disappointed. I thought of avoiding her forever, but I had her two bracelets like two stones in my pack. I spent that night in the café with only a blanket between me and the floor.

I tidied the café in the morning, straightened the chairs, mopped the floor, cleaned the window and swept the entrance. Once home, I planned a day of resting and avoiding everybody, but at midday Rabbia came to see me.

'Here you are!' she shouted, with no charm or greeting. 'Mrs Malani should have either unveiled herself a long time ago or taken her pledge to the grave. I wish my mother had been honest!' she burst out. 'It is certainly stupid for you to cross the sea with Mr Ali, but does Mrs Malani need to go that far to prevent you from going with him?' she asked me in anger and frustration.

Restless and shaken, I went to Mrs Malani to hand her the bracelets. It was late, but not dark yet. Outside her house in the front yard, picking more sticks to put on the fire, she saw me leave the main path and walk up her long, narrow walkway.

She stood for a while and came to meet me. Her face looked red and unusually agitated. She kept walking until she came face to face with me.

'Guess what I have here?' I asked, waving the pouch.

'Tell me,' she said.

'Your bracelets! I pried them out of a crocodile's mouth!'

'Would you accept them if I were to give them to you?'

'What would I do with them?' I answered without thinking.

'Give them to your wife as a gift from me.'

'I might not get married.'

'I hope you will get married. I think you will.'

'I am going abroad.'

'I know you're going away.' She melted into tears and the conversation died. With a low voice, hardly audible, she said, 'You are my son. I want you to have these bracelets.'

She put her arms around me and embraced me for the first time. Dumbstruck, I reached to hug and comfort her. I felt instinctively that I had always been her son and she had always been my mother. I found myself hugging and comforting the most loving and caring woman I had ever known, and *she is my mother*! But I couldn't expect to be treated like a baby, for it was too late and I was too old. I pulled back to have a fresh, new look at her, different from all the other times I had seen her. We parted, she to her house and I to my home. *I left home this afternoon, motherless, just to drop off two bracelets, but now I am going home with my mother alive.* Unable to handle my emotions, joy and sorrow, I was too preoccupied to open the café for the night trade.

I slept in the next morning, stayed home, and went to see

Rabbia as the sun set. I walked in the moonlight and hoped to talk to her, hoping her anger might have subsided, but she wasn't at home, though it was late. I found her husband pacing outside the house, waiting for her; he looked angry and worried.

I felt sorry for Rabbia's husband. I had gone there for a change and a talk with Rabbia, but not finding her, I shuffled back home.

That night, I pulled out Sarir's diary and put it beside my envelope-thin pillow for Mrs Malani to see the following morning. I wondered if she had ever been aware of his journal.

Sarir had broken the pact. My mother had handed me to him and his wife Sabah, and the pledge had been that the light would never shine upon the truth.

My purchasing the seat in Mr Ali's yacht to cross the Mediterranean Sea had severed my mother's nerves, and she had broken the pledge herself, but many years later. Maybe she did it because Sarir and Sabah were both dead.

I tried to sleep that night, but my eyelids refused to close. Excited and nervous, my mind went wild. Pictures of my mother moving up and down between Makran and Tassamat mountains picking herbs, looking at them in the sunlight, kneeling on her knees to smell their essence without disturbing them, cluttered my mind.

The sun's rays through the big window flooded over me and ended my sleepless night. I jumped up like a child on Christmas morning. I waited until mid-morning to pop in on my mother, the notebook in my hand.

It was a clear, sunny morning, but the sun's heat and the

cold wind blowing from the east were in equal measure. Working through their collusion, I felt fresh and energised. Passing the enormous fig tree, I wondered if it still held some of its late-ripening figs. Approaching my mother's house, I found the front door closed, and it looked still and lifeless. Closer to the main door and listening with both ears, I heard the dog inside barking in distress. The door was not only closed, but locked with the traditional bolt, a deep hole in the wall and a long, thick stick inserted into it to stop the door from being pushed in from the outside.

Inserting a stick and my finger through the space between the door and the wall, inching the bolt from the right to the left, I managed to dislodge it, dropping it with a sharp bang to the floor. The door opened, and the dog barked again. It was docile despite the noise it was making, so I inched into the courtyard. I called, 'Mrs Malani! Mrs Malani!' repeatedly, but got no answer. The bedroom and kitchen doors were open wide.

Stepping into the kitchen, to my horror, I found Mrs Malani lying in a foetal position against the wall. I could discern no visible movement, but her right leg was immensely swollen and covered with blood. I put my hand on her sweaty forehead and immense heat emanated.

Heart heaving, I shouted 'What's happened?!'

There was no answer, but her eyelids fluttered slightly. Uncle Mimoun jumped into my mind and I ran straight to him. He was outside his house, sleeves up, a hoe in his hands, digging and loosening the soil around the base of the olive tree.

'Mrs Malani . . . Dying!' I shouted, unable to make intelligible sentences.

Seeing every cell in my body trembling, Uncle Mimoun could have been in no doubt that something horrible had happened. We raced side by side to Mrs Malani's house. Uncle Mimoun was surprisingly fit. Behind us was Mimount, just as fast and just as fit as we were.

We arrived all together and poured into Mrs Malani's kitchen where she was lying. 'What have you done to deserve that?' shouted Mimount, tears pouring down.

Mrs Malani was just the same as I had found her, but sweating heavily from every part of her body. Mimount grabbed a ball of wool from Mrs Malani's bedroom, soaked it in water, and squeezed it into her mouth. A sign of hope, she blinked.

'To the hospital! To the hospital!' I shouted to Uncle Mimoun.

'Right!' he retorted. I unshackled Mrs Malani's donkey. We tried to get her on the donkey and failed. A big yell was heard from Mrs Malani's bedroom.

'Snake! Snake! *Kattala!*' shouted Mimount, shaking Mrs Malani's bedcovers. The snake had jumped at her, but she had swerved and the snake took refuge in a corner where there was a little hole, but it couldn't get through. I took off one of my shoes and hurled it at the snake, hitting it squarely. *Kattala* was killed and put in a basket to take along to the hospital.

All three of us struggled to put Mrs Malani on the donkey, but it was a Herculean task to keep her on. I jumped up behind her to keep her from teetering.

Mrs Malani ran out of luck. Twenty minutes later, she began vomiting and died. The speed of the donkey was no match for the venom of *kattala*.

Dead, Mrs Malani got heavier and heavier, impossible for me to hold on the donkey. 'When a man gets ill, his weight doubles, and when dead, it triples,' said Uncle Mimoun, tears on his chin, looking at me, miserably sad, tears running hopelessly.

We stood still in the road waiting for any help that would pass. Mr Isa and his wife Nonut, on their way to visit their daughter, stopped to help. Other passers-by stopped and offered as well.

With the help of the generous crowd, Mrs Malani was taken back to her home – dead. From mouth to ears, news of her death spread like a wild wind. From near and far, burly farmers and neighbours flocked to the cemetery to help dig the grave. Some had pickaxes, others hoes or shovels. The crowd swelled as the day went on. Everyone in the community had been touched by Mrs Malani at some point.

Burial had to be quick, but couldn't be after one o'clock in the afternoon. Mrs Malani, lying dead in her home, was not yet ready. The long white cloth to wrap her after the ritual washing needed to be bought, and it was already three o'clock.

'It's up to me now to take care of my mother,' I said to Uncle Mimoun. 'She took care of me. When I was alone on the mountain in the hand of snakes and foxes, she was there watching over me, albeit from far away,' I declared with a quivering voice.

Listening to me, Mimount dropped her face into her hands

and sobbed. Unexpectedly, so did Uncle Mimoun. Leaving him to talk to the mourners, I went to the village to purchase the white cloth. Sadly, no shop stocked such cloth. Nador was the closest city where it could be found, so I hired a taxi. There, I bought the material and didn't come home until two o'clock in the morning. Uncle Mimoun and Mimount were there waiting for me.

That morning, I asked Rabbia to perform the ritual diligence of washing Mrs Malani. She refused so Mimount did it. Hundreds of mourners, shocked by the news, turned out to offer their last respects to Mrs Malani when she was buried in the local cemetery, Thahamrit.

Devastated and emotionally paralysed, I couldn't handle the loss of my mother so soon after discovering her. When I awakened the following day, I wondered if it had been real or a dream. I didn't open my café for three days.

The next day, Uncle Mimoun came with a subpoena from the police. *I must be a suspect*, I assumed. Feeling like a criminal, I went to the police station to find out why I had been called.

The station was full of bustling people, and I waited my turn. I was called in and sat on a small chair. An officer came and handed me a letter.

'Your sister has been here, and this is her confession,' he told me.

With a shattered heart, I read Rabbia's confession:

I arrived late, guided only by starlight, but Mrs Malani was delighted to see me.

'*May I take this basket from you?*' she asked.

'*No, thanks,*' I answered. '*I have a bad cold. I need the towel.*'

Though Mrs Malani realised I was very late, she made nothing of it and probably thought I had had words with my husband, as I was tense.

Mrs Malani disappeared into her kitchen, broke sticks, struggled to light a fire. I went to her bed, the basket under my arm. I picked up the bag and spun it over my head for most of the time Mrs Malani was busy boiling the kettle and making tea. The snake was disoriented, not willing or able to move. With extreme care, I freed the snake and tucked it into the foot of Mrs Malani's bed.

It was a quick visit with pleasant conversation. I left, and Mrs Malani said she felt sorry for me. She was convinced something had happened between me and my husband. This was not unusual; she had seen it happen again and again.

'*That was a quick visit,*' *my husband said when I returned home.* '*I thought I would go to bed on my own, like a widower,*' *he told me.*

I knew when Mrs Malani jumped into her bed and stretched her feet, the snake would be waiting. It would take revenge for being disturbed and bite more than once. She would have had only enough time to put on her dressing gown and hobble to the kitchen before collapsing into a heap on the floor.

I gasped and put my head in my hands. I had always known Rabbia was tough, cruel and audacious, but never to the point of murdering Mrs Malani and depriving me of my only source of love.

Feeling like a stranger in my own life, I now knew why I had never fit into my family, why I had always felt alone even though surrounded by people, and why I must leave.

Then I prayed. *Lord, take me from this fearful pit and this miry mud. Put a sweet song in my mouth and lay a solid path for my life.*